YOUTH RESISTANCE RESEARCH AND THEORIES OF CHANGE

D1571959

Youth resistance has become a pressing global phenomenon, to which many educators and researchers have looked for inspiration and/or with chagrin. Although the topic of much discussion and debate, it remains dramatically under-theorized, particularly in terms of theories of change. Resistance has been a prominent concern of educational research for several decades, yet understandings of youth resistance frequently lack complexity, often seize upon convenient examples to confirm entrenched ideas about social change, and overly regulate what "counts" as progress. As this comprehensive volume illustrates, understanding and researching youth resistance requires much more than a one-dimensional theory.

Youth Resistance Research and Theories of Change provides readers with new ways to see and engage youth resistance to educational injustices. This volume features interviews with prominent theorists, including Signithia Fordham, James C. Scott, Michelle Fine, Robin D.G. Kelley, Gerald Vizenor, and Pedro Noguera, reflecting on their own work in light of contemporary uprisings, neoliberal crises, and the impact of new technologies globally. Chapters presenting new studies in youth resistance exemplify approaches which move beyond calcified theories of resistance. Essays on needed interventions to youth resistance research provide guidance for further study. As a whole, this rich volume challenges current thinking on resistance, and extends new trajectories for research, collaboration, and justice.

Eve Tuck is Assistant Professor of Educational Foundations and Coordinator of the Native American Studies Program at the State University of New York at New Paltz, USA.

K. Wayne Yang is an Assistant Professor in the Department of Ethnic Studies, as well as an affiliate of the Urban Studies and Planning Program and the Department of Education Studies at the University of California, San Diego, USA.

Critical Youth Studies
Series Editor: Greg Dimitriadis

YOUTH RESISTANCE RESEARCH AND THEORIES OF CHANGE

Edited by Eve Tuck and K. Wayne Yang

Routledge
Taylor & Francis Group

NEW YORK AND LONDON

www.youthresistanceresearch.com

First published 2014
by Routledge
711 Third Avenue, New York, NY 10017

and by Routledge
2 Park Square, Milton Park, Abingdon, Oxon OX14 4RN

Routledge is an imprint of the Taylor & Francis Group, an informa business

© 2014 Taylor & Francis

Library of Congress Cataloging in Publication Data
   Youth resistance research and theories of change/edited by
   Eve Tuck and K. Wayne Yang.
   pages cm. — (Critical youth studies)
   Includes bibliographical references and index.
   1. Youth—Attitudes. 2. Youth—Political activity. 3. Youth movements.
   4. Educational change. 5. Social change. I. Tuck, Eve, author, editor of
   compilation. II. Yang, K. Wayne, author, editor of compilation.
   HQ796.Y624 2013
   305.235—dc23   2013023307

ISBN: 978-0-415-81683-0 (hbk)
ISBN: 978-0-415-81684-7 (pbk)
ISBN: 978-0-203-58507-8 (ebk)

Typeset in Bembo
by Swales & Willis Ltd, Exeter, Devon, UK

I was twelve years old and had run from the school four times. The moons were whole. The assiduous government agents were waiting, waiting, waiting generation after generation without fail for the defeated tribes to stop running. The agents, hired hunters for the givers of government, captured me once as me and three times as a bird and ran me back four times from the sacred cedar.

The first time, to teach us all good lessons not to run with the tribes and good visions of inner birds and animals, the agents forced me to wash floors and clean toilets for two months.

The second time back, from the sixth grade then, being in the vision of a cedar waxwing, the cruel and mawkish federal teachers pushed me naked into the classrooms, me and the bird in me, and whipped us for our avian dreams.

The third time back as a blue heron from the shallow rivers we were led on a leash to the classrooms and chained at night to a pole in the cowshed . . .

The fourth time back to school, listen now in this darkness, handcuffed and bruised, the last time as a bird, we learned to outwit and outlive government evil.

Gerald Vizenor
Wordarrows: Native states of literary
sovereignty (2003, pp. 117–18)

CONTENTS

ACKNOWLEDGEMENTS

In making a book like this, there are so many casual expressions of gratitude along the way. A thank you at the end of an email or phone call, a note sent through the mail, a lunch after a delicious conversation. Now that we have seen everything up close and in full, the book as a book, our gratitude abounds, exponentially.

To our series editor Greg Dimitriadis, thank you for the multiple, scalular contributions you made to this volume. Your expert advice and co-envisioning saw us all the way through. To Catherine Bernard, our brilliant editor at Routledge, thank you for your enthusiasm for this project, and the insights you brought to its design. Madeleine Hamlin was a capable guide through this process.

To each of the scholars who were interviewed for this volume, we extend our ardent appreciation. Michelle Fine and Pedro Noguera have been our mentors for many years, but to learn from you in this way was a treat we will long remember. Meeting Signithia Fordham, Jim Scott, Robin Kelley, and Gerald Vizenor was an honor and a thrill—and we have felt profoundly fortunate to work with those we have always admired so much. We have been mentored by your generosity and humility, your thinking and your writing.

The authors who contributed to this volume are also our teachers. Each of you has inspired us with your radical reimagining of youth resistance research, your steadfast commitments to justice, and your elegant theorizing of change and possibility. We are so grateful that you put your energies toward this work.

We acknowledge the support of our colleagues at the State University of New York at New Paltz, especially those in the Department of Educational Studies, and in the Ethnic Studies Department of the University of California San Diego. Graduate student Kondwani Jackson served as research assistant for this project.

This book was preceded by a panel at the annual meeting of the American Educational Research Association, and a special issue of the *International Journal of Qualitative Studies in Education*, both called *Youth Resistance Revisited: New Theories of Youth Negotiations of Educational Injustices* (September, 2011). We acknowledge the wonderful contributions that informed this book by: Jessica Ruglis, Maddy Fox, Brett Stoudt, Kathleen Nolan, Jen Weiss, Greg Dimitriadis, Tracy Friedel, Cindy Cruz, Jingjing Lou, Rubén Gaztambide-Fernández, David Alberto Quijada Cerecer, Caitlin Cahill, and Matt Bradley, Nicole Hidalgo, Stephanie Springgay, Nikki Hatza and Sarah O'Donald, Maisha T. Winn and Chelsea A. Jackson, Laura L. Terrance, Lydia R. Otero, and Julio Cammarota.

There are many colleagues and friends we turn to for wisdom and nudges toward the finish line: Kathleen Nolan, Patrick Camangian, Daniele Maeder, Kate McCoy, Julie Gorlewski, Michael Smith, Karanja Keita Carroll, Adria Imada, and our students. JoAnn Schmier and Kaitlyn Schmier, Hardeep Jandu and Kiik A-K took care of us and our families.

Our most heartfelt thanks is reserved for our families. Eve's extended family, and Kevin, Kieran, Melody, Beverly, John, Justin and Sarah, and Wayne's family, chosen family, Ree, and Junobi have sustained us both. We have so many people in our corners that we need more corners.

1

INTRODUCTION TO YOUTH RESISTANCE RESEARCH AND THEORIES OF CHANGE

Eve Tuck and K. Wayne Yang

In 1895, 19 Hopi men were incarcerated in the prison facility on Alcatraz Island, "because," as reported by a San Francisco newspaper, "they would not let their children go to school." The U.S. Federal Government had enacted policies in Orayvi and across Hopi lands that were designed to limit Hopi sovereignty and facilitate settler colonialism. The new policies divided shared land into individual tracts, removed Hopi people from mesas, required new agricultural practices, and demanded that Hopi children attend faraway boarding schools (Sakiestewa, 2010). In the lead up to the arrest of the 19 men, white settlers had drawn a false dichotomy between Hopi who were "Friendlies" and "Hostiles"; hostiles were those who refused to give up collective planting of wheat in favor of individual-ized farming practice, those who refused to adopt Washington ways, and refused to turn over their children. A nearby Mormon/Navajo land dispute involving bloodshed added to settlers' fearful exasperation over the Hopi refusals.

The 19 men, deemed hostiles, were rounded up, and marched by foot, horse, train, and eventually boat to the San Francisco bay, a journey that took more than a month to complete (Holliday, n.d.). When the captured Hopi men arrived, they were sensationalized by San Francisco newspapers as a "Batch of Apaches [sic]" imprisoned "until they have learned to appreciate the advantage of educa-tion" (*ibid*). They were kept on Alcatraz from January 3 to August 7, 1895.

Hopi refusals to send (or more often agreeing to send but never sending) their children to remote boarding schools became emblematic of Hopi resistance to set-tler colonialism and the settler colonial state writ large. This stand about schooling, justice, continuity, sovereignty, and the future of Hopi people is one that has con-tinued to frame conversations about schooling there ever since. Ten years after the return of the 19 men, Hopi schooling again became one key site of struggle over the very terms of educational resistance—to what degree to participate in or reject settler schools—but that's another story (Sakiestewa, 2010).

This book is about youth resistance to educational injustice, research on youth resistance, and the theories of change that undergird youth resistance. Resistance to educational injustice sometimes takes shape as resistance to state schooling in total, as evidenced in the story of the Hopi incarceration, above. At other times that resistance takes form in order to make a claim to schooling and dignity in schooling. Often, resistance to educational injustice is about demanding more from institutions than they were ever designed to do.

For example, Ana Julia Cooper's (1892) *A Voice from the South* entreated schools to enable "racial uplift," challenging them to bring racial discrimination to an end despite being devised to promote stratification. Cooper, writing as a formerly enslaved Black woman, insisted that schools be sites for justice even when the state was aggressively unjust. In *The Mis-education of the Negro*, Carter G. Woodson (1933), not only identified the reasons to resist schooling but also presented theories of how to change the conditions of anti-Black America through schools and out-of-school education. Cooper received her doctorate at the Sorbonne for examining the complex relationships between organizations in French civil society, American and British antislavery movements, and the Haitian Revolution, the only slave rebellion to found a modern state (see Lemert & Bhan, 1998). Woodson was a teacher, then school director, in the military-run U.S. colonial schools in the Philippines. From these vantage points, Cooper and Woodson could see the simultaneity of U.S. imperialism alongside its internal colonial tactics. Schools, they told us long before we would come to know it for ourselves, are sites of both social reproduction, and possibility.

As this book explores, youth resist educational injustice in multiple, sometimes simultaneous and contradictory, sometimes self-injuring, sometimes triumphant ways. In many cases, resistance to educational injustices takes aim against testing, curriculum, school rules, police surveillance in schools, homophobic policies, and disrespectful personnel; just as often resistance to educational injustices can diagnose inadequate facilities, resources, funding, teachers—the stuff of schooling. Youth have called into question the white supremacist and settler colonial projects of schooling, the school to prison pipeline, and subjugation of children via compulsory schooling. Still for others, resistance to educational injustice has meant a rejection of schooling in total. This may read as a truism at first, but classic and recent works on school dropout (Fine, 1991; Ruglis, 2009) and school pushout (Tuck, 2012) have asked probing questions not only about who exits school early, but the significant costs for those students who stay in demeaning schools.

In May 2013, Mayor Rahm Emanuel succeeded in closing 48 elementary schools and one high school in Chicago's poorest neighborhoods, an unprecedented wave of closings for any city (Ahmed-Ullah, Chase, & Secter, 2013). The closings overwhelmingly affected students and families of color, leaving white families virtually untouched. An Op-ed issued the same month by Leslie Fenwick, the Dean of the School of Education at Howard University, insists that urban school reform (such as massive school closures) is rarely about children but in most counts, is actually about urban land development (2013). She argues that programs like Teach for America and charter schools run by venture capitalists are not designed to address root issues, but instead, "are designed to shift tax dollars away from schools serving Black and poor students; displace authentic Black educational leadership; and erode national commitment to the ideal of public education" (Fenwick, 2013, n.p.). Pauline Lipman made a closely related argument in 2003 and again in 2011, pointing to the ways in which Chicago's Renaissance 2010 program was determined to clear Black and brown families from neighborhoods that would be valuable to white professionals.

In the final lines of her Op-ed, Fenwick writes:

> As the nation's inner cities are dotted with coffee shop chains, boutique furniture stores, and the skyline changes from public housing to high-rise condominium buildings, listen to the refrain about school reform sung by some intimidated elected officials and submissive superintendents. That refrain is really about exporting the urban poor, reclaiming inner city land, and using schools to recalculate urban land value. This kind of school reform is not about children, it's about the business elite gaining access to the nearly $600 billion that supports the nation's public schools. It's about money. (Fenwick, 2013, n.p.)

It is crucial to see the critique of education reform as land grabbing alongside the Hopi refusal to send their children to boarding schools in the late nineteenth century. One of the primary reasons for Hopi resistance to settler schools was to thwart the land grabbing of Native territory by the U.S. Federal Government. In this long view, neoliberalism and the corporate invasion of new "frontier" education markets including testing, evaluation, text books, charter schools, remediation programs, and career education "reformers" are just the most recent iterations of settler colonialism.

★★★

Images of youth resistance thread through popular media and the public imagination. Many of those images romanticize youth rebels—the bad boys of London punk rock, James Dean or the Fonz at the jukebox—often gendered, raced, and cast(e) as disaffected working-class white males. Other images convey the smallness of youth bodies (and power) in the face of the state, as in the widely circulated image(s) of Palestinian children aiming stones as Israeli tanks—sympathizing portraits of weak, noble, brown and hopelessly overwhelmed victims. (The only time resistance does not appear masculine is when it depicts victimry.) Then there is resistance portrayed as shockingly loud—as black, masked and masculinized—inviting us to re-experience the cinematic audio-confrontations with the Public Enemy or NWA soundtrack. Beyond these iconic images, however, news of youth and student resistance to educational injustice is more available than ever. The StudentNation blog hosted by *The Nation* distributes bi-weekly reports that catalogue acts of student resistance against unjust policies, racism and austerity across the United States. Student Unions in Philadelphia, Chicago, Providence and in cities all over the country have organized student walkouts. Youth everywhere are opting out of state tests which have narrowed curricula and taken up too much instruction time, most notably the current Seattle city-wide boycott of the Measures of Academic Progress (MAP) test.

In making this book on *youth* resistance research, we are aware that the descriptor "youth" is deployed in multiple ways. Usually youth connotes a social location: Youth are those who society regards as underdeveloped people not quite ready for self-determination. However, we are far more interested in *youth* as a structural (and historical, generational, political) location. Youth is a legally, materially, and always raced/gendered/classed/sexualized category around which social institutions are built, disciplinary sciences created, and legal apparatuses mounted. "Youth" has implications for identity and social life, of course, but its salience as a category is deeply connected to compulsory schooling (in the U.S. and Canada) or other legal apparatuses.

"Youth" became a category of concern warranting academic study during the Progressive Era in the United States (1890–1920s), coinciding with the rise of social science, the development of eugenics policies, compulsory schooling, the universalizing of high school in particular, and the extension of the U.S. settler nation into global empire. Kwon notes: "Developments in social and life sciences that focused on adolescence as a topic of inquiry and object of research converged to cement adolescence as a distinct life stage in need of intervention and social control" (Kwon, 2013, p. 29). The desire to mark some youth as "at-risk" gained prominence in the late 1980s, and a 1992 Carnegie report titled, *A Matter of Time*, shifted the nonprofit and academic fields by asserting that "at-risk" youth of color, when supplied with non-school programs in youth development, could become proper neoliberal subjects, escaping the residuum of "those populations designated as irredeemable and unworthy under neoliberal governance and positioned as, to use Katharyne Mitchell's words, resting 'outside of risks'" (Kwon, 2013, p. 48).

Because youth as a structural location is conflated with youth as a developmental category, youth resistance often gets special treatment, gets made precious. When youth resistance is treated like a precious thing, the real theories of change being theorized through youth resistance get trumped by a larger theory of change around youth as pre-adults. We maintain that there is nothing unordinary about youth resistance or resistance. Resistance is happening all the time, and anyone can be called to resistance at any time. Indeed, in the examples of Hopi incarceration, mass-closures of Chicago schools, and boycotts of the MAP tests, youth resist, their families resist, their communities resist, and the powerful resist too. Resistance, "doesn't go in the directions that we anticipate it will go. Resistance is not just something that low-power youth do toward justice, but also is what high-power youth do to secure the longevity of their privilege" (Tuck & Yang, 2011, p. 526). To understand youth resistance we cannot hold it apart from the particular conditions under which it occurs, conditions which include the actions of other "youth" and "non-youth" actors.

Unlearning Youth Resistance Theory

As we have learned in talking to foundational authors in youth resistance research, most if not all roads in the field lead to Paul Willis' groundbreaking and paradigmatic ethnography. *Learning to Labor*, released in 1977 and reprinted in 1981, followed 12 working-class boys in a working-class town of 60,000 (only 8% of the town were professional middle class) who attended the local Hammertown school. Willis' study details the ways in which "the lads'" resistance to schooling, especially to their classroom teachers (who were mostly women), was an assertion of oppositional working-class culture they inherited from their families and neighborhoods, but also an assertion of their masculinity against the distinctly feminine connotation of intellectual labor (Aronowitz, 2004, p. ix). "Ironically," Willis observes, "as the shopfloor becomes a prison, education is seen retrospectively, and hopelessly, as the only escape" (1977, p. 107). Twenty-five years later, Willis posited:

> It is perfectly possible that I caught "the lads" at the last gasp of a certain kind of real, if always subordinated working-class power and celebration in England; almost from the moment the book was published the conditions got worse. In the late 1970s and early 1980s the United Kingdom became the first industrialized country to experience massive losses of the manual industrial work that had previously been available to the working classes. This trend is now firmly established across the old industrialized world. In the United Kingdom over half of the manufacturing jobs that existed in the 1970s have been destroyed, with a slightly larger reduction in related trade union membership. At the same time, there has been a virtually epochal restructuring of the kinds of work available. Taken together, the new customer service call centers and the hotel and catering industries now employ more than double the number of workers as the old "smokestack" industries—cars, shipbuilding, steel, engineering, and coal mining. (2004, p. 182)

We take Willis' own re/thinking about the specificity of the lads' working-class resistance within the context of now-disappeared factory work, as critical in understanding what we need to re/think and what we need to remember about theorizing of resistance to education(al injustice) for a neoliberal context. Quoting Willis again:

> For many working-class youth [in the UK and in the US], the choice is now workfare, being forced into low-wage labor, or street survival with jail as the likely terminus. This is a state mandated attempt to regulate and reform the labor power of the working class wholesale, attempting to make "idleness" impossible just as work disappears. (*ibid*, insertion ours)

In some ways, an older cousin to this book is *Learning to Labor in New Times* (2004), edited by Nadine Dolby and Greg Dimitriadis. The volume marked the 25th anniversary of the release of Paul Willis' *Learning to Labor: How Working Class Kids Get Working Class Jobs*. In *Learning to Labor in New Times*, Michael Apple employs Ian Ramsey's (1964) distinction between "pictorial models" which might show the world as it really is, but in ways that are reified, and the far more rare "disclosure models" which "enable us to see the people and processes in wholly new and considerably more dynamic ways" (2004, p. 61). Willis' book, Apple insists, is one of those rare works of disclosure.

We believe that Willis' book made (at least) three invaluable moves that build upon one another, and disclose insights for how resistance is punished (especially by the state), insights for thinking about agency within poststructural analyses, and admonitions against analyses that foreclose responsibility. These moves, along with informing the work of practically all of the participants in this volume, inform the commitments of this book:

1) Attending to the Pyrrhic Victories of (Youth) Resistance

The lads in *Learning to Labor* achieve several Pyrrhic (roughly meaning: something achieved at such a large cost that it may outweigh the benefits) victories via their resistance to the modes and mechanisms of schooling (Dolby & Dimitriadis, 2004, p. 5). In his attention to those pyrrhic victories, Willis' work established a new benchmark for research on and with youth. Works that follow that example seek to lift up the nuances of negotiating the costs of dignity in inhumane and undignified circumstances, the ways in which decisions of self-determination can be punished, and the textured acumen that accrues over the lived life (see Fine, 1991; Tuck, 2012; Ruglis, 2009; Nolan 2011). For example, Jessica Ruglis has re-theorized school dropout as biopower—embodied political strategies and contestations—so that dropout "is a physiologically/psychically health-protecting act responsive to injustice" (2011, p. 634).

individual & collective forms   opposition to the popular structuralism

2) Attending to Human Agency within Poststructuralist Analyses

While many celebrate *Learning to Labor* as a critical ethnography, it also was a text that anticipated the questions of agency and desire that would motivate poststructuralist theory (Arnot, 2004). As Deleuze and Guattari ask again and again in their two volumes on capitalism and schizophrenia (1983, 1987), how is it that we desire

Agency: thoughts & actions initiated by people which reflect their individual power

our own oppression? Willis' rendering of the lads performs a sort of rejoinder to that question. "Rather than treating the lads as passive subjects deprived of agency, Willis contended that the lads were not simply channeled into jobs but rather were actively (if not defiantly) embracing their future in the realm of 'unskilled' labor" (McLaren & Scatamburlo-D'Annibale, 2004, p. 42). In anticipating the poststructural turn in social science, Willis' attention to "the profane complexity of cultural experience" (Willis, 1990, p. x) encourages contemporary researchers to emphasize what desire and human agency do, especially when they don't do what we want.

saying same thing true inf different words

3) Refusing Tautologies that Shut Down Feelings of Responsibility and Possibility

Finally, Willis pushed back against the tendency to see tightly regimented structural antagonisms as impossible to intervene upon. Such antagonisms can operate as tautologies whereby resistance results in domination; however, seeing the world in terms of despairing tautologies is "a theoretical as well as a political failure," just an excuse to shirk responsibility to take action (Willis, 1977, p. 186, quoted in Skeggs, 1992, p. 182).

> If we have nothing to say about what to do on Monday morning everything is yielded to a purist structuralist immobilising reductionist tautology: nothing can be done until the basic structures of society are changed but the structures prevent us making any changes. . . . To contract out of the messy business of day to day problems is to deny the active, contested nature of social and cultural reproduction: to condemn real people to the status of passive zombies, and actually cancel the future by default. To refuse the challenge of the day to day . . . is to deny the continuance of life and society themselves. (*ibid*)

What we learn from Willis' writings (as we have learned from the other foundational scholars that we interviewed for Part I of this book) is that what he takes away from his own theories of resistance is often different from the ways in which his work has become canonized. Willis highlights what we need to unlearn about youth resistance theory, and what we need to relearn about resistance, in order to theorize change.

Resistance Is Real, Not Ideal

In our article "Decolonization is not a metaphor," we analyze the problematic ways the term decolonization is deployed in educational research (Tuck & Yang, 2012). We begin with a discussion of the ways in which settler colonialism is different than other forms of colonialism, especially because settlers make their home on the stolen land of Indigenous people, using the labor/bodies of peoples stolen from *their* homelands. Following Fanon (1963) our insistence is that there can be no generalized theory of decolonization, because decolonization is always local and *remedy for wrong*

specific. It is always an acute redress. Thus, we posit that decolonization—because of the specific form of settler colonialism maintained in the U.S. nation-state—will necessarily involve repatriation of Indigenous land and abolition of slavery in all of its forms (Tuck & Yang, 2012).

Here, we wish to draw a parallel between decolonization and resistance insofar as theories of resistance also cannot be generalized. Resistance is always in context, in a place, between real people—even when some of those people embody the state. Resistance is always in real time too, and what is possible in one time and context is unthinkable in another time and context (see Vizenor, Chapter 8, this volume).

Thus, one of the critiques this book offers about the current discourse on *hardened* youth resistance is that its rendering of the specificity of resistance has calcified in recent years, meaning that many of the salient components of resistance—the *important* spatial-temporal context, the people, the strategies, the contingencies—are collapsed into idealized models. As Greg Dimitriadis points out in Chapter 2, the tendencies towards calcification might have always been true of the field. Yet, we are troubled by the efforts of advocates and scholars who churn out models of youth development that attempt to domesticate youth resistance.

Indeed, it is our observation that youth resistance models have bled into youth development models, whereby scholars and educators construct a model of resistance they find most desirable, an *ideal* form, and then hold it up as a meter stick to analyze *real* resistance. The funny thing is that we also observe that resistance doesn't care what our models want from it. Resistance does what it does.

Sarah Zeller-Berkman (2012) remarks that youth development initiatives typical of the last several years are laden with notions of youth as in crisis, especially in regard to being "behind." Zeller-Berkman appraises new policy initiatives concerning out-of-school hours designed to bring certain youth "up to speed." Indeed, the goals of these initiatives seem to be to "fix" young people (p. 748). Such approaches reveal a teleological understanding of young people, in which some are in the right time and place, and others are lagging behind. These approaches place youth along a line of progression that moves away from being "behind," toward a fully functioning, fully well-adjusted and acclimated (adult) person.

Soo Ah Kwon (2013) discusses how the "expansion of nonprofits in the latter half of the twentieth century is tied to the steady incorporation and professionalization of activism," which has the net effect of domesticating youth resistance into civil forms of political participation. This growth in the youth development nonprofit industry has occurred alongside the wide scale adoption of neoliberal governmentality, such that "social disinvestment and corporatization overburden public nonprofits that offer social services, while increasingly situating these organizations as important sites of care for marginalized groups" (Kwon, 2013, p. 5). To understand the work of "empowerment," Kwon argues, we have to understand how these are also forms of management of youth people that resonate with the state's project of care and control:

"Empowerment" operates here as a strategy of self-governance to make the powerless and politically apathetic act on their own behalf, but not necessarily oppose the relations of power that made them powerless. . . . This relationship of government operates through affirming and empowering traditionally marginalized populations, such as "at-risk" youth of color, allowing them to govern and improve themselves through their voluntary and active participation in community programs set up to help them. (Kwon, 2013, p. 11)

In other words, youth development models want youth resistance to look like "empowerment" within the circuits of conventional political participation, and the rubrics of self-discipline and self-governance. Thus youth voice and visibility coincide with sounding and looking like good citizens.

In the contrived combining of youth development models with youth resistance, at least such models explicitly communicate their expectations for what resistance does, what it should do. Yet, in much of youth resistance research, the expectations for resistance—what it does, what it should do, and *why* we want it to do that—are implied. It is the latter that this book seeks to address. Indeed, we hope to intervene upon the expectations placed on resistance. In the discussion that follows, we theorize the disappointment with which observers regard youth resistance.

Uprisings and Youth Resistance Movements

Recent uprisings in Tunisia, Egypt, Libya, and Palestine, massive student protests in Europe and Quebec, the Occupy movement in the United States and elsewhere, and youth protests against police violence have prompted a flood of media images of young people taking to the streets. Though these images of crowded public squares and boldly worded banners are widely circulated, thoughtful discussions about the forms of resistance and theories of change enacted by youth movements are far less common. Western media treat youth uprisings and resistance movements as though they are spontaneous eruptions, emerging out of nowhere as overflows of pure affect. So, the protests that filled (at first) U.S. news programs (before fading from public interest) always received ahistorical coverage, eliding the fact that global youth resistance has reshaped nations not only over the past few years, but in the decade before that, the decades before that, and the decades before that. Beneath the sometimes celebratory, sometimes alarmed discourses on youth resistance are buried theories of change, which when unearthed, reveal unquestioned assumptions about youth, communities, and social transformation.

Resistance is at once a pressing global issue and an ever-present fact. Yet the public gaze on resistance already posits it as a developmental and educational issue: the un-interrogated hope in most youth resistance research is how resistance might lead to progress, frequently imagined as the development and education of youth, communities, and nations. Resistance is also often romanticized. In such formulations, it is regarded as raw force to be harnessed and disciplined on a pathway into responsible democratic civilization (in the case of nations), and into responsible democratic adult citizenship (in the case of youth). Therefore, in this moment of global appropriation of youth resistance, it is all the more pressing to re-engage a critical discussion on the complexities and sophistication of youth resistance and the relative opacity of theories of change within youth resistance research.

For example, in late 1998, students in Serbia formed *Otpor* (translation: Resistance), an anti-Milosevic-government movement starting with a small group of middle-class students that soon spread across the entire country. Drawing aesthetic influence from *Monty Python's Flying Circus* and rock music, *Otpor* established a template that would be followed by *Kmara* (translation: Enough) in Georgia and *Pora* (translation: It's time) in Ukraine—using similar branding, music, fashion, pranks, public performances, sticker campaigns. The template included: A small faction that would grow into a subversive network, non-violence, goals of democratic renewal, marketing, branding, internet and mobile technologies, graphic design, desktop publishing; all of this made resistance look fashionable (Collin, 2008, pp. 3–5).

Organizers from one movement provided training to organizers in other movements. They understood the need for meticulous strategic planning. "'It won't happen without a strategy, without structure, without unity,' a young Georgian explained. 'You need, well, it's like Lenin said, its all about organization, organization, organization'" (quoted in Collin, 2008, p. 5). Core features of Otpor's strategy included the mobilization of middle-class youth and a decentralized leadership structure.

> "None of us was poor," says Milja Jovanovic, the daughter of a writer and a professor, and the only woman in Otpor's inner circle. "We were middle class, we had enough money to sustain ourselves, or our families supported us. We didn't need to go out to work to buy food or pay for electricity. I think that was really important because otherwise we couldn't have committed to Otpor 24 hours a day like we did. We could afford to do it." (*ibid*, p. 15)

Otpor had a decentralized structure with sovereign chapters carrying out autonomous actions. Public leaders could be taken out or discredited—something they learned in student protests of 1996–97 (*ibid*).

In Georgia, youth organizers of *Kmara* sought to confront the "manufacturing of apathy,"

> [Shevardnadze's regime] was saying, "Relax, nothing's going to change and if you do speak out there will be bloodshed and chaos here again—do

you want chaos, don't you remember what happened here in the past?" They were not trying to win the hearts and souls of the people, or make out that they were good—no, they knew that was pointless. They were just saying that it's all the same shit and it doesn't matter, it's just better to accept the way it is. Our job was to challenge the manufacturing of apathy; to show the government's real face and say that we couldn't just sit back and watch. (*ibid*, p. 70)

It may initially read as ironic to readers in the United States that the George W. Bush administration and other Republican organizations provided funding to youth resistance movements across the former Soviet states. Bush paid a visit to Tbilisi in 2003 praising the Georgian Rose Revolution in Georgia and the Orange Revolution in Ukraine, seeking to identify himself with the people power movements of the twenty-first century (*ibid*, p. 62). Of course, the United States has always subsidized resistance and infiltration—only somewhat behind the scenes—as part of foreign policy. This particular case represented a convergence of capitalist, Cold War, and local interests in which the movement desires were compatible with the neoliberal goals of the Bush administration, and also aroused the interests of oil investments and Western transnational corporations.

Most striking about these movements in the first decade of the new millennium was their wildfire reach and speed. Other movements were ignited in Kyrgyzstan, Azerbaijan, and Belarus with harsh acts of containment and force against protesters (and would-be protesters) by the targeted governments.

(T)he television pictures from the Orange Revolution and the instant global access provided by the internet had enthused young democracy activists everywhere. All they needed, it seemed, were the principles of non-violent resistance, a smart logo, some inspiring slogans and enough money to print a few colorful t-shirts. Some of them, however, would quickly discover that it wasn't that easy. Newspaper articles reduced it to a formula: how to bring down a dictator in a few easy lessons. But in many places, the formula just didn't work, at least not immediately; real life proved more complex than a set of simple rules and catchy slogans. Repressive governments were also reading those same articles, and learning. (*ibid*, p. 167)

The "results" of these movements were varied—Otpor, Kmara, and Pora succeeded in overthrowing authoritarian regimes, and in some cases, formed political parties in the new governments. As parties, however, the movements had short shelf-lives and they folded into other parties. Yet, the movements inspired actions in 2005 in the Zvakwana/Sokwanele (translation: Enough) groups in Zimbabwe (where protesters distributed condoms with Bob Marley lyrics on them), Kefaya (translation: Enough) in Egypt (where protesters tried to prevent Mubarak taking a fifth term), and in the Cedar Revolution of Lebanon (where protesters set up a camp in Martyrs Square in Beirut to protest the 15,000 Syrian troops stationed there) (ibid).

In some ways, the story of these movements fits the quintessential bill: Youth inspired each other to challenge authoritarian governments through youth arts and culture, ultimately overthrowing those governments and getting a seat at decision-making tables. Yet there are many parts of this story that don't appeal to the public imagination: The youth were middle class, supported by their parents, they wanted their countries' democracies to look more like the West, they also wanted access to Western consumerist markets, they were buoyed by Republicans in the United States, the G.W. Bush administration, and other government bodies like USAID.

These are stories of resistance, but they may not satisfy the public hankering for *good* stories of resistance, in that they cannot be idealized into a generalizable model. Good generalizable resistance stories have uncompromised working-class heroes, identifiable leaders, linear starts to finishes. Yes, they may not be good resistance stories, but our call is not to only pay attention to the good stories. We must pay attention to what these stories reveal about the gap between the expectations we have for resistance movements, and resistance in the real. This hankering for a good story is part of the sense of disappointment with which many have regarded what happened after the Arab Spring.

Waiting to Fail, Expectations and Disappointments in Resistance Movements

Along with many of the contributors to this volume, we are curious about the disappointment that follows spectacles of resistance—especially disappointment with verifiable movements, such those collectively called the "Arab Spring," Occupy Wall Street, even the U.S. Civil Rights movement. The Arab Spring is faulted for its mix of democratic and fundamentalist results; Occupy is faulted for its mixed messages and internal white privilege; the Civil Rights movement is faulted for its failure to extract the roots of racism and oppression. We suspect that the fault-finding and disappointment both are and are not about those movements. What goes unanalyzed are the varied expectations for resistance movements. In moments of disappointment, the mainstream media, the different publics who are watching, the intellectuals, the pundits, are all silently applying a theory of change to which movements can never avail. In this respect, disappointment becomes another one of the tautologies that Willis warned us about, in that we expect that a movement should do what we want it to do, and it won't, and therefore we are disappointed enough to believe no real change occurred; further, the disappointment concludes that real change is not possible.

Does resistance need us to believe in it to work? In theorizing the revolutionary efficacy of desire Deleuze and Guattari (1987) prompt us to realize that change happens whether we are disappointed or not (see also Tuck, 2010). Following Deleuze and Guattari, resistance is effective in that it produces a new reality, a new condition from which to resist (according to Kelley in Chapter 6, it changes the conditions in which one resists). It "works" even by not doing what we want it do. It works by breaking down (see Deleuze & Guattari, 1987, p. 31 on desiring-machines). Resistance has an impact, or maybe the word is an aftermath, whether we are disappointed or not. Resistance doesn't care that we regard it with disappointment.

As we have already hinted, we think that part of the disappointed expectations in resistance and resistance movements has to do with incompatible theories of change. A theory of change refers to a belief or perspective about how a situation can be adjusted, corrected, or improved. If a resistance movement does not properly fit within a theory of change that is recognized by the public imagination, it will always register as a failure. Yet, theories of change and their relationships to how resistance is enacted are rarely scrutinized in research on resistance.

Deep Participation

In late 2012, an Indigenous environmental and sovereignty movement, Idle No More, began near Saskatoon, Canada. It was started by four (3 Indigenous and 1 non-Indigenous) women with a teach-in on the consequences for First Nations sovereignty inlaid in Prime Minister Stephen Harper's Bill C-45, an omnibus bill that would diminish environmental protection laws. Soon, Idle No More would find support throughout Canada, expressed through round dances, protests, and other displays of resistance.

In December 2012, Ogichidaakwe Theresa Spence went on a hunger strike, consuming only fish broth for six weeks. Anishinaabeg writer Leanne Simpson (2013) remarks upon fish broth:

> It carries cultural meaning for Anishinaabeg. It symbolizes hardship and sacrifice. It symbolizes the strength of our Ancestors. It means survival. Fish broth sustained us through the hardest of circumstances, with the parallel understanding that it can't sustain one forever. We exist today because of fish broth. It connects us to the water and to the fish who gave up its life so we could sustain ourselves. Chief Spence is eating fish broth because metaphorically, colonialism has kept Indigenous Peoples on a fish broth diet for generations upon generations. This is utterly lost on mainstream Canada, as media continues to call Ogichidaakwe Spence's fast a "liquid diet" while the right winged media refers to it as much worse. (Simpson, 2013, n.p.)

Simpson's writing reveals that there are multiple levels to the activities of Idle No More. There is the surface of explicit political participation, for example, a hunger strike as a challenge to Bill C-45. There is also the deep participation, in Eve's words, "bone-deep participation," of Ogichidaakwe Spence's survival on bare sustenance and the Indigenous witnessing, thinking, and discussions of its meaning far off screen (see Tuck, 2013).

Inspired by Ogichidaakwe Spence's hunger strike, on January 17, 2013, six young people—Travis George, Stanley George Jr., Raymond Bajo Kawapit, Johnny Abraham Kawapit, David Kawapit, and Geordie Rupert from Whapma-goostui First Nation—began a 1,600-kilometer walk from their homeland that would conclude on Parliament Hill. They called it the Journey of Nishiyuu (translation: Human beings). The youth were joined by about 200 others along their journey, and they were greeted by an estimated 5,000 people when they arrived more than two months later on March 25, 2013. Their walk was for recognition as sovereign peoples: "We just want to be equal, we just want Algon-quin and Cree, all the reserves . . . to be known and to be treated equally," said Jordan Masty, who joined them on the walk (Barrera, 2013, n.p.).

Idle No More events and teach-ins spread throughout North America, and across the globe, especially among Indigenous peoples in other settler colo-nial nation-states, including the United States, New Zealand, Australia, and Palestine/Israel. Many in North America have scrambled to draw comparisons between Idle No More and Occupy, presumably because the open structure of the movements invites others to make it their own in their own contexts. Yet this comparison seems to also invite predictions of the public's future disappointment in the movement—Occupy was not able to achieve the change it sought, so why should Idle No More? Bryan Brayboy (p.c., April, 2013) has insightfully observed that a more appropriate comparison might be to the Arab Spring because Idle No More is an Indigenous refusal of settler policies and practice. The Arab Spring, as noted, has also accrued its own disappointed audiences: Is Idle No More doomed to disappoint? Will it never be able to meet the expectations the public holds for resistance movements? Maybe. Probably. But, again, we believe this says much more about public expectations for resistance than resistance itself.

Resistance is resisting even when we think it is not doing anything, even when we're not looking. Resistance creates highly visible moments, like Ogichi-daakwe Spence's hunger strike and the conclusion of the Journey of Nishiyuu—but there were many unseen moments in the long weeks of fasting and walking that happened as the rest of the world went about its business. The fasting and the walking were profound acts of deep participation, bone-deep participation, acts that would change the lives of participants and the lives of those around them. In this respect, deep participation doesn't necessarily deliver a new policy, a new regime, a political victory. It might re/new an epistemology. Sometimes it can deliver a movement. Other times, it forms nodes and networks and pathways to be activated episodically for more explicit political participation. "Once a person has engaged in deep participation, her bones will remember it, and will expect it, and set about creating it in other situations" (Tuck, 2013, p. 13).

Resistance can also generate a literal remapping of place and territory (see also Goeman, 2013; Brooks, 2008). On May 22, 2013 at 5pm, First Nations Peoples restored the peak of Mount Douglas to its original name, *PKOLS*. Tsawout, Songhees, and W̱SÁNEĆ nations participated in the reclaiming actions, including the installment of a new sign, a walk, and drumming. Participants held signs that said, "Reclaim, Rename, Reoccupy" (Lavoie, 2013, n.p.).

Finally, as we discuss in the next section, resistance makes networks, rhizomes really, of communication, of linkages between ideas, experiences, ideals, aspirations. Even when the actions are over, when the pace of tweets and emails slow, those pathways, like a dry riverbed before the next rain, are waiting.

The Paths of *Most* Resistance

A little more than a year after a group of protesters began to occupy Zuccotti Park in September 2011, the Occupy Wall Street message boards and twitter feeds were quiet, especially compared to the lively debate and activity taking place at the outset of the movement. The lines of communication that were so integral to the physical and representative occupations in New York City and elsewhere were like ghost towns— everything still in place, but not populated. If this is where the story of Occupy stops, and many would indeed stop it there, the resistance was a disappointment.

But, when Hurricane Sandy struck the U.S. East Coast in October 2012, causing major loss and destruction in and around New York City, the Occupy Wall Street (OWS) message boards and social media feeds sprang to life again. In the days and weeks after, while the national media had moved on to other spectacles and many New Yorkers (like others all along the East Coast) were without power and clean water, the OWS networks were invaluable modes of communication and aid. The network could put out word that water or supplies were needed in a particular neighborhood, and within an hour several dozen volunteers might appear.

Youth resistance researchers have documented the importance of youth networks in organizing youth walkouts (Weiss, 2011; Otero & Cammarota, 2011; Yang, 2007). Youth resistance actions that appear to be spontaneous in the media are made possible by rhizomes of youth communication facilitated by cell phones and social media. Many of these rhizomes are formed illicitly—using cell or internet devices not allowed in school, or memberships to social media hidden from parental view. Some adults catch on to this and attempt to capitalize on these existing tunnels, trying to use them or create new ones to hawk products and lifestyles; these rarely work, either because they are trying too hard, or the technological moment has moved on.

These instances draw our attention to the power of resistance networks (the paths of most resistance) but also the specificity of resistance, and the importance of where stories of resistance end. In a study on the 2006 mobilizations for immigration rights through social networks and text messaging, Wayne describes how what appears to be "fast organizing" is actually quite slow (Yang, 2007):

> Youth fast organizing has been mistaken for ephemeral and spontaneous activity, rather than the outcomes of intentional and continuous organizing . . . spontaneity is an illusion generated by fast-technology, and can mask deeper structures of organized behavior (p. 19)

that took countless hours, days, years of participation to develop. The channels for collective resistance to flow are deepened over time, like trained neural pathways through which the repeated movements become body memory. The resulting

> collective unconscious is the composite of thousands of individual messages among networks of youth—like synapses firing in the background of a collective cortex. (*ibid*, p. 18)

What this means is that deep participation forms well-trodden paths of most resistance that make mobilizing faster the second time around. In the case of youth digital networks,

> [V]irtual space provides otherwise un-propertied youth with a durable, malleable site of identity formation, social organization, and collective memory. . . . That radicalizing moment of protest and crisis was preceded and succeeded by durable changes in ideology and social organizing—as remembered and lived through MySpace. These low-rent organizing halls and offices in virtual space can facilitate political activity, even formal political parties, that could mature into transformative urban movement. (*ibid*, p. 25)

The organizing systems are latent in deep participation structures, and as one youth organizer pointed out to Wayne, the next mobilization can happen anytime (*ibid*).

Researching Youth Resistance

In the existing literature, with important exceptions, resistance only seems to register, to "count," if it includes certain activities and not others. Some forms of youth resistance are celebrated as positive, as developmentally or educationally progressive. Youth resistance is represented as going in one direction (from disempowered to empowered) and as a building block in the formation of social movements. Presumably, theories of resistance stand in contrast to theories of social reproduction, in which opportunities for social transformation are neutralized by the powerful structural forces that remake inequity generation by generation. Indeed, theories of resistance can rely upon theories of change that are so regimented that they are just as over-determined as theories of reproduction are critiqued to be. These are the expressions of youth resistance that are most legible, but there are many other expressions of youth resistance that are not as easy to characterize as positive youth development. The emphasis on resistance as positive youth development in educational research obscures understandings of youth resistance which may not align so neatly with established assumptions about civic participation and social movements; that is, forms of resistance that rely upon alternate theories of change. Implicit in the existing literature is that social movements are the avenue of social progress. Yet it is our assertion that youth resistance offers other forms of survivance, decolonial possibilities, agnosticism with progress, and desires for dignity that would enrich the currently paltry discussion on theories of change.

As noted, in research youth resistance is often masculinized, theorized through and onto the male body—when it is theorized through women's bodies, it is specific to their bodies, made un-universal. Because of the focus on masculinized forms of labor, and of resistance, theories of resistance and their attendant theories of change might already be masculinized unless explicitly queered. Two generations ago, resistance theorists (at least scholars acknowledged as resistance theorists) were all men (nearly), and yet one thing we find exciting is how new resistance research does not assume a masculinized nor a straight lens (and is often conducted by women/and/queer scholars). Still, when we pause to think about who is writing theory/theoretically about power and change, the authors that first come to mind are usually men, and they often are theorizing power and change from a masculinized lens.

For these reasons, the discourse on youth resistance is ripe for an intervention/reinvention—a major aim of the book you are now reading. Contributing authors discuss youth resistance to educational injustices as a fluid and dynamic construct, employing findings of new original research to deepen its complexity. As a whole, the volume is concerned with revamping, elaborating, and even sometimes agitating existing motifs of youth resistance in the literature—such as cultural resistance, everyday acts of resistance, youth resistance as youth development, and social justice frameworks of resistance. It tries in earnest to answer the questions that go unanswered in the existing literature: What does resistance really do/produce? What are the various/competing theories of change at work in contexts of youth resistance?

This Book

This book approaches discussions of youth resistance research so that nothing is out of reach for doubt, for reflection, for remaking, for re-incorporation. In our interviews with foundational authors, in our collaborations with others, in the chapters by contributing authors, the core operating categories of this book—youth, resistance, theory, and change—are constantly made and unmade; assessed, distressed, compressed; sometimes resurrected, sometimes discarded, sometimes renewed. Driving it all is an ethic of responsibility to young people, to communities, to justice, and away from allegiance to tautologies, sentimental nostalgias, and grand theories.

There are three innovative features in these pages:

1) Interviews with Foundational Resistance Theorists

Part I of this volume features crafted transcribed interviews conducted by the editors with prominent and influential authors on youth resistance. We asked foundational resistance theorists to reflect upon their now-classic works and their initial discussions on youth resistance and educational injustice. One thing we learned, and hope readers take away, is how Michelle Fine (Chapter 3), James C. Scott (Chapter 4), Pedro Noguera (Chapter 5), Robin D.G. Kelley (Chapter 6), Signithia Fordham (Chapter 7), and Gerald Vizenor (Chapter 8) already complicate and reclaim their own theories of resistance and change. They highlight what they have rethought, unthought, continue to think. They explain where readings of their work resonate with their own thinking, and ways in which they seem to be misread, and ideas that matter to them but to which readers seemed to have paid less attention or missed.

Like Willis, these foundational theorists have

> sharpened our collective understanding of the ways individual groups resist dominant cultural, material, and social imperatives . . . [and] allowed us a much deeper understanding of how individuals and groups negotiate oppressive circumstances not of their own making. (Dimitriadis, 2011, p. 649)

In addition to revisiting their work, they discuss contemporary contexts of resistance around the globe, such as the recent uprisings in North Africa and Western Asia, the Occupy protests, DREAMer movement, and student protests across Europe and in Quebec.

An introductory commentary by Greg Dimitriadis (Chapter 2) provides a critical historical overview of the emergence of the construct of youth resistance to educational injustice, locating the significance of the work of the interviewed authors and analyzing the distortion of theories of youth resistance in recent years.

2) Discussions of the Relationship between Youth Resistance and Theories of Change

Observing the ways in which some approaches to researching youth resistance have calcified the binary between reproduction and resistance in recent years (Dimitriadis,

2011), and have relied upon unexamined theories of change (Tuck & Yang, 2011), Part II of the book presents several discussions of needed interventions to youth resistance research from multiple perspectives. There is a crucial relationship between a theory of change and the form that resistance takes. That is, a theory of change might inform youth resistance; it might arise from how youth resist; it might prescribe how youth ought to resist; it might be contradicted by how youth live resistance. Thus, the aim of Part II is to highlight, make, and excavate theories of change that are embedded in assumptions about youth lives and youth resistance.

The four chapters in this section discuss the importance of the role of theories of change in understanding and researching youth resistance, and caution against ascribing overly romantic notions to youth resistance. In *Thinking with Youth about Theories of Change* (Chapter 9), an innovative, crowd-sourced chapter, eleven educators/researchers/activists share short insights from their own learnings from working and *thinking with* youth about change. Jennifer Ayala, Kristen Buras, Caitlin Cahill, Justice Castañeda, Jeff Duncan-Andrade, Valerie Futch, Rubén Gaztambide-Fernández, Patricia Krueger-Henney, Django Paris, David Alberto Quijada-Cerecer, and Sarah Zeller-Berkman comment on change as they have felt it, rethought it, doubted it, and helped foment it with youth collaborators from New Jersey to California, in towns and cities of New Orleans, New York, Newark, Madison, Oakland, Toronto, San Diego, Salt Lake City, Sarasota, and Charlottesville, Virginia.

In *The Politics of Coming Out Undocumented* (Chapter 10), Lisa (Leigh) Patel and Rocío Sánchez Ares write about how the DREAMer movement has engaged the state, and how the state has responded—analyzing the mutual engagement of the state and youth resistance as a "conversation" whereby the struggles for immigrant rights are framed and reframed by activists and the state. Antwi Akom, Allison Scott and Aekta Shah in *Rethinking Resistance Theory through STEM Education* (Chapter 11) posit a theory of change within the context of STEM education and STEM labor. By seeing STEM industries as a route to both economic mobility and for correcting eco-apartheid (Akom, 2011), they identify how to target institutions as a site of social change for Black and brown working-class communities in the SF Bay Area. J. I. Albahri, in *Hands Clasped Behind her Back: Palestinian Waiting on Theories of Change* (Chapter 12), offers a "meditation on youth, resistance, and change" that is situated in the context of the *nabka*, or "catastrophe": The displacement, dispossession, and decimation of indigenous Palestinians by the state of Israel beginning in 1947 (p. 123, this volume). Albahri presents different theories of change at work in boycotts of American firms engaged in settler colonialism in the Occupied Territories, in the activist representations of Palestinian youth resistors, and in the desires for Palestinians for return and repatriation of their lands.

3) New Studies in Youth Resistance Research

In Part III, contributing authors Tracy Friedel, Cindy Cruz, Daysi Diaz-Strong, Christina Gómez, Maria Luna-Duarte, and Erica Meiners supply dynamic descriptions of youth resistance to educational injustices in diverse contexts. Authors present new critical ethnographies and participatory action research projects which explore the possibilities and limitations of theories of youth resistance in educational research, and present new and expanded theories of youth responses to injustices in schooling.

Part III opens with a chapter by Monique Guishard and Eve Tuck (Chapter 13) that describes innovative methods in youth resistance research, and important ethical problems in resistance research. In what we hope will be an exceptionally useful chapter for researchers devising new projects in youth resistance, Guishard and Tuck provide pointers, anecdotes, and examples that highlight critical methodologies, youth participatory action research (yPAR), a re(en)visioning of research ethics, and the role of refusal in research.

In *Outdoor Education as a Site of Epistemological Persistence: Unsettling an Understanding of Urban Indigenous Youth Resistance* (Chapter 14), Tracy Friedel unsettles the very premises of urban Indigenous youth disconnection and resistance. Examining the case of Nêhiyawi (Cree) and Âpihtawikosisân (Métis) youth on the Canadian prairies, particularly their engagement with outdoor and place-based learning, Friedel shows how orality goes beyond the disruption of hegemonic curricula, serving to highlight cultural persistences that exist in the present. Echoing Robin Kelley's statement that to understand the 2012 movement in Egypt, we have to understand the decades of resistances and practices preceding it—we feel that Friedel's chapter, written before the Idle No More movement, provides valuable insights about the depth of urban Indigenous youth connections to land and intergenerational struggle—re-envisioning persistence as a theory of change.

LGBTQ Street Youth Doing Resistance in Infrapolitical Worlds (Chapter 15) is a rethinking of the embodied agency of LGBTQ street youth. Cindy Cruz observes that the often violent intersections of the body, race, gender, and sexuality, are where the "tight spaces" of youth resistance are engaged. This chapter examines how queer street youth create collective spaces *through* resistance and in order *to* resist. These are spaces of resistant sociality where youth can talk back just beneath the gaze of authority.

Daysi Diaz-Strong, Christina Gómez, Maria Luna-Duarte, and Erica Meiners collaboratively research and participate in the undocumented student movement. *Out for Immigration Justice: Thinking through Social and Political Change* (Chapter 16) examines in particular the public and intimate politics of "coming out" as a mode of resistance exercised by some of the 1.8 million undocumented youth that currently reside in the United States. They attend to the "*intellectual* and *dynamic* work" (p. 227, this volume) of social change, understanding how public discourse shifts, and how state repressive systems accommodate, retreat, and retaliate. They present a theory of change that, like many of the contributors in this book, highlights the capacity for organized people to respond to changing systems of domination.

We are extremely grateful and honored to have an Afterword by Ruth Wilson Gilmore. This Afterword is in part built upon a May 7, 2013 livestream discussion between Ruth Wilson Gilmore (in Europe at the time) and Laura Pulido (in Los Angeles) (see the recorded discussion at this link on http://inq13.gc.cuny.edu/module-12/). The discussion was part of a Participatory Open Online Course (POOC) called *Inq13: Reassessing Inequality and Reimagining the 21st Century, East Harlem Focus* facilitated by Wendy Luttrell, Caitlin Cahill and other faculty at The Graduate Center, The City University of New York. Gilmore urges us to reintroduce "that richness of resistance in many aspects of life back into the front of our consciousness." Her call to "bring the good thinking of *resistance is everywhere* back, without falling prey to the notion that all you have to do is point at something and say *it's resistance* and be done," resounds.

Final Words Before All of the Other Words

Over the course of this book project, we fell in and out of love and back again with (theories of) resistance; we understand why Michelle Fine (Chapter 3) told us the story of her relationship with resistance theory as though it were a love affair. Each of the many, many conversations that it took to bring forth this book left us with a different sense of resistance, some heart-wrenching, others uplifting. If resistance can be anything, why distinguish it from other human acts? If resistance is everywhere, why look in certain places? Conversely, if resistance only counts or matters if it is intentional, then how do we think about all of the other refusals of injustice that humans engage? These are the questions that seem to be the persistent ones, but they may also be the wrong questions.

Resistance has proved to be a complex concept, a fugitive subject. Drawing from Fred Moten (2008), the "fugitive movement is stolen life, and its relation to law is reducible neither to simple interdiction nor bare transgression" (p. 179). The lessons about change to learn from resistance's fugitive desires are quite complex. We hope that complexity prompts readers to engage resistance in ever more nuanced and attentive ways. We hope readers are inspired to find new and reclaimed ways of mapping resistance and the theories of change that animate resistance. We hope that this volume will ignite new love affairs with resistance, even though resistance doesn't much care if you love it or not.

Works Referenced

Ahmed-Ullah, N.S., Chase, J., & Secter, B. (2013, May 23). CPS approves largest school closure in Chicago's history. *Chicago Tribune*. Retrieved August 5, 2013 from http://articles.chicagotribune.com/2013-05-23/news/chi-chicago-school-closings-20130522_1_chicago-teachers-union-byrd-bennett-one-high-school-program

Akom, A. (April 01, 2011). Eco-Apartheid: Linking environmental health to educational outcomes. *Teachers' College Record*, 113, 4.

Apple, M. (2004). Between good sense and bad sense: Race, class, and learning from Learning to Labor. In N. Dolby & G. Dimitraidis (Eds.). *Learning to labor in new times*, pp. 61–82. New York: RoutledgeFalmer.

Aronowitz, S. (2004). Foreword to *Learning to labor in new times*. In N. Dolby & G. Dimitraidis (Eds.). *Learning to labor in new times*, pp. ix–xiii. New York: RoutledgeFalmer.

Arnot, M. (2004). Male working class identities and social justice: A reconsideration of Paul Willis' *Learning to Labor* in light of contemporary research. In N. Dolby & G. Dimitraidis (Eds.). *Learning to labor in new times*, pp. 17–40. New York: RoutledgeFalmer.

Barker, M., & Beezer, A. (1992). *Reading into cultural studies*. London: Routledge.

Barrera, J. (2013, March 26). Journey of Nishiyuu walker' names now "etched" into "history of this country." Aboriginal Peoples Television Network National News, n.p., March 26, 2013. Last accessed online on March 27, 2013 at http://aptn.ca/pages/news/2013/03/26/journey-of-nishiyuu-walkers-names-now-etched-into-history-of-this-country/

Brooks, L. (2008). *The common pot: The recovery of Native space in the Northeast*. Minneapolis: University of Minnesota Press.

Carnegie Council on Adolescent Development. (1992). *A matter of time: Risk and opportunity in the nonschool hours*. Washington, D.C.: Carnegie Council on Adolescent Development.

Collin, M. (2008). *The time of the rebels: Youth resistance movements and 21st century revolutions*. London: Serpent's Tail.

Cooper, A. J. (1892). *A voice from the South*. Xenia, OH: Aldine Printing House.

Deleuze, G., & Guattari, F. (1983). *Anti-Oedipus: Capitalism and schizophrenia*. Minneapolis: University of Minnesota Press.

Deleuze, G., & Guattari, P.F. (1987). *A thousand plateaus: Capitalism and schizophrenia*. Minneapolis: University of Minnesota Press.

Dimitriadis, G. (2011, January 1). Studying resistance: Some cautionary notes. *International Journal of Qualitative Studies in Education (qse)*, *24*, 5, 649–654.

Dolby, N., Dimitriadis, G., & Willis, P.E. (2004). *Learning to labor in new times*. New York: RoutledgeFalmer.

Fanon, F. (1963). *The wretched of the Earth*. New York: Grove Press.

Fenwick, L. (2013). http://www.washingtonpost.com/blogs/answer-sheet/wp/2013/05/28/ed-school-dean-urban-school-reform-is-really-about-land-development-not-kids/

Fine, M. (1991). *Framing dropouts: Notes on the politics of an urban public high school*. Albany, NY: State University of New York Press.

Goeman, M. (2013). *Mark my words: Native women mapping our nations*. Minneapolis: University of Minnesota Press.

Holliday, W. (n.d.). Hopi prisoners on the Rock. National Park Service. Last accessed May 25, 2013 at http://www.nps.gov/alca/historyculture/hopi-prisoners-on-the-rock.htm

Kwon, S.A. (2013). *Uncivil youth: Race, activism, and affirmative governmentality*. Durham, NC: Duke University Press.

Lavoie, J. (2013, May 22). It's Pkols, not Mount Douglas, marchers proclaim. *Times Colonist*, May 22, 2013, last accessed May 27, 2013 at http://www.timescolonist.com/news/local/it-s-pkols-not-mount-douglas-marchers-proclaim-1.228920

Lemert, C., & Bhan, E. (1998). *The voice of Anna Julia Cooper: Including* A voice from the South *and other important essays, papers, and letters*. Lanham, MD: Rowman & Littlefield.

Lipman, P. (2003). *High stakes education: Inequality, globalization, and urban school reform*. London: RoutledgeFalmer.

Lipman, P. (2011). *The new political economy of urban education: Neoliberalism, race, and the right to the city*. New York: Routledge.

McLaren, P. & Scatamburlo-D'Annibale, V. (2004). Paul Willis, class consciousness, and critical pedagogy: Toward a Socialist future. In N. Dolby & G. Dimitraidis (Eds.). *Learning to labor in new times*, pp. 41–60. New York: RoutledgeFalmer.

Moten, F. (2008, June 6). The case of Blackness. *Criticism: A Quarterly for Literature and the Arts, 50*, 2, 177–218.

Nolan, K. (2011). *Police in the hallways: Discipline in an urban high school.* Minneapolis: University of Minnesota Press.

Otero, L., & Cammarota, J. (2011, January 1). Notes from the Ethnic Studies home front: Student protests, texting, and subtexts of oppression. *International Journal of Qualitative Studies in Education, 24*, 5, 639–648.

Ramsey, I.T. (1964). *Models and mystery.* London: Oxford University Press.

Ruglis, J. (2009). Death of a dropout: (Re)theorizing school dropout and schooling as a social determinant of health. Ph.D. Thesis, City University of New York, 2009.

Ruglis, J. (2011, January 1). Mapping the Biopolitics of School Dropout and Youth Resistance. *International Journal of Qualitative Studies in Education (qse), 24*, 5, 627–637.

Sakiestewa, G. M. (2010). *Education beyond the mesas: Hopi students at Sherman Institute, 1902–1929.* Lincoln: University of Nebraska Press.

Simpson, L. (2013, January 16). Fish broth and fasting [blog post]. Divided No More [blog]. Last accessed May 13, 2013 at http://dividednomore.ca/2013/01/16/fish-broth-fasting/

Skeggs, B. (1992). Paul Willis, Learning to Labour. In M. Barker, & A. Beezer (Eds.). *Reading into cultural studies.*, pp. 181–196. London: Routledge

Tuck, E. (2010). Breaking up with Deleuze: Desire and valuing the irreconcilable. *International Journal of Qualitative Studies in Education, 23*, 5, 635–650.

Tuck, E. (2013). Locating the hope in bone-deep participation. In T.M. Kress & R. Lake (Eds.). *We saved the best for youth: Letters of hope, imagination, and wisdom for 21st century educators,* pp. 11–14. Rotterdam, Netherlands: Sense Publishers.

Tuck, E., & Yang, K.W. (2011). Youth resistance revisited: New theories of youth negotiations of educational injustices. *International Journal of Qualitative Studies in Education, 24*, 5, 521–530.

Tuck, E. & Yang, K.W. (2012). Decolonization is not a metaphor. *Decolonization: Indigeneity, Education and Society, 1*, 1, 1–40.

Weiss, J. (2011). Valuing youth resistance before and after public protest. *International Journal of Qualitative Studies in Education, 24*, 5, 595–599.

Willis, P.E. (1981). *Learning to labor: How working class kids get working class jobs.* New York: Columbia University Press.

Willis, P.E. (1990). *Common culture: Symbolic work at play in the everyday cultures of the young.* Milton Keynes: Open University Press.

Willis, P.E. (2004). Twenty-five years later on: Old books, new times. In N. Dolby & G. Dimitraidis (Eds.). *Learning to labor in new times*, pp. 167–196. New York: RoutledgeFalmer.

Woodson, C.G. (1933). *The mis-education of the Negro.* Philadelphia, PA: Hakims.

Yang, K.W. (2008, March 7). Organizing MySpace: Youth walkouts, pleasure, politics, and new media. *Educational Foundations, 21*, 9–28.

Zeller-Berkman, S. (2012, May 1). Occupying youth development: The pitfalls and potential of literacy policies and youth development. *Journal of Adolescent & Adult Literacy, 55*, 8, 748–750.

PART I

The History and Emergence of Youth Resistance in Educational Research

Introduction to Part I

Eve Tuck and K. Wayne Yang

One of the most exciting features of this volume is the following section, filled to the brim with chapters crafted from interviews with foundational authors in youth resistance research. To create the chapters, we traveled around the United States to meet with authors to discuss their trajectory-setting works, their thinking on resistance then and now, and other musings big and small on change and possibility.

We crafted each chapter using a transcript from interviews with each author. We tried very hard to keep the writing sounding like their voices sounded to us, to keep a cadence to the writing that reflects the swiftness and generosity of their thinking.

We met Michelle Fine in her office at The Graduate Center, The City University of New York in midtown Manhattan. Our questions prodded her to tell us the story of her thinking on resistance, which resulted in the crafted chapter titled *An Intimate Memoir of Resistance Theory* (Chapter 3). Indeed, the chapter reveals a love story between Fine and resistance theory, spanning more than three decades to the very early works in the field. Fine shares why she fell in love with those early works, worries over the conflation of resistance as a way of looking at and theorizing human behavior, and resistance as a mobilization against injustice—"Both are stunningly important," she told us, "but they are not the same" (Fine, this volume, p. 47). Fine's emphasis that "resistance is an epistemology, a line of vision" (p. 49) is a profound contribution (a reminder, really) to the field and to this volume. So too is her call for resistance researchers to engage with youth and communities about what could be, that is, a radical re-imagination for educational justice.

On our drive from New York to New Haven to meet and interview James C. Scott, we were desperately curious about how he would answer our questions pertaining to others' interpretations of his works, especially with regard to intentionality. He greeted us warmly to his office on the Yale campus, and we made ourselves comfortable as he shared with us backstories and insights about his expansive ideas on resistance, change, anarchy, and the explosive power of the first public declaration of the hidden transcript. Though Scott's last direct analysis of resistance was completed in 1990, his conceptualizations circulate forcefully through the field of youth resistance, albeit not always accurately. The chapter crafted from our interview, *Leaking Away and other forms of Resistance* (Chapter 4) addresses some of the misconceptions about Scott's work, but also, more recent ideas related to seeing (not) like a state, living outside the state, and the (non) ethicality of resistance. Especially helpful in Scott's crafted chapter is his differentiation between system-compatible resistance—those that make demands that are "digestible by the political system"—and system-incompatible resistance, that which happens beyond the spectrum of the state and funding agencies (p. 65). For the most part, in Scott's view, youth resistance takes place beyond that spectrum of visibility and recoverability/absorption into the practices of the state.

Our interview with Pedro Noguera took place in his office at New York University, also in Manhattan. We were profoundly impacted by Noguera's observations about organizing, a theme he returned to again and again in the interview. It took us several times to really hear him, it seems, because at first we thought he was telling us about the power of social movements. More than midway through the conversation, it dawned on us that—Noguera was (patiently) teaching us to pay attention to organizing as what matters in social movements, in social change. We came away from that interview with an understanding of the significance of organizing in theories of change that prioritize social movements, but also the hollowness of theories of change regarding social movements which *do not* take the significance of organizing seriously: Without theorizing organizing and what it does to support and enact social movements, we might inaccurately attribute the effectiveness of some movements over others to a random perfect storm of conditions (e.g. reduce the actions of Rosa Parks to being in the right place at the right time, and ignore her training at the Highlander Center); or we might foreclose ordinary people's influence in state affairs through a reliance on elected leaders (see Noguera's discussion of the Obama administration in the chapter). *Organizing Resistance into Social Movements* (Chapter 5) brings those same insights to the page.

We met Robin D.G. Kelley in his light-filled home in West Hollywood, and seated around his family's table we learned about what history knows about resistance. Kelley's interview, crafted into the chapter called *Resistance as Revelatory* (Chapter 6), was wholly generous and connecting, at once an autobiography and a genealogy of resistance. The questions that he has returned to time and again are: Why do so many people not resist? Why does consent work so well? He describes the need he saw to move away from a post-industrial framing to a neoliberal framing in order to document "neoliberalism's conscious, active privatization and commoditization of people's misery through the expansion of prisons" (p. 86). He emphasized the diagnostic power of resistance, to indicate locations of desire, pain, trouble, confusion. In this way, resistance is revelatory, but not necessarily capable of doing anything to make needed change. Thus, he taught us, "our job as historians, scholars, theorists, as social interpreters [is] to find out what these acts are telling us" (p. 87).

When Eve and Greg Dimitriadis entered Signithia Fordham's campus office in Rochester, New York, they were immediately enveloped by her hospitality. After introductions, we dug in to a fascinating conversation, which resulted in the crafted chapter, *What Does an Umbrella Do for the Rain?* (Chapter 7) Fordham told the origin story of her influential acting-white hypothesis, stressing the significance she saw in the burdens of acting white. She spoke to the simultaneous desires of people on the margins away from failure and toward success—one might think of those as one and the same, but as we learned in our conversation, there are different motivations at work. Fordham spoke to the humanness of resistance, while also expressing feelings of frustration with resistance. Likening resistance to an umbrella in the rain, she observes, "It doesn't change the rain, it doesn't keep the rain from falling, it does nothing to the rain" (p. 102). She wondered if transformation is the more compelling frame, and spoke to the limitations of resistance.

Gerald Vizenor's beautiful home in Naples, Florida was a serene setting for our interview. Vizenor's concept of *survivance*—resistance/active presence/the transmotion of Indigenous sovereignty—has been taken up and embraced by all corners of the Indigenous world. His interview took us behind the scenes of his works in theory, fiction, and poetry. Vizenor's articulation of the power of language as resistance flexed our prior understandings. He told stories, stories within stories, while at the same time theorizing stories as "holograms," "a kind of visual memory that depended on the situation and circumstances" (p. 110). His stories dramatized the need for resistance even and especially within mass movements. He was magnanimous when our questions revealed that we didn't quite understand how to hear the stories, and prodded us away from the questions that were false paths. Several of the stories Vizenor told us appear in the crafted chapter, *Resistance in the Blood* (Chapter 8), but several do not. As the day grew late and we continued our conversation over dinner, we made peace with the idea that too much was said to ever convey it with justice. We appreciated the parts of the conversation that were just for us.

The very first chapter in Part I is by Greg Dimitriadis, called *Resistance: The Anatomy of an Idea* (Chapter 2). In it, Dimitriadis engages the writings and interviews with all of the authors, in order to provide a context of the significance of their works, but also a rendering of the emergence of the field of youth resistance research. Dimitriadis begins with resistance theories that were coming out of Post-WWII France delineating the tendency or underbelly to resistance that seems to hanker for a kind of rigidity or calcification. He concludes with a discussion of the responsibility for imagining, not rigidity, that is at the heart of our work as youth resistance researchers.

As you will see, each of the authors elaborated their own definitions of resistance. Each crafted chapter represents a different unpacking, nay, a different *unboxing* of resistance, so that reading across doesn't allow an analogous reading. It isn't possible to say, for example, "Well, Fordham defines resistance as this and as going in this direction whereas Vizenor defines it as this with this trajectory." The chapters are in conversation, yes, but they do not always correspond; in fact they rarely do, in thought-provoking ways. The authors' theorizations are sometimes cross-referential, but even in so doing, they work with each other's ideas in ways that are wholly creative and generative, are made their own. In entering these chapters, we enter the thought worlds of each theorist, forsaking all others, just for the length of time it takes to read and revisit the chapter. In this way, your reading might be like our experience of conducting the interviews—not something to easily synthesize or categorize and file away, but an education to keep reflecting upon in the years to come.

2

RESISTANCE

The Anatomy of an Idea

Greg Dimitriadis

As Tony Judt (2011) argues in *Past Imperfect: French Intellectuals, 1944–1965*, the notion of "resistance" came largely to define intellectual life in France after World War II. In the wake of Germany's occupation of France, writers and other intellectuals developed a keen moral language about the intellectual's commitment and responsibility to human freedom. Part of this had to do with France's anxieties about its own intellectual life under occupation. Who had collaborated? Who had resisted? Was the latter always explicit or were the cues more subtle? Judt writes:

> The source of this unique vulnerability on the part of France's post-war intellectual community is to be found less in wartime experience itself than in the vocabulary, the moral language that it has inherited from this experience. (p. 48)

He continues:

> The experience of occupation and resistance, however one has behaved, thus taught the overwhelming importance of choice and commitment and the weight that could attach to the way in which one expressed these. (p. 57)

No one stakes out these issues more clearly than Jean Paul Sartre, perhaps the major French intellectual of the era. According to Sartre's well-known essay "What Is Literature?" "literature throws you into battle. Writing is a certain way of wanting freedom; once you have begun, you are committed, willy-nilly" (Sartre, 2001, p. 277).

Postwar France is but one place to begin to interrogate the question of resistance—including the ways it can be "calcified" and linked to versions of social change that remain rigidly dogmatic. There are many other origin stories one might draw upon to understand resistance and many other trajectories that could have been traced in this discussion. The notion of "resistance" is a large and conceptually protean one. The interviews that follow focus on several key, contemporary figures—Michelle Fine, James C. Scott, Pedro Noguera, Robin D.G. Kelley, Signithia Fordham, and Gerald Vizenor—all of whom have their own stories, their own starting points, and their own lineages to draw upon. As you will see, lines can be traced from W.E.B. DuBois to Grace Lee Boggs, from Antonio Gramsci to Paulo Freire, from struggles in the global North (such as the Civil Rights Movement in the U.S.) to those in the global South (such as the revolution in El Salvador). As Michelle Fine notes, resistance is linked to what Marcuse called "the great refusal"—"a great refusal of false consciousness, of passivity, of conformity"—of the press to see people as dupes of systems they cannot hope to understand. Gerald Vizenor's work has theorized resistance through the development of his concept of survivance, the active presence of Indigenous life in the face of colonization. Resistance has become both a diagnostic tool—a prism through which to understand complex social and political events—as well as a style of intellectual activity. A central concern of this volume is the work we ask the concept of resistance to perform—and if, perhaps, as argued by Signithia Fordham, we ask it to do too much.

In this chapter, I will reflect on some contemporary currents around the role and importance of "resistance." As I will argue, work in the area has highlighted the often-unacknowledged stream of everyday activities that can gird large-scale political movements. This chapter discusses how resistance has emerged as an orientating construct in the field, as well as how several luminaries have struggled in powerful ways with its possibilities. I will also point out some tensions in this construct—tensions around the role of the intellectual as well as the dangers of theoretical rigidity. As I will show, the construct is always in danger of reification or "calcification," and it has been employed in recent years to refer to an increasingly narrowed set of practices and activities. Researchers and activists face an ongoing struggle to treat resistance as a fluid and dynamic construct. In sum, this chapter offers a critical diagnosis of "resistance" and its uses past, present, and future.

I have chosen to begin this essay in post-War France as it crystallizes many of the complexities and anxieties around the notion of "resistance" as an explanatory tool and rhetorical device. (But, again, I could have chosen others, as noted above.) The notion of "resistance" here was wed to a high-stakes struggle between two Manichean world-views as well as a teleological approach to historical change. In the emerging Cold War landscape, the world was increasingly defined for Western intellectuals between the USA and the USSR. The former represented a triumph of capitalism, the latter a triumph of communism. Or perhaps most accurately, the USSR represented the best real world hope for a committed socialist world revolution while the USA represented the final death of that vision. In this case of French intellectuals, commitment to communism and the USSR became a litmus test of one's political bona fides. Allegiance to the USA meant a broad (and unforgivable) sympathy with the forces of reactionary anti-communism. One either supported the USSR even in its violent excesses or one didn't. There were no other choices.

What emerged was a highly charged language of moral and political commitments. The notion of "resistance" carried a tremendous weight in the intellectual imagination—one that always looked towards the possibility of "revolution" in virtually all of ones choices and commitments. One's commitment to freedom and "revolution" was a sometimes subtle affair, however, as was the notion of "collaboration" itself. As Judt (2011) writes,

> Collaboration, it seemed, was a state of mind, not merely [or only] a political or social choice. All democratic societies, Sartre asserted, contained "collaborators" in their midst, even (especially) when the collaborator does not realize his (or her) own condition. The solution was not to identify and execute a few "traitors" but to make a revolution. (p. 52)

The work of the intellectual was to clarify and expose those states of mind that could contribute to world revolution and those that could impede it. One can hardly imagine a more audacious and expansive a project for intellectuals to give themselves. Writers, intellectuals, and academics were no longer on the sidelines of world affairs. They centered themselves as arbiters of a complex, high-stakes political landscape.

This stress on "resistance" implied an "all or nothing" approach to social change. It implied, as well, a teleological approach to history. That is, standing for communism meant for many French intellectuals standing on the right side of a forward-moving history of the proletariat. This "all or nothing" approach did not allow intellectuals to remain ambivalent—particularly on the question of the Soviet Union. This became extremely thorny when many of Stalin's abuses (such as the so-called "show trials" of the 1930s) became public knowledge. Many like Sartre demanded a fundamental fidelity to the USSR regardless and were willing to overlook its violence and its excesses. Others like his one-time friend Albert Camus would not toe the party line. Camus wrote that "Marxism as an absolute philosophy" justified and legitimated murder. "In the Marxian perspective . . . a hundred thousand corpses are nothing if they are the price of happiness of hundreds of millions of men" (quoted in Aronson, 2004, p. 89). Friendships were fractured and a "with us or against us" attitude came to mark the left French intellectual scene. If nothing else, the responsibility of the intellectual was put front and center—a theme I will return to at the end of this chapter.

With the scene thus set, I turn now to more contemporary concerns and currents.

Taking Culture Seriously: Cultural Studies and its Responses

One can trace many strands of current academic work on resistance to the Birmingham School of Cultural Studies, born in an era of disillusionment with the British Communist Party. As Michael Berube (2011) notes,

> born at a time of postwar crisis and left realignment in 1956, cultural studies marked the British New Left's break with the calcified orthodoxy of the British Communist Party, aptly symbolized by the latter's defense of the Soviet Union's invasion of Hungary. (p. 38)

He goes on to note that cultural studies "attained its maturity" in the late 1970s when its members undertook a series of studies of subculture and media studies.

Work in cultural studies was largely influenced by theoretical concerns around the contemporary inheritances of Marxism. Traditionally, Marxism treated "culture" as an extension of "class." That is to say, all behavior and action were determined by capitalism "in the last instance," to echo the (then) enormously influential Louis Althusser. Drawing on the work of Antonio Gramsci, cultural studies saw culture as a site of struggle, with young people both actively resisting and reproducing the class positions in which they found themselves. Scholars like E.P. Thompson, Stuart Hall, Raymond Williams and Richard Hoggard all opened up important questions about the role of "culture" in the lives of young people—work extended by Paul Willis, Dick Hebdige, Angela McRobbie, and others.

Learning to Labor: How Working Class Kids Get Working Class Jobs (1977) was one of the very first books to take seriously notions of youth agency and resistance. In this study, Willis followed a group of about 12 working-class youth in a depressed, industrial town he calls Hammertown. Willis followed this small group throughout their school and work days, attending classes and leisure activities and, at points, accompanying them onto the shop floor. These working-class boys created a culture of resistance that largely defined the group.

> The most basic, obvious and explicit dimension of counter-school culture [was] entrenched general and personal opposition to "authority." This feeling [was] easily verbalized by "the lads" (the self-elected title of those in the counter-school culture. (p. 11)

This oppositional culture inverted dominant values. "Diligence, deference, and respect" are all emptied of value—indeed, are actively resisted (p. 12).

Willis reads this resistant, counter-culture in nearly all of the everyday cultural practices of these youth, a "style" that was "lived out in countless small ways which [were] special to the school institution, instantly recognized by the teachers, and an almost ritualistic part of the daily fabric of life for the kids" (p. 12).

These boys spent their days "dosing, blagging, and wagging." Above all else, "having a laff" was key.

> Opposition to the school [was] principally manifested in the struggle to win symbolic and physical space from the institution and its rules and to defeat its main perceived purpose: to make you "work." (p. 26)

For the lads, carving out their own space in this school was a daily struggle, filled with small victories. It was not only that the lads drank alcohol, for example. They made a point of drinking it on school time, during lunch. The lads saw school as a meaningless delay on their way to the world of real work. Importantly, the oppositional culture that these youth enacted was a culture mirrored on the "shop floor" they saw themselves heading towards. This was a world of physical, manual work—a world where aggressive, everyday camaraderie reigned supreme. Just as the lads tried to "get over" on their teachers and carve out their own quotidian autonomy, shop floor workers did the same with their bosses.

> Shop floor culture also rests on the same fundamental organizational unit as counter-school culture. The informal group locates and makes possible all its other elements. It is the zone where strategies for wrestling control of symbolic and other space from official authority are generated and disseminated. (p. 54)

In valorizing work and demonizing school, the lads emulated the lives of their parents and thus their place in the class structure of the United Kingdom. The cultural dimensions of their lives made the decision to work "on the shop floor" a seemingly empowering one. This, in turn, helped them to reproduce their class position. This tension between "reproduction" of and "resistance" to authority would help define a generation of work in critical youth studies.

Willis' great insight here was to explore the importance of cultural dynamics of class reproduction. In many ways, this book was an answer to the riddle with which he opens the book:

> The difficult thing to explain about how middle class kids get middle class jobs is why others let them. The difficult thing to explain about how working class kids get working class jobs is why they let themselves. (p. 1)

Willis underscores a concern central to generations of Marxist scholars—how and why are people complicit in their own class reproduction? Why don't they revolt against the system? One could not only take recourse to the traditional "false consciousness" nostrum—that is, the working classes are somehow "tricked" into operating against their interests. Willis' focus on the cultural dynamics of people's lives was meant to disrupt overly deterministic theories of social reproduction. That is, he intervened in a body of work that looked only to the structures that organize and oppress people. We see this in earlier doctrinaire notions of Marxism that tended to imply deterministic, class-based notions of history and social change. Willis allowed us to see how culture was critical here, as was resistance itself, in why those structures worked. While the language of "resistance" implied something less rigid than fidelity to a particular political party, it still was linked to a Marxist agenda.

Others have approached the question of resistance with a more open-ended sense of politics and political change. For example, James C. Scott's *Domination and the Arts of Resistance* (1990) powerfully foregrounds the notion of everyday resistance in understanding historical change. Scott's work eschews Marxist, tele-ological notions of social change, and his politics are closer to anarchism. As he (2012) recently wrote in *Two Cheers for Anarchism*:

> The condensation of history, our desire for clean narratives, and the need for elites and organizations to project an image of control and purpose all conspire to convey a false image of historical causation. They blind us to the fact that most revolutions are not the work of revolutionary parties but the precipitate of spontaneous and improvised action . . . that organ-ized social movements are usually the product, not the cause, of uncoor-dinated protests and demonstrations, and that the great emancipatory gains for human freedom have not been the result of orderly, institutional pro-cedures but of disorderly, unpredictable, spontaneous action cracking open the social order from below. (2012, p. 141)

In his interview for this volume, Scott underscores how "resistance" can be calci-fied into serving the imperatives of the state, including those driven by a com-mitment to Marxism:

> And almost all of these revolutions that led to changes in the state ended up producing governments that were just as bad or worse than the govern-ment that they had thrown out . . . there was something mistaken about looking to new state structures as the structure for emancipation. (p. 69)

As we will see, Scott offers particularly trenchant critiques of "false conscious-ness" and other cornerstones of Marxist and neo-Marxist thought.

Domination and the Arts of Resistance is an extended argument about the role and function of "hidden transcripts" vs. "public transcripts" in social change. Scott maintains that both the dominant and subordinate groups have developed "onstage" and "offstage" conversations, though elites often have the luxury of having their stories synch in more seamless ways. The oppressed often have to develop more coded or hidden ways to communicate. His notion of "hidden transcripts" is often at direct odds with the notion of "false consciousness"—or that the oppressed are often "duped" into believing and acting in ways that are not in their best interests. According to Scott, this notion of "false consciousness" denies the ongoing wellspring of resistance that is often nurtured in oppressed groups and people—and can find voice at key moments. "[T]he explosive and symbolic power of the first public declaration of the hidden transcript in the face of power . . . is always dangerous, always explosive" (Scott, this volume, p. 63). The moment can be (quite literally) world changing.

Scott offers a particularly powerful and interesting reading of the aforementioned *Learning to Labor*. By contrast to the so-called "lads"—everyday, resistant working-class youth – the "ear'oles" listened to teachers, deferred to school authority and all it represented. As Willis points out, the lads felt superior to the ear'oles, felt they were living their lives to the fullest while these conformist youth were passive and inactive. Scott's reading of *Learning to Labor* alerts us to its perhaps counter-intuitive insights: that the ear'oles pose a much greater threat to the social order. This is a key point. Willis' investment in neo-Marxist approaches to change tended to valorize the role of the lads. Perhaps Scott's less prescriptive theoretical investments opened him up to another possibility—that the conformist youth were the real revolutionaries. He writes, "The system may have the most to fear from those subordinates among whom the institutions of hegemony have been most successful" (p. 107). We see this in the contemporary role of the disenfranchised middle classes in sparking some of the important contemporary revolts and revolutions—including those associated with the Arab Spring or the Occupy Movement. As the political maxim goes, there's nothing more dangerous to an authoritarian regime than those who are unemployed and college-educated.

Race Rebels: Historical Perspectives on Race and Resistance

Robin Kelley's *Race Rebels: Culture, Politics, and the Black Working Class* (1996) picks up many of these arguments about the power of everyday resistance as well as the limits of movement politics. This work is largely informed by Marxist notions of social change—a stress on the "making of new working classes" as they emerge from revolution and resistance (p. 5)—though they are rooted in the struggles and histories of African Americans. For this project, Kelley draws on the works of W.E.B. DuBois and C.L.R. James, noting they are important precedents to texts like Marxist historian E.P. Thompson's *The Making of the English Working Class*. Kelley takes Scott's term "infrapolitics" and connects it to the everyday histories "from below" that often go beyond the purview of "official" histories of politics and political struggles (p. 8). He notes, "I want to suggest that the political history of oppressed people cannot be understood without reference to infrapolitics, for these daily acts have a cumulative effect on power relations" (p. 8). Kelley considerably expands "what counts" as politics here to include a wide range of cultural practices—songs, jokes, stories, as well as everyday resistance to official authority. Taken together, infrapolitcs challenges traditional approaches to historical change:

> Too often politics is defined by how people participate rather than why; by traditional definition the question of what is political hinges on whether or not groups are involved in elections, political parties, or grass-roots social movements. (*ibid*)

Kelley argues that shifting the focus to the "why" question,

> to what motivated disenfranchised black working people to struggle and what strategies they developed, we may discover their participation in "mainstream" politics—including their battle for the franchise—grew out of the very circumstances, experiences, and memories that impelled many to steal from their employer, join a mutual benefit association, or spit in a bus driver's face. (p. 9)

Kelley details the ways everyday workplace practices were sites of subversion and resistance in the Jim Crow South. For example, Southern domestic workers created a "code of ethics" between them, including sharing collective knowledge on which employers were abusive or unfair. North Carolina tobacco workers would employ collective strategies to control the flow of work—including strategically timed slowdowns. On these tobacco stemmers, he writes,

> On the factory floor, where stemmers were generally not allowed to sit or talk to one another, it was not uncommon for women to break out in song. Singing in unison not only reinforced a collective identity but the songs themselves—religious hymns, for he most part—ranged from veiled protests against the daily indignities of the factory to utopian visions of a life free from difficult wage work. (p. 18).

Kelley highlights the ways everyday resistance can be diagnostic of historical change more readily than official histories of organized movements, iconic leaders, etc. His later work has extended this line of critique; in *Freedom Dreams* (2003) he notes that "I spent more than half my life writing about people who tried to change the world, largely because I, too, wanted to change the world" (p. ix). Kelley concedes however that these dreams of a new world—particularly those rooted in Marxism and utopic "third world" visions—never materialized.

Kelley turns squarely to the radical, utopic dreams that have helped constitute the "black radical imagination." These dreams are not constrained by Marxist ideology or particular notions of "the real." For example, looking to "The Marvelous" among diasporic Africans, he notes,

> The surrealists are talking about total transformation of society, not just granting aggrieved populations greater political and economic power. They are speaking of new social relationships, new ways of living and interacting, new attitudes towards work and leisure and community. (p. 5)

Kelley locates traces of this surrealism in the poetry of Aime Cesaire and his "Discourse on Colonialism" as well as the work of bop jazz artist Thelonius Monk. He writes,

> juxtaposing surrealisms and black conceptions of liberation is no mere academic exercise; it is an injunction, a proposition, perhaps even a declaration of war. I am suggesting that the black freedom movement take a long, hard look at our own surreality as well as surrealist thought and practice in order to build new movements, new possibilities, new conceptions of liberation. (p. 192)

Kelley offers a powerful corrective to those who would lock their studies into Manichean struggles between oppressors and resistors—the language of clarity associated with many writers and intellectuals. Most importantly, we see Kelley's own ideas about social change evolve over time—moving from an investment in the teleologies of Marxism and neo-Marxism to more open-ended theories of change.

Education: Perspectives on Resistance

Work on resistance has become particularly important for the field of education—a fact evidenced by this collection as a whole. Willis' study was also foundational in this regard. Resistance has given educators another way to understand youth— not as disobedient or noncompliant individuals – but as active political agents. Resistance has also given educators a way to redefine their own roles away from passive or "objective" spectators in political or historical processes. These intertwined phenomena are worth exploring a bit more.

Much of the earliest critical work in education was interested in questions of economic reproduction. In particular, Bowles and Gintis (1977) defined a trajectory of research concerned with how schools reproduce structural economic inequalities by inculcating compliant mental habits and dispositions. Famously, this work treated schools as "black boxes" and was pessimistic about the potential for education in a capitalist context. "Our approach to US education suggests that movements for educational reform have faltered though refusing to call into question the basic structure of property and power in economic life" (p. 14). In responding to structural Marxists like Bowles and Gintis, a generation of theorists and researchers came to stress "resistance." While work out of the UK like Willis' tended to stress class reproduction and resistance, work in the US tended to take up questions of race and other nodes of inequality. Much of this work took place in education and related fields, where resistance would imply resistance to school.

For some like Ogbu and Fordham, this meant a sharp focus on race. As John Ogbu made clear many years ago, there are crucial distinctions in the US between "voluntary" and "involuntary" immigrants—that is, immigrants who came to this society by force versus those who came by will. According to Ogbu, low achievement among African American youth could be theorized as an "adaption" to their caste-like status as involuntary minorities. In many ways, this failure was a fait accompli of a "Black ecological structure" that "set many of these youth up for failure" (Fordham, 1996, p. 69). By observing a "job ceiling" in their families over time, these youth learn "both to avoid seeking certain categories of jobs" and also "to resist the legitimating of such categories" (p. 69).

Signithia Fordham's work extended these concerns to the "expressive dimension of the relationship between the dominant culture and Black Americans" (p. 69). Indeed, Fordham's book *Blacked Out* explores the ways African American youth "imagine" themselves as part of larger kinship systems—ones that they engage with in different and distinct ways. If Ogbu's work tended to focus on history as an empirical accumulation of persistent marginalization, Fordham extended this focus to human agency in individual and communal expression and imagination.

Fordham's book considers how "success" is experienced and defined by both high-achieving and low-achieving African American youth at a school she calls "Capital High." Her research questions include: "Why do Black students resist school-sanctioned learning?" and "What are some of the costs associated with school success for African American adolescents?" According to Fordham, these youth were engaged in a long process of reclaiming their blackness in an oppressive set of circumstances. Thus, as she clarifies in her interview for this volume, her main interest was understanding the burden of acting white:

> What I remained excited about was the possibility of theorizing *the burden of acting white*. Of course, I recognized this burden and its consequences from my own childhood. But I wanted to understand how classrooms manifest the tension of schools success as acting white and what happens to Black youth who want to achieve in school, but don't want to be turned into the other in doing so. They want to succeed in school, but don't want to do so at the costs of losing membership in an important community. (see page 98, this volume).

While other scholars and researcher have taken on the notion of acting white, they do not always attend to its tremendous burdens—something Fordham has taken great pains to document.

She highlights several groups that emerged from her study: the high achievers, who resisted Otherness by conforming, and the underachievers who refused to "liquidate" their selves. The high-achieving students often "act white" as a strategy of pretending or masquerading as "(an)Other" (p. 238). These students are motivated by two factors. They believe that they can prove racists wrong and will be able to "remain the rightful identity of African-Americans and obtain the same opportunities and rewards as their White cohorts" (p. 328). Second, they want to "avenge the dehumanization of their Black ancestors by appropriating and inverting the myth of intellectual inferiority" (p. 329). Such success often comes at great cost to these youth who have to develop a complicated "double consciousness" to be able to psychically survive. In contrast, the underachievers do not often deploy such efforts to imitate appropriate Otherness. These students see racism as clear evidence that they should "oppose and resist the dominant society's appropriation efforts. Their general response is to shun all efforts perceived as impersonating or imitating the Other" (p. 331). These students reject school often through avoidance.

Work in education has tended to use resistance as a way to understand and unlock data. According to Fordham, "resistance" was the key to helping her struggle with this data. She notes that her initial observations of the school tempted her to label the underachieving students as somehow deficient or lacking access to middle-class values. Yet failure as lack was not an adequate explanation—and she turned to "resistance as an explanation for academic failure . . . as well as a form for agency for dominated populations" (1996, p. 339). Fordham's writing is very clear that this was a personal struggle for her—one in which she was deeply implicated. She was very much intertwined in the lives of these young people. In the end, she was able to offer a discussion of "blackness" as a highly contested construct—one struggled over, linked to imagined communities and fictive ties.

Michelle Fine's *Framing Dropouts: Notes on the Politics of an Urban Public High School* (1994a) takes up similar such concerns and is another example of a school-based ethnography that deploys resistance as an organizing trope. Fine discusses the phenomena of young people "dropping out" at a single urban high school she calls Comprehensive High School (CHS). As she reports, only 20 percent of incoming students end up graduating from this school. Fine steps back and asks the question—how do we "frame" or understand this problem? How do we "frame" dropouts? As Fine argues, schooling works largely to "silence" youth. Authentic and vibrant participation is not validated. In some sense, success equals silence. As she writes, "*Silencing* provides a metaphor for the structural, ideological, and practical organization of comprehensive high schools." She continues,

> Although the press for silencing is by no means complete or hermetic. . . . low income schools officially contain rather than explore social and economic contradiction, condone rather than critique prevailing social and economic inequalities, and usher children and adolescents into ideologies and ways of interpreting social evidence that legitimate rather than challenge conditions of inequality. (p. 61)

This complex problem of silencing is at the heart of life at CHS. Those who are silenced typically graduate. Those who aren't typically don't. Both options entail great costs—the former, mostly psychological, the latter, mostly social.

As Fine shows, charged topics such as health, sexuality, crime, racism, and economic inequality are not taken up in their multi-faceted complexity. Students are often asked to think about such issues within prescribed and limiting confines, in ways that don't often make sense. Contrary or disruptive talk is not rewarded. Critical discourse—talk which often contains the "seeds" of incipient and powerful social critique—is averted. She writes,

> These adolescents live in communities in which the rhetoric that stresses education as the route to social mobility is subverted by daily evidence to the contrary, and they are as suspect of the economic prospects of a diploma as they are cynical about the social distinction between "legit" and "illegit" ways to make a living. (p. 107)

Young people often develop complicated and contradictory ideas about such issues—and have no place to explore them. "They know no safe, public sphere in which to analyze, mourn, and make sense out of these contradictions" (p. 107). When compounded by personal problems, including problems at home, many see leaving school as the most logical choice. All of these forces thus conspire to force many young people to "drop out"—often with the goal of getting a GED, joining the military, or entering a professional or proprietary school of some kind.

As in Willis' study, many of these youth experience dropping out as an empowering moment—a moment when they can reclaim their own dignity. In fact, Fine argues that many who do resist in this fashion are the most psychologically healthy. Those who submit to the silencing often do so at great cost to themselves. Like Fordham, Fine is interested in the "cost of success" and the power of opting out of school structures and cultures. She notes, "Dropouts failed in traditional academic terms. But perhaps, ironically, they retained intact some connection, even if problematic and temporary, to community, kin, peers, and racial/ethnic identity" (p. 135). In counter-distinction, those academic success stories

> seem to deny, repress, or dismiss the stories of failure, and resist undaunted in their personal crusade against the odds. The costs to graduate, in terms of their psychological vulnerability, disrupted connections to kin and community, and fragmented racial identities, remain undocumented. (p. 134)

Resistance and Activism

Resistance has functioned as an effective diagnostic tool for understanding youth (in particular, to keep them out of "deficit spaces") as a well as a trope for academics looking to redefine their own roles in more active and politicized ways. Fine and others have pushed work on resistance in order to redefine their own role both "in the field" and "at the desk." The notion that we can take on multiple such roles was developed in Fine's well-known book chapter, "Working the Hyphens: Reinventing the Self and Other in Qualitative Research" (1994b) from the *Handbook of Qualitative Research*—a chapter that serves to explore and extend same of the methodological issues which gird *Framing Dropouts*. As Fine argues in this noted article, research subjects are typically "othered" in qualitative research. Following Clifford, Pratt, and others, Fine observes that research participants are made into neat fictions—often flattened-out characters in the ethnographer's imagination.

Yet, Fine maintains here that this self/other dichotomy needs to be continually worked out and through, thought and rethought. Researchers need to work not to "other" all those who do not fit some imagined, dominant mainstream. Among other strategies, she suggests academic work that looks towards social change. This need to be done without further romanticizing the groups one works with—a particular danger in work on resistance. Researchers today are facing new, ethical demands from nearly every direction and quarter. The notion of the disinterested, neutral observer has been called inextricably into question, forcing researchers to take new kinds of responsibilities for their work, both in the field and at the desk.

I would like to briefly explore one such response to this moment—Youth Participatory Action Research (YPAR). Contributions by both Michelle Fine and Pedro Noguera have been key in this response. YPAR is a particular method of researching with youth. But it also reflects a more basic set of assumptions about how knowledge is produced and created. As Tuck and Fine (2007) write, YPAR has the following characteristics:

> the design is collaboratively negotiated and co-constructed; research questions are co-constructed; there is a transparency on all matters of the research, from administrative details like institutional review board approval to the budget to the theory and reasoning behind practice; analysis is co-constructed; research projects are collaboratively drafted. (p. 165)

A recent collection, *Revolutionizing Education: Youth Participatory Action Research in Education* (Cammarota and Fine, 2008), brings together many important such projects, examples of researchers (particularly and markedly "junior" ones) working with youth around key issues—Torre and Fine on the Brown vs. Board of Education decision and its legacies; Tuck and colleagues on the role and importance of the GED as a credential; Cahill and colleagues on the gentrification of New York City neighborhoods; Romero and colleagues on a social science curricula designed to empower Latina/o youth around issues of educational segregation; Morrell and colleagues on a summer Youth Summit in Los Angeles designed to bring together stakeholders on race and class inequalities. As the editors sum up in the book's introduction,

> YPAR represents a systematic approach for engaging young people in transformational resistance, educational praxis, and critical epistemologies. By attaining knowledge for resistance and transformation, young people create their own sense of efficacy in the world and address the social conditions that impede liberation and positive, healthy development. Learning to act upon and address oppressive social conditions leads to the acknowledgement of one's ability to reshape the context of one's life and thus determine a proactive and empowered sense of self. (p. xx)

In addition, Pedro Noguera's collection, *Beyond Resistance* (2006) co-edited with Shawn Ginwright and Julio Cammarota, provides a powerful argument about the need to go beyond diagnosing resistance to work towards active change. From New York City to Los Angeles, university classrooms to afterschool centers, high schools to community centers, the volume's contributors offer a sweeping view of youth activism today and its potential to inform debates in education.

Pedro Noguera (with Chiara Cannella) concludes the volume with reflections on the status of "resistance." As they note, the notion of resistance has allowed educators to go past delimiting and debilitating notions of youth—the often-oppressive stereotypes educators have about urban youth, for example. Drawing on several generations of work, they argue that taking young people's agency seriously means seeing them as active authors of their own lives.

> Social scientists have characterized young people as passive participants in larger events, as spectators, ground troops, and victims, but rarely as actors with the ability to influence the course of events. (p. 334)

Noguera aims at a corrective. But he also stresses that the job of educators today is to create a sharper language around resistance. That is, much of this work fails to draw sharp distinctions between oppositional behavior and "behavior that is rooted in a deliberate critique of one's circumstances" (Noguera & Cannella, p. 335). The latter is increasingly important to understand as we begin to craft more effective and efficacious pedagogies with youth. We have a responsibility to not only recognize oppositional behavior as resistance but to work with youth towards social change. This means a conscious commitment to more socially just forms of social policy—policy that takes seriously the voices and needs and perspectives of youth.

In the interview for this volume, Noguera highlights his own history as an activist and how it informs his own work:

> You have to go where the action is. There are insights you gain from being directly involved that you may not as an outsider looking in. This is especially true with people who study social movements. (this volume, p. 80)

What he sees as the step after often inchoate resistance is the need to organize around change:

> To me, organizing is the highest form of resistance. When we decide, "We're going to focus on a particular issue, and we're going to plot a strategy to address that issue," then we are engaged in genuine praxis. . . . We would work on cultivating robust organizations. We would develop a media strategy. We might develop a sustainable citywide strategy, some of which might include a legal strategy, combined with a political strategy. . . . But it would be tactical. It wouldn't be simply sitting around and talking about how screwed up the policy is, or having a rally and saying, "The policy sucks." (p. 75, this volume)

In his book, *City Schools and the American Dream* (2003), Noguera discusses the various roles he has taken in efforts for change—from working in the Mayor's office to teaching in local public schools to researching in the university. Throughout, he is concerned with the ways young people are made into one-dimensional caricatures, as "underachieving" or "failing" or even "violent." Taking the perspectives of youth as a starting point, he discusses efforts to listen to youth and develop policies with them, for example, working with youth to understand the underlying causes of violence, to create a climate of respect and mutual trust, as well as to create multiple ways for students to participate and perform well in school. He does not take "violence" as resistant opposition full stop. It is a starting point for more fruitful engagements with youth.

The question of activism of course permeates this volume. The cautions of Gerald Vizenor in this regard seem appropriate in helping to draw this section to a close. As Vizenor notes,

> I have been drawn into mass movements several times, but never trusted the energy. I must have developed early in my life a sense of the resistance in my blood to collective resistance movements. I have never trusted mass movements. I don't know how that mistrust was first realized, but as a boy I can remember knowing the difference between the approval and disapproval of my friends, and the need for acceptance, from the frenzy and anonymous excitement of a mass movement. (p. 116, this volume)

He goes on to describe both the excitement of meeting at Pine Ridge Reservation to discuss the American Indian Movement's occupation of Wounded Knee in 1973 as well as his own need to separate himself from the developing group. Vizenor offers appropriate cautions about the temptations to move quickly into mass movements, to feed off of their energies in ways that can overwhelm the self.

The stories told by Gerald Vizenor in the interview for this volume reveal some of the limitations of movements, of activism in addressing the symptoms of oppression. His emphasis is on language as resistance, as a site of confrontation:

> My strategies of resistance have always involved transforming language and language play. Obviously there is a great power in language, and in using it powerfully you could pay a real price for it, but also build a sense of presence. . . . I am more convinced about the power and resistance of language than I am about the power of mass movements. (*ibid*, p. 110)

Vizenor's interview highlights stories about language as resistance, ranging from social work and a youth play to a federal courtroom on a Native land claim. Most pressing is his insistence on resistance, even against or within mass movements. His observations serve as counterpoints to many of the laden assumptions of how change happens, and where the power to make change is located.

Conclusions

In this chapter, I have looked to understand resistance as an evolving construct. As noted, different theories about change gird different approaches to resistance. These approaches to change are often not made explicit in the work itself but thread throughout nevertheless. Making this discussion more explicit might help inform future work in the field. For example, many researchers have come to read their own hopes for "freedom" and "social change" on to disenfranchised populations. This can be a powerful use of the research imagination. Of course, the impulse here is to tell counter-narratives to dominant ones—to give special priority to the perspectives of those most hurt by dominant social, cultural, and material imperatives. The goal is to give new life and meaning to the otherwise degraded and disparaged stories. Another impulse, as Vizenor cautions in his interview for this volume, may be to romanticize the experience of being part of a mass movement; Noguera offers parallel cautions about the perceptions of spontaneity that are attributed to social movements.

I offer some of my own cautions here—in particular, the caution not to valorize the experiences of youth in irresponsible ways, or to remain locked into particular ideas about how historical change should happen (recall here the earlier discussion of French intellectuals). This is particularly dangerous for those of us who do not have to live with the consequences of such decisions in the long term. For example, the lived experience of under-employment, over time, can work to level the ways resistance to school is sometimes valorized. The lives of these youth do not necessarily follow a historical teleology that will lead to broad, social change as many early Marxists believed. In fact, as Signithia Fordham points out in her interview, the very nature of academic work often precludes the kind of longitudinal vision that would allow us clearer understanding of resistance and its implications over long periods of time. The world is not bound by the parameters of research projects, which have (by necessity) to have beginnings, middle, and ends. Too often, we read the future into the lives of our participants, informed largely by our own ideas of change and historical teleology. At the very least, we have the responsibility to avoid making our stories neat—to create heroes and imagine happy endings for them and the world they are supposed to represent. Indeed, while social scientific texts of resistance remain powerful, we must never forget that the "imagining" at the heart of this project comes with important responsibilities. This is one of the unavoidable challenges ethnographic researchers face today.

Works Referenced

Aronson, R. (2004). *Camus and Sartre: The story of a friendship and the quarrel that ended it.* Chicago: University of Chicago Press.

Berube, M. (2011). *The left at war.* New York: NYU Press.

Bowles, S., & Gintis, H. (1977). *Schooling in capitalist America.* New York: Basic Books.

Cammarota, J., & Fine, M. (Eds.). (2008). *Revolutionizing education: Youth participatory action research in motion.* New York: Routledge.

Fine, M. (1994a). *Framing dropouts: Notes on the politics of an urban public high school.* New York: SUNY Press.

Fine, M. (1994b). Working the hyphens: Reinventing self and other in qualitative research. In N. Denzin & Y. Lincoln (Eds.). *Handbook of qualitative research*, pp. 70–82. Thousand Oaks, CA: Sage.

Fordham, S. (1996). *Blacked out: Dilemmas of race, identity, and success at Capital High.* Chicago: University of Chicago Press.

Ginwright, S., Noguera, P., & Cammarota, J. (Eds.). (2006). *Beyond resistance! Youth activism and community change.* New York: Routledge.

Judt, T. (2011). *Past imperfect: French intellectuals, 1944–1956.* New York: NYU Press.

Kelley, R. (1996). *Race rebels: Culture, politics, and the Black working class.* New York: Basic Books.

Kelley, R. (2003). *Freedom dreams: The Black radical imagination.* New York: Beacon Press.

Noguera, P. (2003). *City schools and the American dream: Reclaiming the promise of public education.* New York: Teachers' College Press.

Ogbu, J.U. (1978). *Minority education and caste: The American system in cross-cultural perspective.* New York: Academic Press.

Sartre, J. (2001). *Basic writings.* (Ed.). Stephen Priest. New York: Routledge.

Scott, J. (1990). *Domination and the arts of resistance.* New Haven: Yale University Press.

Scott, J. (2012). *Two cheers for anarchism.* Princeton: Princeton University Press.

Thompson, E.P. (1963). *The making of the English working class.* London: Gollancz.

Tuck, E., & Fine, M. (2007). Inner angles: A range of ethical responses to/with Indigenous and decolonizing theories. In N. Denzin and M. Giardina (Eds.). *Ethical futures in qualitative research: Decolonizing the politics of knowledge*, pp. 145–168. Walnut Creek, CA: Left Coast Press.

Willis, P. (1977). *Learning to labor: How working class kids get working class jobs.* New York: Columbia University Press.

3

AN INTIMATE MEMOIR OF RESISTANCE THEORY

Michelle Fine with Eve Tuck and K. Wayne Yang

NEW YORK, NEW YORK

Michelle Fine is a Distinguished Professor of Social Psychology, Women's Studies and Urban Education at the Graduate Center, CUNY and is a founding faculty member of the Public Science Project (PSP). A sampling of her most cited books and policy monographs includes *The Changing Landscape of Public Education* (with Michael Fabricant, Paradigm Press, 2013); *Charter Schools and the Corporate Make-Over of Public Education* (with Michael Fabricant, Teachers' College Press, 2012); *Revolutionizing Education: Youth participatory action research in motion* (with Julio Cammarota, Routledge, 2008); *Muslim-American Youth* (with Selcuk Sirin, New York University Press, 2008); *Becoming Gentlemen: Women and law school* (with Lani Guinier and Jane Balin, Beacon Press, 1997); *Working Method: Social research and social justice* (with Lois Weis, Routledge, 2004); and *Framing Dropouts: Notes on an urban high school* (SUNY Press, 1991). Her classic collaboration, "Changing minds: The impact of college on women in prison" (2001) is nationally recognized as the primary empirical basis for the contemporary college in prison movement.

Falling in Love with Resistance Theory

I am a social psychologist by training. The intellectual grandchild of Kurt Lewin—a founder of action research, I am also an academic cousin to Phil Zimbardo, who conducted the Stanford Prison experiments, Stanley Milgram, who authored numerous obedience to authority studies and Solomon Asch, famous for his conformity studies.

My field, social psychology, delights proudly and problematically in a long history of experiments that claim to demonstrate the human capacity for passivity, conformity and submission to authority. Yet, even within those very contrived experimental settings, one can discern substantial unacknowledged evidence of resistance, questioning, angst, ambivalence and challenge. The omission is curious and pernicious, raising epistemological questions about the intellectual and political project of psychology as a discipline and psychologists as disciplinary—deeply implicated in Guantanamo, Iraqi and Afghanistani torture exercises. Searching for the ghostly evidence of resistance within psychology and education has been my life's work. Luckily it's not hard to find.

My own activist history in anti-war, feminist, labor and racial justice struggles, combined with fortunate moments/friendships with Henry Giroux, Stanley Aronowitz, bell hooks, Madeline Grumet, Linda Powell, Lani Guinier, Derrick Bell and Paulo Freire, have fed my interest in critical resistance theory. In 1981 I was a beginning assistant professor at University of Pennsylvania when Paul Willis' *Learning to Labor* was released. Bowles and Gintis (1976) had been writing on reproduction for a decade and a half when ideas about critical youth and educator resistance were just beginning to circulate in critical educational studies, critical race and feminist theory.

Resistance as an epistemology was superbly appealing to me. Straddling the two fields hugely implicated in justifying social hierarchies—psychology and education—I was moved by Herbert Marcuse's commitment to the Great Refusal. Those early works on resistance supplied theoretical tools, and then we generated methodological and organizing strategies, to unhinge the grip of hegemonic concepts including false consciousness, passivity, internalized oppression and conformity. Resistance theory recognized that people—educators and youth in particular—understood in deep, complex, contradictory and embodied ways, the very systems which were oppressing them. Resistance theory recognized that oppression births structural violence but also critical resistance, despair, anger and also desire.

In those early years, I fell in love with resistance theories even as I worried the limits and contours.

In retrospect, we were all vulnerable to a naïve belief that educational struggles of resistance could be mobilized and sustained *outside of* and *free from* the dynamics of reproduction. We understand now that resistance movements are always intimately and dialectically *embedded* in and *disruptive of*, cycles of reproduction and transformation. By no means a binary with reproduction, resistance slows down, disrupts and creates new transgressive possibilities, within a theatre of reproductive dynamics. That is, there is never a final victory, but always a struggle to be waged, in solidarity across the power lines of race, gender, class, position and zip code, across the borders of youth, educators and communities.

Early on there was a confusion, and conflation actually, about resistance as a way of looking and theorizing human behavior, and resistance as a mobilization against injustice. Both are stunningly important, but they are not the same.

In those early years, resistance theory as deployed by Willis, Giroux, Freire and a bit later for me in Audre Lorde's 1995 *Cancer Journals*, offered frameworks for theorizing how people make sense of injustice, in mind, body, spirit, movements, and political gestures. This line of analysis did not assume that youth carried an informed intent to disrupt systems, nor that they were guaranteed a political victory. The writings of Robin Kelley describing the collective performance of African American youth taking up space and voice on public transit; James Scott's chronicles of the hidden transcripts of resistance; Janie Ward's analysis of Black families "raising resisters" among their daughters around the dining room table, and Signithia Fordham's writings on "those loud Black girls" offered transformative scenes of resistance theorizing. These scholars did not presume that young people had fully catalogued an inventory of political readiness to take on systems. They did, however, recognize that affectively and ethically, young people embodied an appetite for justice and dignity, and would thereby retreat from and/or challenge social relations, institutions and dynamics that, in the language of Du Bois, were designed to "eat our young."

I so appreciated the epistemological possibilities that assumed conviction and intentionality, not passivity and conformity. I was thrilled to hang out with writers and frameworks that would insist that we interrogate the conditions under which, and the capillaries through which, oppression moves under the skin, into the soul and onto the tongue; how oppression is negotiated, challenged, queered, swallowed, rejected, and sometimes indeed internalized.

The Limits of Young Love: Romanticizing Resistance in the Late 1980s and Early 1990s

In 1991, in *Framing Dropouts* I argued for a theoretical understanding of dropping out (being pushed out) as an act(ion) of racialized and classed political resistance; a refusal to be miseducated. Challenging the then-classic conception of dropouts as struggling students, scarred by low self-esteem, depression and little ambition, these young people narrated critique, ambition and desire. They were leaving high school prior to graduation with only partial knowledge of the politics and structural conditions that were evacuating them; but a deep sensory response to the pollen of historic and structural oppression. They sniffed the toxicity, tripped onto an exit strategy and sadly no one got in their way to say, "Where do you think you are going?" While these students knew in their bodies that something was wrong, neither they, nor I, knew at the time how relentlessly they were being prepared as *excess*, as *disposable*, in an economy and housing market that didn't need them; nor that the prison industrial complex had been tagging their bodies for deportation. But they knew the promise "Stay in school and you'll get a good job" rang hollow.

The reception to *Framing Dropouts* was outstanding, in a frightening kind of way. Dropouts were elevated as deeply informed, working-class heroes; resistance was romanticized. Fans on the Left celebrated the act of dropping out, and more mainstream critics would ask me after a lecture, "Do you really think it's a good idea to drop out?" Of course I didn't. While I appreciated the passion of their flight, the educational thirst narrated by these young men and women, and their contestation of what Ignacio Martin-Baro would call the "collective lie," I also worried the economic, educational, psychological and reproductive consequences of their decisions.

Willis' volume *Learning to Labour*, like *Framing Dropouts* became fast classics. A radical chic backpack stuffed with varied enactments of youth rebellion, the construct *resistance* was beginning to swell to incorporate too many varied forms of fightback, opposition, refusal and transformation, losing specificity and political utility. The cheap ideological thrill of resistance was particularly alive in the U.K. and the U.S., if less so in South Africa and South America where resistance was always understood as individual and collective, rooted in place, consciousness and sacrifice, embodied, spiritual, and dangerous. But in the U.S., the resistance of youth seemed a vibrant and convenient projective canvas for Leftist academics. Relatively (un)comfortable in our own privilege and security, we valorized their risks a bit too much. I place myself at the center of this retrospec(ula)tive-critique.

There grew a kind of hero worship, a fawning over James Dean, the "lads" in England and the drop outs in the U.S. Romancing the bad boy and worshiping his/her bold opposition, there was too little attention to consequence. Although young people's resistance clearly derived from political, relational, embodied and sometimes quite intellectual recognition of what was happening around them, their forms of resistance may have been good for us, but in deeply material and existential terms, not always good for them.

When young women run from sexual abuse in their homes, they are indeed resisting. But they often run straight into the arms of older men eager to sell their bodies. And in that dark alley, the thrill of resistance meets up with the ghosts of reproduction. When adolescents flee miseducating high schools only to be recruited by proprietary schools with deceptive promises, the relief of early exit mingles with the thirst to be educated. Both are quickly sabotaged by the weight of defaulted loans and lingering debt.

When adolescents of color are confronted with aggressive policing and other forms of state violence, they may refuse or they may get on their knees and surrender because they want to avoid being killed; because they have to pick up their baby from child care. They may promise themselves to write down his badge number or they recognize that it's not worth a fight today, it's only Monday. These after-shocks, as Michelle Billies would argue, from surveillance threat are all forms of resistance; aspirations for dignity in the language of Arjun Appardurai.

Resistance is an epistemology, a line of vision, theorizing and analysis; it does not require intent and it does not guarantee victory, it simply presumes the human yearning for dignity and action. Acts of resistance, in the language of

Pierre Bourdieu, reflect our human capacity to demand what should be, especially when transformation in the moment seems so improbable.

And yet "failure"—not smashing capitalism, overthrowing racism, undermining patriarchy or eradicating homophobia—cannot be mistaken as the absence of resistance. The allure of profit, the dynamics of neo-liberalism, the footprint of patriarchy and the choke-hold of racism haunt, and exploit, the vulnerable and lonely child/youth fleeing home, school, abuse, police, foster care, surveillance and exploitation, hungry to be-long, thirsty for justice, yearning to be educated with dignity.

A representational problematic of early resistance theory can be found, ironically, in the spot-light featuring of the resistant youth and the correlative whiting out of structural, institutional and political landscape in his/her surround. Resistance theorizing so fully pivots our attention onto the wisdom of young people that our gaze may be detoured off of the adults, the policies and politics of finance inequity, miseducation, racial recruitment into the prison industrial complex. The bold and resistant youth is sketched, sitting alone center stage, a feisty re-enactment of Rosa Parks misread as tired and solitary. Resistance frameworks bring sharp precision to portraits of the youth but typically sketch blurry atheoretical, homogenized and simplified profiles of adults—bystanders, witnesses, and administrators—as if they mindlessly facilitate reproduction. In *Framing Dropouts* it was too easy to read my words as an indictment of teachers as passive, or active, agents of a repressive state—except for the labor hero in the book who ends up being Peter Steinberg (who actually is a hero, by the way).

After publishing the book, and receiving several challenges from educators who felt badly "framed" by the text, I went through a long period of intense self-criticism for my theoretical whitewashing of teachers; that is, painting youth as embodiment of resistance and educators more or less as dupes of the system. Soon after publication of *Framing Dropouts*, I began to take up critical participatory work with educators, parents and youth, to avoid what Thomas Teo would call epistemological violence; painting teachers or social workers as stooges of the State, reproducers of race/class hierarchy, lubricants of stratification, in ways that denied their complex subjectivities and negotiations (Fine, 1991).

Two more troubles with resistance theory, in its infancy, need to be noted. First, I fear that analyses of resistance are often totalizing; neglecting a lesson from Bakhtin, that youth, like the rest of us, speak in marbleized tongues, braiding discursive currents of critique and fear, desire and ambivalence, a yearning to exit and a profound wish to be-long. Resistance is never pure, never simply oppositional or rejecting; it is often enacted with an affective bouillabaisse of anger, disappointment, sense of injustice, desire, yearning and ambivalence.

Finally, early resistance studies suffered from an atemporality. We now know that it is crucial to track the biography of resistance over time; not only at the moment of eruption. The mo(u)rning after resistance is central to understanding the sustainability, and evaporation, of movements for social change. A few projects have brilliantly tracked how critical young people, engaged in youth organizing over time, sustain lives of civic engagement, dedicated to social justice (see Mediratta, Shah, & McAlister, 2009; Torre et al., 2012). In other contexts, however, individual acts of resistance, particularly absent a community of politically engaged peers, can degenerate to self-blame and despair over time.

When conducting research for *Framing Dropouts*, I interviewed young people immediately after they left school. They were full of energy and critique, headed to Catholic schools in New Jersey with newborn babies. I then interviewed young people who had left high school three or four years prior, and their sense of energy and aspiration had deflated; their apartments were filled with smoke, diapers and bills. I had planned to do 40 of those interviews but I stopped at 25 because I felt like I got the story: The line of social resistance had self-impaled, reduced to "I shouldn't have played cards in 7th grade. I shouldn't have cut Algebra." At the same time the world had colluded with those regrets so that, for most of them, their lives were in fact pretty constricted. They were led to believe it was their fault. I got to see the biography of critique. Youth resistance can last for a lifetime (see Fox et. al., 2010; Mediratta, Shah, & McAlister, 2009; Torre et al., 2012) or it may spoil after a short shelf life when the world is aligned in deeply reproductive, and punishing, ways. It's not to say these young people forgot the critiques they had engaged at the time of leaving school. The social critique was still there, but it was covered over by a whole set of cumulative setbacks for which society—and ultimately the young adults—were ready to blame themselves.

After *Framing Dropouts* was released, I was often asked, "So, you think dropping out is *good*?" At the time I could only respond, "No, of course not; that's a troubling misread of the argument. Given economic, educational, criminal justice and reproductive after-life of push out/drop out, no one can celebrate the consequences."

But, then and now, it would have been a mistake to argue that the desire to exit was entirely misguided even if the consequences were brutal. I was trying to shoe-horn into the dominant ideological straitjacket that young people's leaving was not irrational, despite the structural punishments most would endure. But my response was unsatisfying to me—and to my questioners.

The outstanding research and publications of Eve Tuck (2012) and Jessica Ruglis (2011) have advanced and complicated this debate. With distinct theoretical and methodological orientations, both Tuck and Ruglis document the adverse effects of early exit as well as the psychic and physical dangers of remaining in toxic school environments. Elegant and politically penetrating, their works reveal that early departure from high school reflects a search for health and sanity, an enactment of embodied intentionality informed by a field of structural and historic dynamics that encourage racialized and classed exile, with responsibility loaded up on the bodies of young persons and deflected by the very systems that are squeezing them out.

A Quarter Century Later: The Privatization and Commodification of Critique and Resistance Today

Today, 25 years later, critique and resistance have become radical Right wing chic. Michelle Rhee sees herself as a freedom fighter. While a quarter of a century ago it was important not to romanticize resistance, today it crucial for theorists, researchers, educators, activists and youth to contest the appropriation of critique, the commodification of resistance and expose the move to privatize social justice—that is, to make money off of racial/ethnic/class-based pain and cumulative oppression.

For more than 30 years I have collaborated with friends, allies, youth, women in prison, activists, researchers, policy makers, on social justice research, policy work and organizing. We document the profound possibilities of small schools, college in prison, performance-based assessment and the structural violence of high-stakes testing, the prison industrial complex, State policies that gentrify the academy. . . .

Today, however, we notice a weird echo in our work groups, like when you think you are being followed down the street by a stranger, this time well-dressed and with a tape recorder. An industry of neoliberal, corporate, State and sometimes philanthropic "reformers" have swallowed and distorted our words and analyses, folded them into a neoliberal agenda, and circulated ideological frameworks for educational "reform" that undermine racial justice, community control, critical inquiry, parent/community governance, the wisdom of educators and the vibrant spirit of youth; a framework that trashes, starves, privatizes and then whitens all things public, criminalizing or demonizing the bodies left behind. All this in the name of "choice," "accountability," "saving the children" and of course "civil rights."

Progressive educators, activists and researchers find our best ideas appropriated by Districts or philanthropy and turned into a mandate, a reform, more aptly a de-form: individualized, privatized, and stripped of racial justice or equity. The critique has been appropriated by the Right to dismantle and privatize public education; declare "crisis" in order to punish educators, unions and districts, close schools and usher in charters, vouchers and online/technology-based educational "alternatives" (see Fabricant & Fine, 2012; 2013). Progressive movements have been appropriated by philanthropy and ripped from their activist roots (Noguera & Fine, 2011). Two examples may help unpack these dynamics in the real-world politics of education in communities and in prison.

In the 1990s, in New York and Philadelphia researchers, activists and educators documented the academic and civic power of small schools, designed and governed by collectives of educators, parents and sometimes students. Within a decade of the movement, Gates Foundation also fell in love with small schools, not as a movement fueled by inquiry, participation, community/educator determination and messy democracy, but small schools as a philanthropically funded initiative that could be mass produced and "brought to scale." They funded hundreds of small schools in cities around the country; commodities that could be "replicated," decoupled from community, educator or student ownership, stripped of participation and designed from the top.

In 2007, at a meeting organized by the editors of *Rethinking Schools* on small schools, a colleague from Milwaukee told me, "They're mandating that we create small schools and they're handing out your article." In response, I published a piece in *Rethinking Schools* called "Not in Our Name," clarifying that the small schools movement was never about size, but was intent on creating democratic, warm, and intellectually provocative schools nestled in communities (Fine, 2008). I've learned too often that the radical roots and participatory vision of progressive reforms are often severed in the second generation, as the reform becomes a commodity that can be situated anywhere, by anyone, at any time. Indeed, the philanthropic small schools movement laid the ground work for the similarly twisted history of the charter school movement—another movement born in the soil of social justice activism, corrupted by a neoliberal State agenda and a privatizing educational reform industry (Fabricant & Fine, 2012; 2013).

A second example of the commodification of progressive educational reform comes from our work in prisons (Fine et al., 2001). For two decades, a collective of researchers, prisoners, and now formerly incarcerated women and men, have worked together to document the abuses of mass incarceration and the positive effects of college in prison. You will remember that then President Bill Clinton signed the Violent Crime Control and Law Enforcement Act of 1994, which withdrew Pell grants from prison. Since that time, we have been gathering data, and mobilizing, to restore Pell grants for women and men in prison (see Fine et al., 2003).

In the last few years since the recession of 2008, State legislatures have "discovered" that they don't have much money in the budgets because they have so deeply invested in the prison industrial complex. They are now eager to learn what might be done to stem the flow of prisoners in, and to support prisoners upon release so that they do not return to prison. While the Federal government has been quite reluctant to even consider restoration of Pell grants for prisoners, they have turned to foundations to determine how college in prison might be subsidized without public dollars. In 2012, at a meeting of foundations interested in re-entry and strategies to reduce recidivism, the conversation turned to college in prison. Surprised and thrilled to see such widespread interest, I felt whip-lashed when the now-familiar dynamic of reform-commodification reared its head.

The foundation representatives were, no doubt, sincere in their desire to support college in prison. Unwilling to challenge the long, racialized reach of mass incarceration into communities of color, they wouldn't, as a group, agree to advocate for strategic public investment in Pell grants, nor would they advocate a more equitable tax structure for the top 1 percent and corporations. They were, and remain, dedicated to a philanthropic campaign for college in prison by placing computers in prisons and supporting a small—but wonderful—collection of college-in-prison programs. A young man from the Gates Foundation projected a Powerpoint spreadsheet that showed us the cost/benefits of placing hundreds of computers in prison to deliver a college curriculum to prisoners. There would be no discussion of strategic investment by the Federal or State government; no discussion of the power of bringing educators and volunteers into the prison, building curriculum through participatory inquiry and critical pedagogy with women/men in prison; no reference to the power of critical classroom dialogues, participatory student cultures or any of the elements of prison in college that work.

It is as if corporate reformers and venture capitalists follow progressives to the gardens of radical creations, and decide: "That's a beautiful rose. I think I'll cut it off and reproduce it," rather than understanding that these beautiful flowers grow in the soil of community with the sunlight of social movements. Those small schools were started by educators and parents with an aspiration of educational justice; college in prison was resuscitated by women at Bedford Hills Correctional Facility, borne of commitments to educational justice and collective self-determination.

We can no longer be surprised at the appropriation of progressive critique or the commodification of social justice strategies by the neoliberal state or by corporate interests.

Tithing Resistance Across Place: Documenting and Provoking Circuits of Resistance

Resistance is an epistemological stance by researchers, activists, practitioners and educators recognizes the individual and collective, embodied and spoken desire, pain, inquiry and lust for justice in the lives of youth. Resistance offers a lens for social analysis, engaged pedagogy and organizing; a critical journey toward interrogation and mobilization of the affects, desires and despair that lay beneath the surface, behind the performance, under the rage. To tap resistance is to keep open the possibility that there is something deeper; to understand that things might be otherwise; resistance insists on denaturalizing, indeed, queering social arrangements and provoking the social imagination for what else is possible (Greene, 2000).

Resistance is entwined with critical education, organizing and crafting ethical, pedagogical and political nests where people engage in difficult dialogue about troubling issues; participatory research challenges the dominant conceptions of school failure, stop and frisk and incarceration; where transgressive texts and evidence are analyzed and developed, debated, interpreted, written, revised and performed. Resistance theorists/researchers/educators/activists have an obligation to document spaces that feed our collective capacity for critical inquiry and action, and particularly within institutions that breed structural violence, legitimate stratification and choke the much-too-forgiving souls of young people living in poverty and surrounded by racism (see also Cammarota & Fine, 2008; Mediratta, Shah, & McAlister, 2009).

In New York, at the Public Science Project at The Graduate Center, CUNY, activists, youth, researchers and educators have launched a series of studies-for-action on what we call *circuits of dispossession, privilege, and resistance* (Fine & Ruglis, 2008). A consortium of researchers, policy makers and community activists PSP produces critical scholarship "to be of use" in social policy debates and organizing movements for educational equity and human rights. Across time and place, we document with community members the impact and braiding of high-stakes testing, charter schools, stop and frisk, mass incarceration on youth and communities, tracking the policies and flows of capital that move opportunities out of marginalized communities of color and into wealthier, whiter communities, assessing the bodies and aspirations left behind, and documenting always the forms of resistance generated within and across zip codes (Fox et al., 2010). We gather activists, youth, researchers, educators and policy makers from across sites, in New York and beyond, to explore the common base of structural (dis)investment and the shared vision for educational and racial justice.

Several years ago, we sponsored a cross-city conversation/campaign on school closings and brought together youth and adults from Denver, Boston, Chicago, New York, Newark, Philadelphia and San Francisco. It was stunning for young people to realize it's not just that we have this nasty superintendent in Philadelphia, or corrupt politicians in Detroit, or mayoral control in New York or privatization on steroids in Newark (all of which were true). Circuits of dispossession, the blueprint of neoliberal reform, could be discerned across, as could the circuits of resistance. At first, the cross-city conversation was careful and tentative. Youth researchers from one city were checking out the youth researchers from another city. Then, a young person from Arizona observed that Special Education was held in the basement of her school. "Really?" said a youth researcher from New Jersey, "Our schools too." A prec(ar)ious solidarity was borne in the wretched air of special education classrooms, buried in high school basements linked across the country.

A shared analysis of the architecture of privatization, stratification and dismantling of the "public" forced a different kind of conversation for strategic action, within and across cities. A few months later, when allies in Detroit were confronting the first rash of school closings, they called for help, and many of us from Cleveland, Chicago, Newark and New York showed up for a mobilization in Detroit to figure out our common and distinctly local dynamics, forms of resistance, mobilizations and how to frame school closings not as a way to "save local schools" but to sever the precious strands that link local communities to their last public resource. Most recently, activists from many of these cities boarded buses to Washington, DC on the Journey to Justice to voice outrage and demand a moratorium on school closings particularly in communities of color. Without a cross-city/context analysis of these circuits, resistance stories remain too localized, and too easy to defeat. Organizing and documenting both dispossession and resistance across site—what Cindi Katz would call a counter-topography of global dynamics within, and across, place (see also Fine, Tuck, & Zeller-Berkman, 2008; Katz, 2004)—helps prepare the grounds for national and global social movements.

Provoking a Radical Re-imagination for Educational Justice

Our obligation, then, today, as theorists, researchers, activists, educators (and tweeters —you, not me) is that we must be vigilant on critique, design spaces to cultivate inquiry, resistance and radical imagination, and circulate images of what could be, beyond resistance. The real work of resistance, now, is to offer critical alternatives so people can imagine what's possible. Maxine Greene (2000) speaks of releasing the imagination, or provoking radical images of what must be. Du Bois (1903) argued with William James, and ultimately left the university because he (Du Bois) sought a social science that was both critical of what is but also inspired toward an ethical alternative for what should be.

Resistance studies have, no doubt, contributed enormously to documenting damage, outrage and injustice, but haven't sufficiently provoked, I fear, radical imaginaries for what might be.

In our small part of the world, at the Public Science Project, we host summer institutes for critical participatory praxis with collectives of activists and researchers, and during the year we collaborate on a range of critical participatory action research projects, with community-based organizations, schools, movements, universities, artists, performers, lawyers, activists, youth, formerly incarcerated and currently imprisoned women and men, policy makers . . . working together to critically analyze and challenge the structures, dynamics and policies of oppression that might otherwise seem so natural; to contest policies, distributions and social arrangements that seem so fixed, cemented and immutable; to generate evidence for court cases, organizing and policy reformulation. These projects release a collective refusal; insist that injustice is anything but natural, and together with community-based allies we build fragile bridges across community and university, activism and research, what is and what could be.

The Public Science Project is designed as a gift from, and a gift to, those young men and women who were willing to speak to me, 25 years ago, with words, bodies and actions, pleading for us to recognize that injustice is intolerable; that miseducation is anything but natural. Those young people fled their schools and most, I am sure, paid a price. Indebted to their legacy, we must honor resistance, build nests to gather solidarities of critique and imagination, and muster the collective courage to advocate for a more just tomorrow.

Works Referenced

Bowles, S., & Gintis, H. (1976). *Schooling in capitalist America*. London: Routledge & Kegan Paul.

Cammarota, J., & Fine, M. (Eds.). (2008). *Revolutionizing education: Youth participatory action research in motion*. New York: Routledge.

Du Bois, W.E.B. (1903). *The souls of Black folk*. Chicago: A.C. McClurg & Co.; Cambridge: University Press, John Wilson & Son.

Du Bois, W.E.B. (1913). *The Crisis Magazine*, 6, November, 339–345.

Fabricant, M., & Fine, M. (2012). *Charter schools and the corporate makeover of public education*. New York: Teachers' College Press.

Fabricant, M. & Fine, M. (2013). *The changing politics of education: Privatization and the dispossessed lives of those left behind*. Boulder, CO: Paradigm Publishers.

Fine, M. (2010). Participatory evaluation research and structural racism. *Critical Issues Forum: Marking Progress / Movements Toward Racial Justice*. 3, July 2010. Washington, D.C.: Philanthropic Initiative for Racial Equity.

Fine, M. (2012a). Resuscitating critical psychology for "revolting" times (Lewin Address). *Journal of Social Issues, 68*, 2, 416–438.

Fine, M. (2012b). Disrupting peace / provoking conflict: Introduction to special section on school closures. *Peace and Conflict: The Journal of Peace Psychology, 18*, 2, 144–145.

Fine, M., & Ruglis, J. (2008). Circuits of dispossession: The racialized and classed realignment of the public sphere for youth in the U.S. *Transforming Anthropology, 17,* 1, 20–33.

Fine, M., Tuck, E., & Zeller-Berkman, S. (2008). Do you believe in Geneva? In N. Denzin, L.T. Smith, & Y. Lincoln, *Handbook of critical and Indigenous knowledges*. Beverley Hills, CA: Sage Publications. Also in C. McCarthy, A. Durham, L. Engel, A. Filmer, M. Giardina, & M. Malagreca (2007). *Globalizing cultural studies*. New York: Routledge, pp. 493–525.

Fine, M., Torre, M.E., Boudin, K., Bowen, I., Clark, J., Hylton, D., et al. (2003). Participatory action research: Within and beyond bars. In P. Camic, J.E. Rhodes, & L. Yardley (Eds.). *Qualitative research in psychology: Expanding perspectives in methodology and design*. Washington, D.C.: American Psychological Association, pp. 173–198.

Fox, M., Mediratta, K., Stoudt, B., Ruglis, J., Fine, M., & Salah, S. (2010). Critical youth engagement: Participatory action research and organizing. In L. Sherrod, J. Torney-Purta, & C. Flanagan, *Handbook of research on civic engagement in youth*, pp. 621–650. Hoboken, NJ: John Wiley & Sons.

Giroux, H. (1983). Theories of reproduction and resistance in the new sociology of education. *Harvard Education Review, 53*, 3, 257–293.

Greene, M. (2000). *Releasing the imagination*. New York: Jossey-Bass.

Katz, C. (2004). *Growing up global*. Minneapolis: University of Minnesota Press.

Lorde, A. (1995). *Cancer journals*. New York: Aunt Lute Press.

Mediratta, K., Shah, S., & McAlister, S. (2009). *Community organizing for stronger schools: Strategies and successes*. Cambridge, MA: Harvard University Press.

Noguera, P., & Fine, M. (2011, May 9). Don't blame the teachers. *The Nation, 292*, 19, 6.

Powell Pruitt, L. (2011). *Changing minds, changing schools*. Richmond, VA: Leaven Press.

Ruglis, J. (2011). Mapping the biopolitics of school dropout and youth resistance. *International Journal of Qualitative Studies in Education, 24*, 5, 627–637.

Torre, M., Fine, M., Stoudt, B., & Fox, M. (2012). Critical participatory action research as public science. In P. Camic, & H. Cooper (Eds.). *Handbook of research methods in psychology*, pp. 171–184. Washington, D.C.: American Psychology Association.

Tuck, E. (2012). *Urban youth and school pushout: Gateways, get-aways, and the GED.* New York: Routledge.

Ward, J. (1993). Raising resisters. In M. Fine & L. Weis (Eds.). *Beyond Silenced Voices.* Albany, NY: SUNY Press.

Willis, P. (1981). *Learning to Labor.* New York: Columbia University Press.

4

LEAKING AWAY AND OTHER FORMS OF RESISTANCE

James C. Scott with Eve Tuck and K. Wayne Yang

NEW HAVEN, CONNECTICUT

James C. Scott is the Sterling Professor of Political Science and Professor of Anthropology and is Director of the Agrarian Studies Program at Yale University. His research concerns political economy, comparative agrarian societies, theories of hegemony and resistance, peasant politics, revolution, Southeast Asia, theories of class relations and anarchism. His books include *The Art of Not Being Governed: An Anarchist History of Upland Southeast Asia* (2009), *Seeing Like a State: How Certain Schemes to Improve the Human Condition Have Failed* (1998, and *Domination and the Arts of Resistance: Hidden Transcripts* (1990).

Listening to Peasant Resistance

I started teaching in Wisconsin during the Vietnam War, so I came out of, in a sense, the wars of national liberation. I decided that I wanted to devote my career, for the time being, to understanding peasants, since they were the most numerous class in world history.

"Peasants" may already read to some people as an abstraction because it's an unfamiliar signifier. The normal definition of peasants is that they are part of a larger, stratified society in which they pay rents, or part of their grain, to a superior class of landlords, aristocrats, or the state. I think a peasant is someone who scratches the earth for a living, who doesn't have a lot of property—maybe a small plot, but nothing that would qualify as wealth or capital. The reason we call a Kansas farmer a farmer rather than a peasant is that he owns his own land outright; aside from taxes because of the government, no one has any superior claim on his product; and he also has a million dollars worth of capital equipment in his machine shed. So, if he liquidated his shed and his land, he'd be a rich man.

Not my first book, but my first decent book was *The Moral Economy of the Peasant*. It was essentially a library work of research of secondary sources and documents, trying to understand peasant rebellions in Vietnam and Burma in the 1930s. Why people would take those risks at that particular time? It had to do with subsistence threats.

Peasants live at the margin, and the whole point of the book was that they organized their social life, their cropping pattern and so on, in an effort to avoid a disastrous year. To avoid starving to death, or having to move out, or losing everything. Minimizing the risk of the maximum loss is the way in which peasants operate. That's not the same for people who have a margin to play with, or who don't live at the edge.

The United States has had peasants, by the way. Black and white sharecroppers, between the wars, in the South—the cotton South–lived from season to season on a tremendous amount of debt. They owed at the store. They owed to the person who owned the land. That was a peasantry. After slaves, we had a kind of serf. We called them sharecroppers, but they fit the description of peasants.

The thing that's distinctive about peasants is not only are they relatively powerless—you could draw some analogies with other people who are relatively powerless—but they are also tied to an annual cycle of crops, and harvest, and planting. In these ways, peasant subsistence is completely different than factory work. There are certain things that peasants may or may not share with other powerless people, but the distinctiveness of an agricultural year and a more dispersed life in the countryside rather than a concentrated, dense city life, is important in considering forms of resistance available to them.

I owe to a small, Malay, rice-farming village, which I call Sedaka, all of my insights into resistance, in a sense. You know, I actually cannot understand abstractions unless I can see them walk on the ground in a particular place and time. The stuff I want to read, that I think I'm going to learn the most from, is not the fifty-fourth gloss on theories of resistance, but research by someone like Paul Willis who spent a couple of years in a classroom trying to understand how it works out in working-class schools. To me, the sort of naïve, wide-eyed, really meticulous, close participant observation is likely to lead to new insights into resistance. In my case, I had to conceptualize resistance their way, by listening to the way they lived it. I had to spend time living in a village—to get to know one peasantry like the back of my hand—so that every time I was tempted to make some stupid generalization, I had a real place to think about whether it made sense.

To my surprise, when I decided to go to this Malay village, a lot of people said, "This is the end of your career, Scott. Nobody is interested in a tiny village of 70 families. Nothing is happening there." They had just introduced combine harvesters, which were essentially taking the jobs of people who cut and threshed and cleaned the rice. It's like the agricultural uprisings in England in the 1830s when they brought in combines for wheat harvests. Except from an outside perspective, there were no politics in this village—not any open politics in the formal sense that political scientists would understand politics.

I'm actually trained as a political scientist, but I think most people, most of my colleagues would think I'm an anthropologist. I'm proud of that actually. I'd rather be an anthropologist. However, one of the problems with political science and anthropology is that we've got no sense of history. We tend to be captive of what happened in the last ten years or so. Yet for every context of resistance that you can come across, there are historical analogs that intelligent people have written about. For me, a book by Armstead Robinson, which I read a draft of when I wrote *Weapons of the Weak* and *Domination and the Arts of Resistance*, discussed the desertion by whites and runaway Black slaves during the Civil War was very helpful. Robinson's book was an incredible historical reconstruction of how the South was undermined by these everyday forms of resistance. In this Malay village, although there were no marches, no demonstrations, no riots, and so on, there was sabotage. There was a kind of war of words, of reputation, of condemnation, of small thefts, and of sabotage of the machines, and so on. There were—what I called—everyday forms of resistance.

I tried to say, "Isn't this the kind of resistance that one finds throughout most of history when people cannot risk open action for fear of retaliation?" They have to muffle themselves, as it were. I wrote about resistance in the forms of desertion from armies, of squatting on land. In the army, open political action would be mutiny, where you take over and replace the commanding officers. Desertion is just leaking away. Squatting is where you run away when the police come, and then, leak back—as opposed to an open land invasion. The idea was to broaden our understanding of politics to include things like poaching of game and wood, and all kinds of things that often pass as crime. Throughout most of history, for most people, everyday forms of resistance have been the safer route. It's only in a crisis that things explode in a big way.

The Intentionality and Materiality of Resistance

The person who invades the Crown Forest, and kills a rabbit, and has rabbit stew—are they just indulging their taste for rabbit stew or are they resisting?

I make two arguments about intention. First, almost all of the resistance that I'm talking about is resistance to the appropriation of labor, time, property, and life chances by a superordinate class. Therefore, we must always expect that there will be a material side. This is E.P. Thompson's argument, too. That is, how dare people criticize the seaman for quarreling over ship's biscuits? This is not trivial. This is what class struggle is about. When appropriation is of daily necessities, of access to property, a pure symbolic act of resistance is not something that one will generally find among large masses of people; it's going to have a material side.

My other point does not directly address intentionality. How do you research intentionality when the success of many forms of everyday resistance depends on concealing and not revealing intention? Ex post facto, when a system collapses, you can get evidence of intentions, when it's no longer necessary for the powerless to conceal intentions. You could probably find journals and letters. But people who resist in such manner have every reason to disguise their purposes and their intentions. My suggestion is that there is circumstantial evidence from which we can infer certain things: When it turns out that for two centuries gamekeepers could never get villagers to testify against other villagers for poaching, for example, I take this to be evidence of shared politics.

Intentions are not trivial. When a slave is ordered to do something and says, "Yes, sir," in a surly way, but just with that edge, and then, the master says, "Were you sassing me?" holding his whip. And the prisoner says, "Oh, no, sir. I didn't mean anything by that." There you have a kind of disavowal, right? Nonetheless, it was slipped in, then disavowed. Intentions are hard.

Ridicule Is a Solvent of the Pretensions of Power

Robin Kelley's discussion of the Zoot Suit is a kind of classic. Robin uses "infrapolitics" to refer to my work on everyday forms of resistance. He put his finger on something that I, in my peasant world, did not: Cultural resistance. People thumbing their noses at, let's say, bourgeois clothing habits, or ways of behaving, or walking, or dressing, or dancing, or whatever. He understood how that kind of resistance has a kind of power. It is similar to the analyses about mods and rockers by Tony Jefferson and Stuart Hall from the Birmingham School for Cultural Studies. We can't understand British youth culture of mods and rockers without seeing it in contrast to the clerk with the furled umbrella and the bowler hat as the standard bourgeois male Londoner. It's the contrast gives a Zoot meaning—you can't think of these things except as in pairs, except as one insulting the other, or ridiculing the other.

The big question is whether these forms of "display resistance" are a substitute for "more serious" forms of resistance? Or do they accompany it, or prepare the way, or increase their likelihood? I think the latter. One form of nonconformity helps you make the next step in nonconformity. Speak back to the teacher once; the second time is a little easier.

Also, cultural resistance, especially if it has its intended effect, drives people crazy. When Indira Gandhi was doing quite terrible things as Prime Minister, hundreds of people in the audience would stand up at the moment she began to speak and turn their back on her. They wouldn't say a word, but they made their contempt visible.

I actually believe that ridicule is the most powerful solvent of the pretensions of hegemonic power.

After the Democratic Convention in Chicago, at the trial of the Chicago Seven, when Rennie Davis got on the defense table, and crossed his legs in the lotus position, and just said, "Om, om, om," it was far more powerful than making a straightforward legal defense. It said, "You know, this is a farce. I'm not participating in it." Resistance that refuses to take seriously the framework for dialogue set up by people in power—the court procedure in this case—it's a powerful solvent. So I'd like to see more work on humor.

There's a great Burmese cartoonist, who's managed for 20 years to evade imprisonment for making fun of the military regime. I think no one in all of Burma, including Aung San Suu Kyi, heroine though she is, has done more to keep the spirits of Burmese up than this cartoonist. Two or three times a week, they can see something that says exactly what they feel about the military creeps who run the place.

Protest Is Not a Weapon of the Weak

What I think was a good title originally, *Weapons of the Weak*, has become a bit overplayed. Again, and again, and again, I'll come across some reference saying, "Oh, that's just another weapon of the weak." Often, the writer is referring to a public act of petition or protest. Yet this is exactly what I'm not talking about, right? Some people, who I think have either not read it, or paid attention, or are not thinking, have carried away the title, *Weapons of the Weak*, to describe anything that poor or powerless people do to protest, whereas I wanted to highlight a particular bandwidth of activity that was not public, and was not openly declared.

I took slavery, concentration camps, serfdom—starker versions of subordination—because I wanted to see in sharp relief forms of resistance and efforts to thwart appropriation. I created this dichotomy between resistance and nonresistance, whereas in fact, a lot of acts are ambiguous and are intended to be ambiguous. There were insights be gained by this sharp dichotomy, and yet, it's less helpful for cases that are more ambiguous, especially in cases which collaboration is in the interest of the subordinate.

The Explosive Power of the Hidden Transcript

One of the things in *Domination and the Arts of Resistance* that I see at work and wonder why it hasn't been taken up to the degree it merits, is the explosive and symbolic power of the first public declaration of the hidden transcript in the face of power. You're familiar with the hidden transcript—the things that people say behind the back of power but they can't say out loud? The first public declaration is always dangerous, always explosive, and yet, in very repressive situations, it's the first indication people have that someone is speaking their very own thoughts, just exactly what they'd felt about this boss, this teacher, this thing.

I use Mrs. Poyser, a tenant farmer in a George Eliot book, as a literary example, where her criticism of the landlord explodes like a cork, in contrast to dribbling out by the sly. Ricardo Lagos' daring criticism of Pinochet on live television was a sensational moment in Chilean history. In places where a kind of silence is imposed, either it is broken by laughter and ridicule or by angry outbursts in which people finally say what everyone has been thinking and, in fact, saying around the kitchen table, but never in the public square. It becomes a political act of defiance.

Resistance Is Medicalized and Criminalized

I last worked on resistance in 1990. I suppose if I were starting fresh, I'd take the world of state categories and social work, which has a whole series of ways of typifying behavior that I would call resistance, but are called delinquency, vagrancy, truancy. In socioanalysis, in Eastern Europe, people were called asocial. That's where Foucault comes in handy, in analyzing the legalization and medicalization of defective human beings. You both medicalize and criminalize a behavior that ought to be seen as resistance. John Zerzan, a theorist for the Black Bloc, makes the argument in *Elements of Refusal* that the rising rates of truancy must be seen as resistance to the school system. Piven and Cloward make that point, too in *Poor People's Movements*. To call it truancy, medicalizes and criminalizes, telling you that they've got a defective human being here. Vagrancy was probably the most prosecuted crime for two centuries in Europe—poaching also. All these criminalized behaviors should be seen as resistance to constraints on movement and to the enclosure of common property. With feudalism, people could no longer access the woods, rabbits, game, fish, and so on. I don't think anyone has quite done justice to that, not since Hobsbawm's *Primitive Rebels*.

Actually, I truly hate the way social work and psychiatric professions take structural problems and medicalize them, so that they give Ritalin to kids who are hyperactive, and in old people's homes, they give drugs just to keep people quiet and have them not complain. They call putting people in a straitjacket, "calming." That's the official therapeutic word for putting people in a straitjacket, which is imprisoning them in their own bodies. There's a whole ideological apparatus working very hard with well-intentioned people to re-label what, I would hope, our readers would regard as acts of resistance.

If you're talking about schools, if you're talking about any institutions that are supposed to be caring for people, the anarchists' take on this is to promote the maximum degree of autonomy and agency and control over one's life world. What I'm trying to do is to figure out how a good anarchist would design institutions to maximize the flexibility, the autonomy, and the agency of the people in it.

The Relationship between Youth Resistance and System Change

In thinking about the relationship between youth resistance and change, the categories I would like to suggest are *system-compatible resistance* and *system-incompatible resistance*. The system always prefers system-compatible.

If a foundation is going to fund something, it needs a group, a formally exist-ing institution, even if it's a youth club or some little social movement. That's fine, and I'm sure there are some organizations that would fit that bill. I suppose, in its early days, the Student Nonviolent Coordinating Committee would have been one of those things. Let me call that system-compatible resistance. Let's say, youth groups making demands for more green space. This kind of thing is the bread-and-butter of normal political systems. You've got interest. You want more. Somebody else wants something else. Let's cut a deal. We'll take this into consideration. How many votes do you have? It's in the interest of foundations, in the interest of normal legislative, normal politics, to encourage that all resist-ance take the form of formal organizations making demands that are, in principle, digestible by the political system.

However, I would argue that a whole lot of youth resistance is system-incompatible resistance. Foundations are not funding truancy. They're not going to fund graffiti gangs—maybe some art shops will if it becomes popular. The problem is—and this is Piven and Cloward's argument that I completely buy—that movement organizations are parasitic, and necessarily so, on actual outbreaks of resistance. They come in afterwards and try to organize them into political demands that are, can be, digested. In doing that they serve a good function, by the way, but 80 percent of what I would understand as youth resistance takes place beyond the spectrum visible to foundations.

To the degree that anarchic, oppositional, subversive behavior can be recov-ered to the normal political process of demand-making interest politics—to that extent, the political system has done its job by taking desires for change and funneling them into an institutional process. My guess is that for any seri-ous demands, such processes probably don't work. It seems to me that serious change has generally taken place only as a result of widespread disruption outside the normal institutional framework, whether it's the Civil Rights Movement, whether it's the Wildcat strikes and riots in the Depression that led to the New Deal, or whether it was opposition to the Vietnam War.

One of Paul Willis' brilliant insights in *Learning to Labour* concerns the kids who are not resisting, the "ear'oles," who do what the teacher tells them, try to get ahead, and get good marks under the promise that they're getting to the promised land of a middle-class job. The openly resistant kids, the lads as he calls them, are already cynical and disillusioned; they don't expect anything from the system. They just want to get through, get to the pub, and put in a bad-faith day at the factory. It's the ear'oles who buy the hegemonic promise and who pay a price every day by not screwing around and suffering the ridicule from the lads. Of course, the system doesn't deliver. The ear'oles become the trade union mili-tants. They become the radicals because they sacrificed for the promises and were betrayed by the system.

Even truer today than 30 or 40 years ago are how the inequalities in institu-tional access and financial power are so enormous that the system is simply not accessible to people who have demands that are even remotely radical. Lobbyists for major corporations and the financial industries don't just have pots of money and lawyers; they actually write the legislation with the loopholes that they want from the very beginning. That kind of access used to be available to unions and the organized opposition to business interests, but now it's not. It's not. And it's certainly not available to your youth resistors, at least of the kind of resistance that I would consider to be substantial in terms of the change it was looking for.

Disruption Is a Precondition for Radical Change

If you take Piven and Cloward's argument seriously that the sieges of welfare offices, the riots, and the Wildcat strikes at the beginning of the Depression were such that people in power genuinely feared a revolution, the result was that proposals that would never have been considered were not only entertained, but also passed: Social Security, unemployment compensation, and so on. The promised disruption, and over the horizon, the revolutionary situation that power feared, led to a substantial revamping of social guarantees for human security that never would have been considered otherwise.

The same thing is true in the Civil Rights Movement, but slightly more complicated because of intra-national and transnational politics. The Kennedys don't want to lose the Democratic South; they're not all that sympathetic to the Civil Rights Movement or they think it's going to cost them if they are. But the Cold War depiction of America as a racist society by the Soviet Union and by the Communist Bloc was really powerful for them. To see the Jim Crow violence unfolding made Russian propaganda look like simply the truth. The Civil Rights Movement itself sort of unraveled Southern society, and required a tremendous amount of violence, such as the federalizing of the Arkansas National Guard. Without that level of disruption, the peaceful NAACP pressuring for school integration and the *Brown v. Board of Education* Supreme Court decision wouldn't have been implemented successfully at all.

I should make it clear that I consider disruption to have generally been a pre-condition, at least in liberal democracies, for any substantial progressive change. It is also true that that disruption can, in certain circumstances, lead to a conservative coup, to military government, to fascism. Disruption is a necessary condition for progressive change, but it doesn't always result in progressive change. However, you won't have progressive change without it.

The state scrambles to maintain control over disruption. Franklin Delano Roosevelt saves capitalism by creating what he thinks are the necessary reforms to get people off the streets, lower the temperature, and contain the disruption. In 1968 in France, Pompidou calls in the Communist Party and he gives all the workers in France a 30 percent raise. Just like that. It never would have happened if there weren't people in the streets tearing up the paving stones and if Wildcat strikes weren't happening all over France. People in power do what they think they need to do in order to contain, and then to bleed off enough of the support for the disruption so that they can regain control of the situation.

With the various urban uprisings in the 1960s, 1970s, 1990s, and more recently in 2012 in the United States, you couldn't co-opt them. There wasn't any leader to talk to. You couldn't say, "Oh, we'll give you A, B, and C, but not D." In the urban uprisings of the 1960s no one was making any demands; they were just tearing the place apart. They don't give you much of a signal about what they want; except they signal what they hate, their desire for consumer goods, and their willingness to burn police cars. It leaves to the imagination of the authorities what they have to do to somehow regain control of the situation. The underclass threatens cities, economic development.

What I don't want to say is that disruption works all by itself. Disruption depends on substructures and connections that people have through schools, and neighborhoods, families, and so on. It's not as if this disruption is structureless; it has a structure, but it tends to be a structure that the state can't easily coopt.

Resistances We Love and Resistances We Don't

The Civil Rights Movement is the movement everyone loves because it occupied the moral high ground. It had to do with the extension of democratic citizenship to Blacks. It was nonviolent. It's the movement everyone loves to love and correctly so.

What people don't love is, let's say, the violence in the Parisian suburbs or in England in the summer of 2012. Whole neighborhoods went up in flames. People attacked the police, they looted, they stole. Or the riots in U.S. ghettoes in the late 1960s and early 1970s. Yet those uprisings resulted in the Poverty Program, and the Model Cities Program in the United States.

Once you ask, "Resistance to what?" it forces you to think about the "what" that's being resisted and whether you think it ought to be resisted. I think one has to make some ethical commitments. On the one hand, I'm thinking of the graduate vegetable seller in Tunisia who didn't get his permit for his vegetable cart and who burned himself, who set himself afire, killed himself, who became the sort of pretext for the Tunisian rebellion. That was an inchoate cry of pain, obviously against the government because he left a letter about why he was in despair, having not gotten a job, harassed even for his little vegetable cart, and needing to pay off all these people. It's easy to say, "Well, this is a rotten government that hasn't done anything." On the other hand, if you think of the Muslim youth in Northern Nigeria who are burning out Christian churches. Or in Eastern Indonesia, Christians who are burning out Muslim mosques. You can't not call it resistance. It happens to be a kind of resistance that I think is unethical, destructive, and non-emancipatory.

You should not fail to understand that acts you hate are also resistance. They lead to outcomes that are worse for human freedom and emancipation, but it's still resistance.

I'm thinking of an example to which I'm quasi-sympathetic. A Dutch social worker was describing to me a working-class Rotterdam couple in their 60s, who've always lived in the same place, who've been poor and unable to move out of their section of Rotterdam, where they've lived for the last 40 or 50 years. The neighborhood around them has become completely Moroccan. Everyone's speaking Arabic or French. All the grocery stores are Moroccan. So, in their life world, it's as if you sent them to Casablanca, right? They haven't moved, but their whole life world has been completely transformed.

They, of course, are furious, vote for the right-wing parties, become right-wing party militants, after having been trade unionists. They're resisting living in a world that's so unfamiliar to them, and they assume hostile as well, and it actually may be. It's important to understand it as resistance—the implication that I draw is that people can't put up with a radical, rapid change in their life world by and large, and you can't expect them to.

Take the 2008 Presidential election and ask yourself, in what places did McCain do better than Republican candidates had in the past? In a general Obama sweep, what places voted even more Republican than they would have historically? And the answer is—these are my people, by the way—West Virginia, Kentucky, Tennessee, Arkansas, Missouri, Oklahoma. What are those places like? Well, as someone said, distance from open water. Coal. My understanding is that these are the largest concentrations of whites, relatively poor whites, who have not participated in the progress of the last 20 or 30 years. The one thing they had going for them, if you like, is that they weren't Black. Now we have a Black president, so it makes them seem just poor. That sort of whiteness doesn't have the kind of cachet that it had before.

My guess is that these people would say something along the lines of: it's not their world; the Blacks and immigrants are taking over; and so on. Their anger that the country is no longer compatible with their values—it's resistance, and it takes an ugly form. It's resistance, and it's racism.

Seeing Outside the State

I did two books on this theme of resistance: *Weapons of the Weak* and *Domination and the Arts of Resistance*. Then, I did *Seeing Like a State*, which is about how states try to order the world for their management, manipulation—good or bad. That led me to my most recent book, *The Art of Not Being Governed*, which is an effort to understand the history of hill peoples throughout Southeast Asia, all the way from Vietnam through Southwest China to India. People who have, over the last two or three thousand years, put themselves purposefully—I argue—at a distance from the state and practiced a form of agriculture that's impossible to appropriate.

One reason why I find myself writing a book on anarchism is that I had great hopes for revolution leading to changes in the state. And almost all of these revolutions that led to changes in the state ended up producing governments that were just as bad or worse than the government that they had thrown out. Now, you could say that's progress, I guess, but it seemed to me that there was something mistaken about looking to new state structures as the structure for emancipation. As a friend of mine put it, which I've adopted as my motto, "Once the revolution becomes the state, it becomes my enemy." I find emancipation through state power to be not irrelevant—I'm not completely against it in terms of French universal citizenship, for example; I see a lot of the gains for human emancipation have come through state action—but just as much horror, destruction and limitations on human freedom.

I became interested in people who avoided the state altogether, practicing slash-and-burn agriculture, moving to the hills, going to the periphery, and having social organizations that can easily fission and disperse to avoid state control. I was looking at how people have historically avoided and intense, direct contact with the state and incorporation into states.

The state, as a nation-state, doesn't exist in any real way until about 1500. The earlier empires, they're little dots on the map—even the Roman Empire or the Chinese Empire. Most of the people in the world live outside state control. Since *Homo sapiens* have been around for 200,000 years. States, even the tiny ones, didn't come into existence until maybe 5,000 years ago. Strong states didn't come into existence until 1500 and, in Southeast Asia, not till after the Second World War.

It seems to me that most of human life has been lived outside the state, and it would be interesting to know how people were able to perpetuate that status of statelessness. It certainly is a change for me to move from the study of resistance to the state, in which the state is taken for granted as the institutional structure in which one lives, to a situation which people have not even crossed that particular Rubicon.

What Resistance Research Means for Resistance Movements

I don't think resistance researchers ought to flatter ourselves that we have much of an effect on the world. People are going to do what they do when they resist, and we try to understand it.

If people who study resistance have an activist life as well, in which they're trying to apply some of these lessons in actual groups and movements, then they can presumably bring a kind of theoretical and analytical understanding to bear. They might actually influence actions to be effective.

I expect that a whole lot of people have read my stuff on resistance, and yet, I don't think it's had any practical effect on the world. I research to amuse myself, but I'm not under any illusions. I had a three-or-four-year activist life as a student leader in the National Student Association, and I didn't like myself in that. It was a world of friends and enemies. I was fighting tooth and nail in intra-leftist struggles with people who, 95 percent of the time, were on the same side of the barricades as I was. And I now wonder why I was fighting with them in the first place. Because I'm so passionate when I get into these things, I recognize that I lose my perspective. I have chosen the life of contemplation on the fourth floor of Rosenkranz Hall to protect myself from doing stupid things as an activist.

Again, it's both wrong and foolish to say, "You should be doing this; you should be doing that. I'm in charge of research here. Don't resist me." People can do what they damn please.

Works Referenced

Eliot, G. (1985). *Adam Bede*. London: Penguin Books.

Hall, S., & Jefferson, T. (1976). *Resistance through rituals: Youth subcultures in post-war Britain*. London: Hutchinson.

Hobsbawm, E. (1959). *Primitive rebels: Studies in archaic forms of social movement in the 19th and 20th centuries*. Manchester: Manchester University Press.

Kelley, R.D.G. (1994). *Race rebels: Culture, politics, and the Black working class*. New York: Free Press.

Piven, F.F., & Cloward, R.A. (1977). *Poor people's movements: Why they succeed, how they fail*. New York: Pantheon Books.

Robinson, A.L. (2005). *Bitter fruits of bondage: The demise of slavery and the collapse of the Confederacy, 1861–1865*. Charlottesville: University of Virginia Press.

Scott, J.C. (1976). *The moral economy of the peasant: Rebellion and subsistence in Southeast Asia*. New Haven: Yale University Press.

Scott, J.C. (1985). *Weapons of the weak: Everyday forms of peasant resistance*. New Haven: Yale University Press.

Scott, J.C. (1990). *Domination and the arts of resistance: Hidden transcripts*. New Haven: Yale University Press.

Scott, J.C. (1998). *Seeing like a state: How certain schemes to improve the human condition have failed*. New Haven: Yale University Press.

Scott, J.C. (2009). *The art of not being governed: An anarchist history of upland Southeast Asia*. New Haven: Yale University Press.

Thompson, E.P. (1964). *The making of the English working class*. New York: Pantheon Books.

Willis, P.E. (1977). *Learning to labour: How working class kids get working class jobs*. Farnborough: Saxon House.

Zerzan, J. (1999). *Elements of refusal*. Columbia, MO: Columbia Alternative Library.

5

ORGANIZING RESISTANCE INTO SOCIAL MOVEMENTS

Pedro Noguera with Eve Tuck and K. Wayne Yang

NEW YORK, NEW YORK

Pedro Noguera is the Peter L. Agnew Professor of Education at New York University, the Executive Director of the Metropolitan Center for Urban Education, and the co-Director of the Institute for the Study of Globalization and Education in Metropolitan Settings (IGEMS). His books include *The Imperatives of Power: Political Change and the Social Basis of Regime Support in Grenada* (1997); *City Schools and the American Dream* (2003); *Unfinished Business: Closing the Achievement Gap in Our Nation's Schools* (2006), *The Trouble with Black Boys . . . and Other Reflections on Race, Equity and the Future of Public Education* (2008); *Creating the Opportunity to Learn: Moving from Research to Practice to Close the Achievement Gap* with A. Wade Boykin (ASCD, 2011); *Invisible No More: Understanding and Responding to the Disenfranchisement of Latino Males* with co-editors Aida Hurtado and Edward Fergus (Routledge, 2011); *Social Justice Education for Educators: Paulo Freire and the Possible Dream* edited with Carlos Alberto Torres (Sense Publishers, 2008); and a co-edited volume, *Beyond Resistance! Youth Activism and Community Change: New Democratic Possibilities for Practice and Policy for America's Youth* (2006).

Activism Informs Resistance

I think that resistance is important because it affirms our humanity, and it reminds us that we can be more than simply victims of oppression or observers of a particular historical moment. By resisting, we affirm our innate human ability to act in the world. And I think that that's why it's so inspiring to write about, to read about, and to see.

First and foremost, my interest in youth resistance comes from direct experience as a young activist in high school, in college, and in graduate school. In high school we were organizing against racism—against layoffs of Black teachers, against disproportionate suspensions—of Black students by the administration. So I came to college already as an experienced activist at 18 years old. I was very active as an undergraduate at Brown, both on campus and in the community, and by the time I got to grad school, I was a veteran activist.

What motivated me, as a young activist, was the belief that we could have an impact, not just on the campus but also on larger events occurring in the world. I became involved in the Anti-Apartheid movement during high school right after the Soweto uprising in 1976. At Berkeley in the mid-1980s, I was elected student body president and created a political party that still exists today. We built a movement that compelled the University of California to divest $4.6 billion in holdings in firms doing business in South Africa. It was by far the largest disinvestment in the country and it set the stage for changing U.S. policy toward South Africa, which up to that time had been characterized by Reagan's policy of "constructive engagement." To see Apartheid fall and Nelson Mandela released in the 1990s, gave me an appreciation for what could be accomplished through collective action. It was also a rare feeling of satisfaction to see something that I had been involved in for nearly 20 years culminate in success at a certain level.

I recently returned from a visit to South Africa, and clearly the struggle continues. Yet Apartheid, at least as a legal and political system, has come to an end.

I was much more radical when I was younger. I believed that there would be a revolution in my lifetime and that I would play a role in making it happen. That was the way I thought at that time, and as I reflect upon it now it seems very naïve. I used to believe that creating fundamental change at the level of state would transform society. I now realize that even revolutionary change is always very gradual. I was in El Salvador in 1984 with students who were actively resisting military repression by not only the Salvadorian government, but also the United States. I also lived and worked in Grenada in 1982 during the revolution where I did the research for my dissertation, which was eye-opening for me. These revolutionary situations in Central America and in Grenada shifted my understanding of how change occurs. I began to realize that sometimes, even in a period of revolution, there is not much change: Former revolutionaries become the new regime and the new oligarchs. They create bureaucracies that you must struggle with. Revolutionary change is never fundamental or instantaneous. It is always incremental.

I also understand that in different periods, what may be possible varies. What was possible in Berkeley in 1984 when we had thousands of people protesting against Apartheid is not the same as what is possible when there is no similar movement. The constraints are real, but the ability to act is also real. It is the ability to identify where are the possibilities for action and resistance lie, where the holes, the weak spots and the degrees of freedom can be found, that provides opportunities and openings where we can push and challenge the power structure.

Although I was excited by the possibilities that might be created I think there was a kind of naïveté when people expected President Obama to be a transformational leader who could deliver such things as an end to war, healthcare, educational equity, and immigration reform. Where was the movement to make him do all these things? If you want Obama to do things, we have to make him. You have to have a movement. Without a movement, a President will not change things. That is not how change happens.

Right now, the young people organizing for the DREAM Act are some of the most inspiring examples of resistance that I see. Here are young people willing to take great risks in order to challenge people in authority, and to draw attention to an issue. I think they are actually succeeding to a large degree. Obama's recent action, DACA,[1] was achieved in part because the DREAMers have been able to keep the issue alive. Otherwise, there would have only been lip service.

Reading History from Below

I think it would be very helpful and inspiring to another generation of young activists to learn from historical work on social movements. The young people who organized SNCC, how did they do it? Why did the Panthers emerge in Oakland? What gets people who are presently acquiescing and accepting their situation to actively resist? How do you generate critical mass and build a movement that goes beyond a few true believers? It is harder in the moment to understand the forces that produce change. Such questions are easier to answer from an historical vantage point. So what we will read about the revolution in Egypt or the Occupy movement will be much more compelling and explanatory in a few years than while we are immersed in the moment.

Historians always have the advantage in the study of social movements, because they do it in retrospect. There is a great book by Theda Skocpol, *States and Social Revolutions*, where she looks at different countries in similar historical moments, in order to ask comparative questions about revolution. Why did France have a revolution, but not England, during a similar period? Why did Germany not have a revolution, but Russia did? Why did China have a revolution, but not Japan? In retrospect, one can see how forces come together, how they are able to capitalize on weaknesses among the elites in power, and how that then results in the possibilities for revolutions to occur.

In the 1960s, one of the questions social scientists asked was, why certain cities experienced riots and other cities did not. Oakland never had a riot, a major riot, like Detroit and Newark did. Why? Were conditions different? If so, in what ways? Social scientists have learned that predicting uprisings or the outbreak of social movements is the hardest thing because they are not simply determined by material conditions. There is a subjective element related to the particular actions taken by key actors that is important. Would there have been a Cuban revolution without Fidel and Che, or a Chinese revolution without Mao? In retrospect in seems clear that individuals really matter in shaping events.

When we started organizing in 1984 in the Anti-Apartheid movement, it was a time when all media accounts were saying, "Students have gotten conservative."

Reagan had just been re-elected and it seemed as though we were in the midst of a very conservative period. Yet, all of a sudden, this movement broke out, not just at Berkeley, but also at college campuses all around the country. It involved workers, churches and even celebrities. The media was totally caught off guard, and wanted to know "Where did this come from?"

Clearly, we were inspired by the events in South Africa. The vivid images of both resistance and the brutal repression of the South African regime were inspiring to the broader populace, not just activists in the United States. That was a huge advantage because it made it possible for us to organize broad support for the movement. Yet, the movement against U.S. intervention in Central America never got as big despite the atrocities that occurred in Guatemala and El Salvador. The movement against U.S. intervention in Central America was robust in certain areas, but it never got massive the way the Anti-Apartheid movement did.

This is why scholars who study social movements and resistance must ask themselves what can be done to resist structural oppression—poverty, marginalization, powerlessness, and how can we make it happen? Despite being nearly 100 years old, Grace Lee Boggs is still working on these questions, writing about things right now, in Detroit. I am really taken by her critical analysis and by what she is saying: We are too caught up in waiting for someone to deliver us. Well, guess what? No one is going to deliver us. No one is going to save Detroit. Obama is not saving Detroit. The people of Detroit have to save Detroit themselves.

Throughout history, ordinary people have at various times asserted themselves by resisting oppression through deliberate forms of activism and organizing. History shows us that it is possible to shape events and not merely be shaped by them. We do not have to defer to elites. Many people adopt a very Freudian way of looking at social change; we are led to believe that powerful people—Presidents, billionaires, Generals—are the only ones who shape events and who set the course of history. But when we read history from below, we learn about movements that come from below. Individuals who seem to be relatively powerless, like a Harriet Tubman, Helen Keller, Fannie Lou Hamer and others whose actions actually have profound political consequences.

Part of what is inspiring about the story of the Civil Rights Movement is that the movement was made possible by people who were not special—they were ordinary. If you read about the work of Fred Shuttlesworth, Ella Baker, and Bob Moses, you can see that they succeeded by mobilizing ordinary folks to act. This is a very different way of reading the Civil Rights Movement than through the study of great men leading marches and giving speeches. I think that's very inspiring.

Critical Pedagogy Is Not the Same as Organizing

I was drawn to teaching because I recognized early on that the pedagogical space is important for encouraging critical thinking. I have seen from experience that when done well teaching can enable young people to become critical thinkers and actors in the world they live in, about their society. When they can see how what they learn can be used to organize in their community, or to confront injustice that is a great thing. However, it doesn't mean they're going become activists or organizers. I don't want to diminish the value and importance of critical pedagogy but I am troubled when I hear it described as "emancipatory or liberatory." To whom? This is a gross exaggeration of what is being done.

To me, organizing is the highest form of resistance. When we decide, "We're going to focus on a particular issue, and we're going to plot a strategy to address that issue," then we are engaged in genuine praxis. Take the stop-and-frisk policy of Michael Bloomberg, the Mayor of New York City. If we were going to work with young people to address that issue, we would have to develop a strategy with them that would have to include building allies. We would work on cultivating robust organizations. We would develop a media strategy. We might develop a sustainable citywide strategy, some of which might include a legal strategy, combined with a political strategy. We would have a very specific goal of getting that policy overturned. But it would be tactical. It wouldn't be simply sitting around and talking about how screwed up the policy is, or having a rally and saying, "The policy sucks."

This is where political education must be critical and sophisticated. If you don't do that work with young people, then they get frustrated when nothing changes after they come out to a rally. I've seen this happening as young people in New York have organized against the school closures. They assemble at a big rally, go to the PEP[2] meeting, and then listen to speakers. It's actually disempowering. The lesson they come away with is, "You mean we did all that, we were all there, we were all angry, and they did what they wanted to do anyway?" I've seen it; I've talked to those same students who feel very frustrated and dispirited. "We did all this work, and they shut down the school anyway." What we should do in advance is say, "Look, this group is a group of puppets appointed by the Mayor so they are going to do what the Mayor wants them to do. We are protesting to demonstrate to Bloomberg, who's not even here, that we're not going to put up with these policies. The important thing is that even after today, when they seem to do as the please anyway, we've got to have a comeback in response to their decision." We must help young people understand the protracted nature of this work.

Organizing Beats Spontaneity

In the Occupy movement, there was very little organizing that went into creating a sustainable strategy. What I liked about Occupy was its spontaneity, but that was also its greatest weakness. Think about it, how long can you occupy a park or some other public space? Bloomberg mobilized hundreds of police and ran the occupiers out of the park. Once they lost the physical space the movement dissipated. They killed it. I spoke to some of the organizers who argued, "Oh, well, people will come back. All we have to do is call them." No, it needed organization. It needed structure, and they were anti-organization, anti-structure.

I had similar disagreements with activists in the 1980s. We worked with the anarchists, who were against organization, were against structure, were against taking a more deliberate, planned-out set of strategies. I don't agree with anarchists. I'm anti-anarchist. Show me in history when people spontaneously rebelled, and when it led to sustainable change. I've never seen it happen.

There were some people who thought the Occupy Movement in New York and other cities would be like the Occupy Movement in Egypt. Clearly this was incorrect. The contexts were totally different, and thus the possibilities for change were different. In Egypt you had a dictatorship that had been repressing people for years. Egyptians had both their own target to focus on, this repressive regime of President Mubarak, plus a model to draw inspiration from, the overthrow of Gaddafi in Libya half a year earlier, and President Ben Ali in Tunisia just weeks earlier. They thought, "Look, if they can do it there, we can do it here."

But you saw what happened in Egypt. It began as a massive, broad-based movement against Mubarak. Then it all splintered. The Muslim Brotherhood came to control the Presidency, because aside from the military, they were the most organized faction in the society. Once it came down to elections, the movement was not strong enough to go against people who were actually organized. Organization beats spontaneity every day.

Organizing Is an Art and a Skill

I know from my own experience that student organizing is too episodic. In a kind of a flash, we might have a rally against some injustice: Stop-and-frisk, Trayvon Martin's killing, school closures in New York—but such mobilizations are not actually focused on winning or even sustaining pressure. To build a movement and to win real victories, you must think in terms of building a campaign that will continue over time. It's not a rally. It's what happens after the rally. You need people who have lists of names that they are going to call; they have meetings; they work on developing a strategy and a plan; they know how to network with people because they *have* a network. As a professor I've seen so many student activists who come to me with energy and enthusiasm who think, "Oh, I'll just put up flyers, and random people will come to our rally or event, and we'll make change." They might come the first time, but they won't come back unless you have a plan to make it happen. If you're a real organizer, when people do come, you're going to say, "Can I get your name, your email address and your number, so we can get back to you?" That's how organizers operate.

Organizing is an art and a skill. Saul Alinsky knew that. All these elements of organizing have to be retaught over and over again. And the possibilities for building movements are even greater now with the advent of social media. I think there's a whole generation of scholars who study social movements but who don't really understand them. They study the manifestation and try to understand it once it's there. They don't understand how things grow and develop.

For example, people who understand organizing know that when making tactical decisions you must sometimes decide between focusing on policymakers or on public opinion; it really depends on the life cycle of the issue. Sometimes, what you really should be striving for is influencing and educating the public, not the policymakers, because the policymakers are indifferent to protest. This is why organizers must also be educators, not in a traditional sense but in a political sense.

With divestment from South Africa, we didn't simply try to influence the policymaking body of The Regents,[3] although we used Regent meetings as a focal point for struggle and for organizing. We focused on changing public attitudes, which succeeded where lobbying did not. Public opinion is the reason why George Deukmejian, who was a Republican Governor of California at the time, ended up voting in favor of divestment because it was a politically popular issue.

We helped to make the issue popular and to keep it alive, just like the DREAMers are doing for the DREAM Act. Those students who walked from Miami to Washington, D.C. risked their lives, and made huge sacrifices to keep the issue alive. I think they were not so much trying to influence the politicians. They were trying to influence the public, by keeping the issue in the media. And that is as important as anything else sometimes.

That's where the political reading of the situation becomes important. You need a view of the long haul, the long struggle.

Resistance Has Gradations and a Subjective Dimension

My own work in schools makes me very cautious about calling every act of defiance or oppositional behavior a form of resistance. I remember my first teaching experience was in Providence, Rhode Island while I was still a student at Brown. I was often asked to work with kids who were getting in trouble. I would could see that their motivations to act out and disrupt classrooms might be due to the fact that they didn't like school, or that they felt the rules were arbitrary, or felt they were treated unfairly, or they were simply "having a laff" in the Willis mode; trying to have a good time in school at the expense of the teachers and administrators. I don't think of all of these behaviors as acts of resistance.

I think Giroux is very good about saying that the subjective element of resistance, the conscious critique, is an important part of it. That's why we can't simply call something resistance just by looking at it. In *The Trouble with Black Boys*, I wrote about how sometimes what appears to be conformity might actually be a form of resistance. When someone is striving to do well in school to counter stereotypes and low expectations to demonstrate that Black children can achieve; that can be a form of resistance.

I describe a situation at a Berkeley High School where kids were required to read *Huckleberry Finn.* Some of the Black students in the class said they would rather leave the class than to have to read the book because they were offended by the use of the word *nigger* throughout the book. Other students chose to conform and basically give the teacher what she wanted. They figured, "School's a game anyway. I'll just play the game and ignore the racism in the book."

But one student I observed made a different choice. She said, "Screw the teacher. I'm going to write what I think, and if she wants to penalize me for it, so be it." She stayed in the class, and she wrote a paper critiquing the way in which slavery and the character Jim is portrayed in the book. If you just looked at her conduct in the classroom you might assume that this is a compliant student. You would have to talk to her and read her writing, to realize this student is actually exhibiting the highest level of resistance of all the students involved.

For some, resistance only seems to count if we like it, if it fits our ideological framework. I'm not willing to go that far. Where a lot of resistance research runs into trouble—what we struggle with as scholars who study it—is the subjective dimension of resistance. That is, how do we know if an action we observe is coming from a conscious, deliberate critique on the part of youth actors? How much is informed by an awareness about what they're doing and how it connects to other issues?

As a high school student, I saw myself as part of a national liberation movement even though I was just active at my school. The local issues were symbolic of larger issues for me. Driving my activism in many ways was critique—an understanding, first of all, of what I'm up against, what we're up against. I knew then that it couldn't just be my understanding of the issues, that it needed to be a collective, shared understanding. In order for political action to be far-reaching it can't be simply be based on how I see things. There must be work done to create a collective consciousness and long-term goals.

However, this perspective may not be true for everyone who is an activist. I can think of many people that I worked over the years, for whom this wasn't true. When the specific issues we worked on were resolved, or when we left high school together, they ceased being activists. Even for people in the same movement, you can't generalize about what motivates them, or how they are reading and interpreting their own actions.

There may be aspects of resistance where the actors may not be able to fully explain what it is they're doing, why they're doing it, and what they're reacting to. This is especially true for children. My granddaughter, who's four, may not be able to explain herself, but what is motivating her actions could in fact be based on some deep sense of injustice about something she sees. That is where the work of James Scott is important because he explores these very subtle forms of resistance.

However, I think it's a mistake to call all forms of agency, "resistance," or all forms of oppositional behavior, "resistance." Because if we call everything resistance, then it starts to lose its meaning and significance. We can no longer appreciate the differences involved in collective organizing, and the differences in collective consciousness that it requires. Micro manifestations of resistance are examples of agency, which demonstrate, to me, the human capacity to resist. At the same time, I want to make a distinction between the capacity to resist, and the work of young people who actually form movements for change.

That is why I take into consideration different levels or gradations of resistance. If a student is angry at unjust policies at their school, and they decide, "I'm going to cut school," or, "I'm going to cuss out the principal," that may be a form of agency but it may not be an act of resistance. But if that same student decides, "You know what I'm going to do? I'm going to organize other students to have a boycott of school," that is clearly a higher level of resistance.

There's a great film called *Bush Mama*, by the director of *Sankofa*, Haile Gerima. He's an Ethiopian-American filmmaker. It's an interesting film set in Watts in the 1960s, and it shows the transformation in consciousness of a woman who goes from being victimized by police to becoming a militant. This is the kind of evolution that I'm speaking to—a higher level of consciousness, with a more developed theory of action. We need to draw distinctions within our understanding of what resistance and what movements look like between these various forms.

In the Los Angeles "uprising," after the Rodney King verdict—we still don't even know what to call it—there were a lot of Central Americans who participated. It was an interesting phenomenon that people didn't understand because the media presented the outburst as a manifestation within the Black community. Many of the Latinos who participated in the uprising had been activists in the revolutions that were occurring in Central America. Some came out of highly developed political organizations in El Salvador. There's an interview that Anna Deavere Smith conducted with one activist, where she asks, "How do you characterize it?" The activist replies, "Well, some people want to call this a rebellion but it's not a rebellion because we've been in a rebellion in my country and rebellions are different from this. I will call this a social explosion. People were angry, and they let off some steam, and now it's over. It's different than a rebellion. What we are doing in El Salvador, that's a rebellion. We are organized. We are prepared to take over the state if we get a chance."

You have to draw distinctions in the level of action. Otherwise, resistance becomes almost meaningless if all actions are regarded in the same manner.

Why Research Resistance?

I think people are drawn to resistance research because we need a sense of hope. There is hope in the belief that by resisting forms of oppression we are not just engaged in fruitless work. When we see that we can actually have an impact on our reality and on the world around us through our actions we begin to believe that change is possible. Such hope is not just delusional. It's real. This is why I never allow my students to only read *Schooling in Capitalist America*. I know that after they read it they will feel, "Oh well, it's hopeless. Nothing we can do here until capitalism's gone." But for people who actually want to do something now, they want something else; they want some sense of the possible that isn't just naïveté. That's why I assign *Schooling and Work in the Democratic State* by Carnoy and Levin. They understand the historical importance of social movements in shaping social reforms.

For people studying youth resistance, I think it's essential to become totally embedded among the people and the movements that you're trying to write about. If you want to study it, you've got to be in it. You've got to know it. You've got to understand it. When not embedded, researchers risk making a lot of projections that miss the mark. We see in research a lot of people who say they're studying youth organizing, but they're really studying youth mobilizations or youth activism. If you are too removed to even understand it, you're like a fan, not a player.

If you were working with the young people organizing around the DREAM Act, you would learn a whole lot about how they're organizing and how they're sustaining their efforts. That could be a very rich area of scholarship for people who are interested in studying resistance. Among a generation of young resistance scholars, there is a growing awareness that you have to look at resistance where it is. You have to go where the action is. There are insights you gain from being directly involved that you may not as an outsider looking in. This is especially true with people who study social movements.

I don't call myself an activist any more, although I do consider myself a scholar-activist. I try to use my intellectual labor to support activist work. I'm doing a press conference tomorrow against the state's education policies. But I don't have any illusions that a press conference will change anything. It might get some press and hopefully remind folks that not everybody agrees with what the state is doing. But I don't believe that's how change happens. For that, we would have to have an organizing strategy. You don't see many groups that actually do organizing any more. Organizing's gone out of style.

What hasn't changed for me is the idea that resistance is not individual; it's collective. It's shaped by historical circumstances, and that's why it's not necessarily transferable. That's why what happened in Egypt doesn't happen in Saudi Arabia.

You have to read your situation to understand what's possible in a particular time and place. For me, agency, collective agency, is resistance in its most potent form. Such agency is critically conscious, in that it is informed by historical and contemporary struggles for justice everywhere. It is farsighted in that it attempts to foresee and foretell a future struggle, as well as a future that is more free. Collective agency is politically sophisticated. It is strategic about locating the pressure points on the system. It is organized.

Notes

1 On June 15, 2012, President Obama signed the administrative memorandum, Deferred Action for Childhood Arrivals (DACA), directing the Department of Homeland Security immigration and border control agencies to practice prosecutorial discretion towards some individuals who immigrated illegally to the United States as children.
2 The New York City Panel for Educational Policy (PEP) consists of 13 appointed members and the Chancellor.
3 The University of California is governed by The Regents, a 26-member board, of which 18 are appointed by the Governor of California.

Works Referenced

Alinsky, S.D. (1971). *Rules for radicals: A practical primer for realistic radicals.* New York: Random House.

Bowles, S., & Gintis, H. (1976). *Schooling in capitalist America: Educational reform and the contradictions of economic life.* New York: Basic Books.

Carnoy, M., & Levin, H.M. (1985). *Schooling and work in the democratic state.* Stanford, CA: Stanford University Press.

Gerima, H., Mypheduh Films, & Facets Video. (1993). *Bush mama.* Chicago: Facets Video.

Gerima, H., Ghanaba, K., Ogunlano, O., Duah, A., Medley, N., Negod-Gwad Productions, & Mypheduh Films. (1995). *Sankofa.* Washington, D.C.: Mypheduh Films, Inc.

Giroux, H.A. (1983). *Theory and resistance in education: A pedagogy for the opposition.* South Hadley, MA: Bergin & Garvey.

Noguera, P. (2008). *The trouble with Black boys: And other reflections on race, equity, and the future of public education.* San Francisco: Jossey-Bass.

Scott, J.C. (1985). *Weapons of the weak: Everyday forms of peasant resistance.* New Haven: Yale University Press.

Skocpol, T. (1979). *States and social revolutions: A comparative analysis of France, Russia, and China.* Cambridge: Cambridge University Press.

Smith, A.D. (1994). *Twilight—Los Angeles, 1992 on the road: A search for American character.* New York: Anchor Books.

Willis, P.E. (1977). *Learning to labour: How working class kids get working class jobs.* Farnborough: Saxon House.

6

RESISTANCE AS REVELATORY

Robin D.G. Kelley with Eve Tuck
and K. Wayne Yang

WEST HOLLYWOOD, CALIFORNIA

Robin D.G. Kelley is the Gary B. Nash Professor of American History at UCLA. His books include *Freedom Dreams: The Black Radical Imagination* (2002); *Race Rebels: Culture, Politics, and the Black Working Class* (1994); and *Thelonious Monk: The Life and Times of an American Original* (2009).

Becoming a Resistance Theorist

I'm a historian. My approach to thinking about these ideas is to tell stories of how resistance and movements have happened. I became a historian because I was a communist. I came to my work in resistance because as a Marxist, questions of resistance in revolution specifically—not just rebellion, not just opposition, but revolution—were very, very important, both politically and theoretically. These questions were at the center of all the work I was doing as a graduate student. My book, *Hammer and Hoe*, put the question of the effectiveness of resistance at the center because it was concerned with a communist movement in antebellum South, in which acts of resistance necessarily had to be underground for the most part.

In the research for that book, I began to attend to the strategies of opposition that hid their tracks. I wasn't initially looking for that, but that's what I found. I began to realize that many of the folks who engaged in acts of resistance and struggle were actually not in the Communist Party, not in the NAACP, and not in the sort of formal organizations we usually think of. That led to the next book, *Race Rebels*.

Inspirations for Early Works in Resistance

My books *Race Rebels*, *Yo Mama's Disfunktional*, and *Freedom Dreams* represent sea changes in my thinking on resistance. *Race Rebels* was about everyday forms of resistance, and people consider it to be my first theoretical and historical contribution to resistance in broader terms. At the time I was reading James C. Scott closely, including *Domination and the Arts of Resistance* and his earlier book, *Weapons of the Weak*. The latter was especially important to my cohort of activists and scholars because it was coming at questions of resistance from a different standpoint than anyone else writing at that time. Scott's theorizing resonated with the work I was doing with the Communist Workers' Party; I was grappling with the questions of why so many people did *not* resist, why so many embraced the system, why did consent work so well?

Antonio Gramsci was the most instructive on all of these questions, which I read as part of a study group we formed in the Communist Workers' Party. I imagine it would have been very different to read Gramsci for the first time in an academic context, but reading it in our CWP study group informed the significance of his ideas with the context of our lived practices. We were trying to really understand theories of resistance in struggle. "How can you translate Gramsci's theories of hegemony? And what position, what maneuver should we try? How do you translate those words on the page into active actual struggle?" These were the questions his work raised and helped us to think through.

Through reading Gramsci, I found myself reading Stuart Hall, and I ran smack into the field of British cultural studies. I had one foot in the academy, one foot in the active movement, and as a historian, I sought to understand these questions from the perspective of the long view, within a particular historical framework. *Race Rebels* reflects the combination of influences from Stuart Hall, James C. Scott, Antonio Gramsci, my experiences in the CWP, and historical scholarship by people like E.P. Thompson; these all informed the way that I theorized the Black working class' own self-activity.

Self-activity is a term coined by George Rawick. I consider Rawick the most important theorist on the question of resistance in the twentieth century. He emphasized the ways in which oppressed people—Black people, slaves, free people, the working class—fight back on their own terms under circumstances which are not of their own choosing; understanding their resistance as still being on their own terms was his critical insistence.

Yo Mama's Disfunktional discusses youth culture in terms of commoditization, the entrenchment of capitalism, and the identification with the system of capitalism by young people trying to get ahead in a post-industrial labor market. *Freedom Dreams*, then, was a recognition of what was missing from the prior texts: how people in struggle *imagine* a different future. In the other books, I put so much emphasis on struggling with the state for resources, that I seemed to be saying that justice was comprised only of struggling against or engaging the state. *Freedom Dreams* asked the questions: How do people think? What do they imagine they are trying to produce? And how do social movements work to activate that imagination? In writing *Freedom Dreams* I had to ask myself, why did I think that the state was at the center of what was possible?

Grace Lee Boggs was one of the people who helped to change my mind about the necessity of the state. She was calling me up, writing me letters, challenging me to think about the difference between rebellion and revolution. She insisted that we do not need the state to provide resources. She was in Detroit working with young people, saying, wait a second, we need to do this for ourselves. *Freedom Dreams* was very much inspired by those debates with her. Those conversations forced me to rethink what resistance is.

Particular books always resonate with particular readers, but each of those books represent a rethinking on my part. There is a set of readers who are interested in everyday forms of resistance discussed in *Race Rebels*. These are scholars and young people who say, "After engaging that book, I now feel empowered to look at cultural forms as precursors to rebellion. Now I know to understand Tahrir Square or Tunisia or London in 2005, I need to pay attention to the kind of cultural expressions that preceded those events." There is another set of readers for whom *Yo Mama's Disfunktional* is most helpful. The articulation of the need for mostly people of color, labor, working class-based forms of struggle to make certain kinds of demands on the state, resonates with them. These readers might include people engaged in the DREAM Act or in struggles against the criminalization of truancy. Finally, there are those who really identify with *Freedom Dreams*, and with the notion that we have to pay attention to not just what's wrong but to what we want. What is it we're trying to produce? I am not the first person to ask this question—this has been part of the discourse since the eighteenth century—but something about the way people read that question in *Freedom Dreams* has mattered to them.

What I'm very, very heartened by is, that among the most important, most dynamic youth-based struggles happening right now are movements that resonate with aspects of all three of those texts. For example, young people who are transgender are dealing with enormous violence and exclusion, but are also producing a cultural sort of reclamation, a kind of cultural renaissance. I have heard from transgender people about connections they see between all of these texts. For them, being able to express oneself is an act of resistance. Obtaining access, whether it is access to bathrooms, access to institutions, access to healthcare, access to the right to be, is a revolutionary act. In their organizing work, they are trying to imagine a future in which homonormativity and heteronormativity are completely redefined—a future in which normativity itself is eliminated.

The Salience of the Category of Youth in Resistance

I have never relied heavily on the category of *youth*. My work looks at forms of opposition across a whole generation, within the broad scope of a class, across racial lines. Where there is resistance and struggle, that's where I'm looking. When I discuss hip hop, resistance on buses in Birmingham, Malcolm X, or the zoot suit, youth figure in prominently for obvious reasons. In each example, we can observe the emergence of a new generation of working-class people who are trying to distinguish themselves generationally and culturally from their fore-fathers and foremothers. That distinction is part of their own self-activity.

To consider youth resistance a discrete category didn't occur to me, in part because the lines around "youth"—where it ends and where it begins—are so unclear. More importantly, it doesn't seem useful to try to say that youth are any more or less resistant or engaged than people who are not youth.

Of course, one of the amazing things about Civil Rights, Black Power, and many of the organized movements in the 1950s and 1960s that I have written about, is that the leadership oftentimes came from the ranks of what we today call youth—young people who are 17, 18, 19 years old. And they are not in a separate youth sub-group, they are leaders in the organization. It is significant that there is no distinction between leadership and youth leadership.

One experience that shaped my thinking about youth leadership was the Black Radical Congress in 1998. There was a heated debate about the existence and role of the Youth Caucus. Part of the discussion had to do with defining who is a "youth"—I made the point that many people in the Youth Caucus were already college graduates, and that in designating their work as "youth work" it was channeling young people's energies and contributions to the side. It was the very contributions and energies of the Youth Caucus that allowed for the elders and leaders of the Black Radical Congress to take the main stage. To say that anyone 25 and younger is doing "youth stuff" and that anyone older than 25 is doing "grown-up stuff" is to block the synergy produced out of collective think-ing through struggle, through strategy and tactics. In some formations, youth resistance is not about thinking at all; it is about participating in actions designed by adults, engaging in identity development, that sort of thing. It is rarely about how young people actually theorize their own forms of resistance, theorize their own circumstances.

I actually argued something similar several years before, in a keynote to a group called Scholars, Artists and Writers for Social Justice (SAWSJ), who had a number of young people doing work under the label of "youth organizers." I told those youth, "You need to be up here running SAWSJ. You need to be running the unions. You need to be fighting for control of the locals because an important part of the work is trying to create a new generation of dynamic think-ers to push labor in a new direction."

Many of the ideas in that keynote were published as a letter to the editor of The *Nation* (June 20, 1998) in response to Eric Alterman's ridiculous attack on me and my speech. I think of that letter as one of the best things I have ever written. Everyone loves youth resistance scholarship as long as the youth resistance is on the page. As long as it's about consumption, cultural expression, rights and rebellions, clothes, language, then it's cool. But when you start to say we're going to implement the idea of youth-led struggle or intergenerational leadership, some people get very bothered by that. As a historian, I know that in each of those spaces in history that are now considered important centers in the struggle for power, youth have played a major leadership role. That is how it has always been. Spaces like the Southern New Youth Congress, the United Farm Workers—many of those organizers were youth, they were just kids. Thus, my theorizing of youth resistance was never separated from their actual, broader movements.

Limitations and Misrepresentations of Earlier Works

My earlier work used a framework of the post-industrial, whereas now I would describe neoliberalism as a much more comprehensive, effective framework for understanding the conditions facing not just young people, but all people. I used post-industrial to convey the idea of capital flight and the disappearance of institutions which kept communities if not together, at least in a structure of a public culture. Post-industrial was a way to get at the erosion of public culture. What I did not deal with in earlier work but now address, is neoliberalism's conscious, active privatization and commoditization of people's misery through the expansion of prisons. Earlier I did talk about prisons and the state, but not in the way that connects with the transformation of capitalism since the 1970s.

One of the frequent misreads of my work is the overemphasis on culture as resistance. I have written about structure and culture, about capitalism, the erosion of institutions and public spaces; I have written about culture as part of all of this, all the while insisting on the caveat that I'm not calling all cultural forms, acts of resistance. I'm not saying that the strategies of self-commoditization are means to overthrow a system. In fact, these acts just raise survival, raising it to reinforce capitalism. When people come away from my work with a focus on culture, I see them coming away with a misread. When too much emphasis is put on culture, people tend to fetishize the cultural form itself, rather than the way cultural forms are really diagnostic of power. Cultural forms matter because of the way people make meaning of them. There is nothing inherently rebellious nor resistive nor radical about a zoot suit, hip hop music, or any other expressive form. The resistance they enact is not self-evident.

For example, Raymond Williams' notion of alternative culture was a way to say that sometimes, people produce cultural expressions not at all meant to be resistant but the state decides that they are. You're just out there having a good time; next thing you know, you're being arrested or beat up by somebody. And you don't even know why. In this way, the state produces resistance; it makes visible cultural expressions that were not forms of opposition until the state interpreted them as resistance. These expressions become oppositional because somehow they challenge the state, even if that's not the intention.

People have mistakenly concluded from my work that everything is resistance and then say, "Well, if that's true, then what's the outcome? What's the effect?

How come nothing has changed?" Paul Willis' *Learning to Labour* had a huge impact on my thinking because the lesson drilled home is that, in the end, these cats are working in the mines. Their resistance produces, indeed reproduces, their proletarianization. They are children of proletariat who are going to become the proletariat again and again and again because their very acts of resistance often-times tighten the noose. Just because you resist authority, does not mean you have any impact on transforming the conditions of your life. The potential may be there, but in the end, you end up reinforcing for another generation terrible wages and working conditions. Part of *Race Rebels* was building on Paul Willis' notion of reproduction, and the work of people like Phillip Corrigan, to say, we have to be careful not to fetishize resistance. Resistance sometimes tightens the noose and makes things worse. That was the most important lesson in *Race Rebels*, but people took the opposite message from the argument. I added an afterword to the paperback edition to make the point about resistance and the noose, and to encourage readers not to overemphasize resistance, but to think and strive for revolution. I also needed to remind readers not to ignore the essential role of organization.

Resistance as Diagnostic

People misunderstand resistance when they think it is just about young people rebelling, and outright rebellion is where the action is in theorizing social change. The most compelling way to think about James Scott's everyday acts of resistance, as Lila Abu-Lughod has argued, is as diagnostic. Everyday acts of resistance are telling you what people desire. They are telling you what causes pain. They are telling you where there are trouble spots. They are telling you where people are confused. Everyday acts of resistance are revelatory, revealing things about social relationships and power. Being diagnostic of power doesn't mean that these acts actually do anything to change those relationships. They can even reinforce them. It is our job as historians, scholars, theorists, as social interpreters to find out what these acts are telling us.

Resistance as Theorizing

Resistance is not just about getting people organized, getting people to pro-tests. It's also always about thinking. One big weakness in scholarship on youth resistance is that it rarely takes into consideration theorizing going on among young people, especially young people who are organized. Being part of an organization like the Communist Party or like Sister Sol, means you are involved with a group of people that have a conscious agenda to change, which is so different from just being pissed off about a situation. Youth resistance scholarship sometimes collapses these as though they are the same thing, like listening to hip hop music is the same as being part of an organization.

The generation of young hip hop artists and activists of the 1990s, and those influenced by the music, proved how wrong that equivalence is by going on to form organizations like Critical Resistance, Prison Moratorium Project, and others. What masses of young people do in terms of class, race, intergenerational struggle—that's one kind of resistance. Young people who actually form organizations, are part of movements that try and make changes—we cannot ignore them just because they are fewer in number. We have to pay attention to them as a particular category because they are theorizing their own resistance through organizing.

Here in Los Angeles, connected to the Labor Community Strategy Center, a group of high school students has been working with an organizer named Manuel Criollo for the past five or six years. Recently, they challenged the number of tickets issued for truancy by LAUSD school police and the LAPD. They found data that over the last several years more *than* 13,000 tickets had been issued for truancy; not a single one issued to a white student. They organized and made public presentations, they wrote in public forums, and they won. They convinced city council to amend the truancy laws to reduce the tickets from around $250.00 to $20.00, to allow for hardship cases, and to relax requirements around parents coming to the court. At a time of budget cuts, when the whole nation is increasingly criminalizing young people by moving even minor so-called crimes into the adult court system, this example shows how organized youth have effectively fought back against these trends.

In post-Katrina New Orleans, Students at the Center (SAC) is an intergenerational group of youth, radical schoolteachers, and poets in New Orleans. The brilliance of SAC lies in its process—collective story-telling and careful listening rooted in non-hierarchical, consensus-building practice that focuses on strengthening community. Teacher Jim Randels and the great poet (and teacher) Kalamu ya Salaam create space to enable young people to not only tell their story but to critique society, to understand why their schools are bad, why developers are pushing them off the land, why opportunities are so elusive, and what is special about New Orleans, its legacy, and the struggle over its future. Their work recognizes that young people are in the lead, and are theorizing the framework of the social movement—theorizing how to transform the United States and its place in the world.

When Michelle Alexander talks about the new Jim Crow, it's young people of color who are at the forefront of struggles to decriminalize their daily lives, in writing circles, theater groups and other organizations: this is what this new civil rights movement looks like. But isn't that how it always is? The very moment of danger, George Lipsitz would say, where everything appears hopeless, is also the moment where you see the most dynamic and revolutionary possibilities emerge. All around us, young people are at the forefront of asking how we imagine a different future, but their theorizing goes unnoticed because youth are still seen as the junior partners of the social movement. This represents a departure from how youth were perceived in prior generations. Then, youth were the future. Now, they are who we need to train to become like us.

Youth Development as Containment

Much work in youth resistance as youth development is actually a form of containment under the guise of preparing young people for democracy and citizenship. Nowhere in that work is an attempt to dislodge the notion of American democracy as the ideal, as the most appropriate way for people to participate and for us to run things. Young people are contained by youth development models in which there's no critique of representative democracy and no embrace of participatory democracy as it was laid out by people like Ella Baker—one of the great theorists of participatory democracy. The Civil Rights Movement would never have imagined using youth resistance simply as a workshop to prepare people for citizenship. Youth in the movement did the theorizing, the interrogation of what citizenship *is*. Instead of youth development, we should look to young people and their self-activity to produce new ways of thinking about how to reorganize our society. Malcolm X insisted that that problem wasn't that Black people were second-class citizens, but the notion of their citizenship at all was a lie. We don't need to prepare youth for active citizenship. They need space for completely revamping and rethinking and interrogating American citizenship and American democracy as they are currently defined. The opportunity is to make educational space to see contemporary youth movements in the United States for what they are, which is a remapping of American society.

This educational space cannot be fully provided within a classroom. It needs to take place in the context of social movements where young people are not just a part of, but lead and run organizations. Even though Occupy got a lot of bad press for the spectacle it portrayed, it was one of these contexts. In *The Empire of Illusion* Chris Hedges writes about how spectacle has displaced critical analysis. The spectacle of Occupy became more prominently circulated than the analysis it offered. The spectacle of unshaven white people, young kids in the park, replaced any discussion of the critique being leveled both within Occupy and against Occupy. If we pay attention to the history of the movement itself, we realize many of the people who gave rise to it were young people of color who participated in the U.S. Social Forum, young people of color who had organized things like Domestic Workers United, Project South, and others. They have envisioned real radical change and have been fighting for a decade for it. And yet, when the stories of Occupy are circulated, those young people don't exist. Occupy got read as spontaneous.

The discourse by, from, and about a movement really matters. There are examples of intergenerational exchanges and collective analyses that happen both in and out of schools, that are not about containment, that are not about preparation. 67 Sueños, an activist group of primarily Latina/o young people, recognizes that only a minority of undocumented youth are covered in the discourse of the DREAM Act. The rest, the 67 percent, do not have access to college nor to deferred action, and enter the labor force with zero protection. 67 Sueños is theorizing the limitations of constitutional democracy and the DREAM Act. They are producing a different framework in order to expand the possibilities of social justice. These kinds of discourses stand outside the bounds of preparing young people for democratic participation. To me, these are revolutionary kinds of claims.

The Expectations Applied to Youth Resistance

In my view, the ways that youth resistance is being theorized in scholarship has reached a kind of bankruptcy. Earlier work in U.S. cultural studies sometimes celebrated forms of consumption that had resistance. Now, when understanding that same consumption within a neoliberalism framework, it seems untenable to claim that any kind of consumption is inherently resistant to a commodity culture. Some cultural studies are holding on to the same old ideas that still fetishize popular culture. It's the new generation of organizers and theorists who are no longer doing that. Young people are theorizing racism as an operative analytic in their lives, despite being constantly bombarded with a consumer culture that says racism is no longer even an issue, that racism doesn't exist. But what does exist is social media, Facebook and Twitter. As much as we can celebrate social media as systems for mobilizing, as we saw in Arab Spring, they are as much part of the conveyor belt for consumer culture.

One of the frustrating things about the media discourse on recent movements in Tunisia, Egypt, Palestine, Quebec and Arizona, is that young people are cast as the inspiration or the energy of the movement, but not as leaders with the capacity to produce policy. Young people get erased as the theorists of the movements. For example, youth leaders of the actions we now call the Arab Spring, were read by the West as incapable of producing democracy. The discourse is that democracy takes a long time to develop, to come up to the standards of the West. Think of Tom Brokaw, who commented on how it would take a long time for the burgeoning democracies to achieve a Jeffersonian democracy: really? That is the expectation we are going to apply to this movement? That is what we think they are trying to achieve? Small farms and "Notes on Virginia"?

To understand the Arab Spring, we have to look at the five or ten years before the uprising in Tunisia, at the students and young people in the labor movement who were trying to create a new form of civil society that opposes U.S. imperialism and opposes fundamentalism. They were imagining a civil society that struggles for women's rights, that struggles for reorganization of the economy based on social justice—and not based on neoliberalism, not based on competition, not based on privatization. These struggles have put the question on the table: What are the tools we need to create to help us understand not only the sources of the uprising and opposition, but also what is required to sustain a real movement?

We cannot decide what resistance is, based on its perceived effectiveness. We have to understand where people are coming from—the limits, the cultures, the experiences, the histories, the memories—and see self-activity as self-active, self-generated modes of struggle. We don't have to like these self-activities. We don't have to think they're great or grand. We miss the point if we only judge them strictly on whether or not they succeed.

Without attending to the theories produced by youth resistance, we run the risk of work on resistance becoming irrelevant.

The Role of Research in Resistance

After *Race Rebels*, I published an article in *The Nation* about resistance on buses. Eric Mann contacted me because he was working with a group forming a bus riders' union, they had read my article, and they wanted talk about how to collaborate. Organized groups do this all the time, they are very active intellectually, they read and want to collaborate with scholars. When the collaboration is initiated by activists, I think it's very successful.

There are also great models of social science research that operated outside of formal institutions, and in collaboration with social movements. One is a wonderful book called *Lessons from the Damned*, put together by a group of welfare rights activists, Black feminists, mainly in Mount Vernon, New York back in the 1970s. The book features essays written by "the damned," working-class, poor, dispossessed people—the welfare recipients, the truants, kids that struggled in school—about what it means to be poor and Black under Nixon. Some might look at this collection and think that it is memoir, but really it is research. The approaches vary, including interview, archival research, but they work together as a collective expression on the lived experience of being poor and working class.

There is another model of collaboration. A think tank model, like those offered by the Mellon Program, can bring in dynamic young people who want to go to graduate school to work with scholars as research assistants to produce some research on young people. This approach can be very, very useful, but the living dynamism of community-based research is missing.

In my view, the most powerful examples of collaboration are those in which the people about whom you are writing have a role in collecting and analyzing data. As part of a study in Central Harlem, Leith Mullings established a community advisory board of people across generation, occupation, class, and status who met to oversee, advise, and critique her research. In one story she tells, they advised her not to focus solely on unemployment rates in the community and instructed her to lead with employment rates. Flip the narrative usually circulated about people in Harlem. Suddenly, what the data communicated was the story not of a Harlem full of jobless people who are potentially dependent, but of a working class employed—still underemployed—but a working-class community. In light of this narrative, the approach to policy on poverty must change.

Mullings tells another story about housing research. The advisory board said to her, "If you just want to know about housing, don't just go to the houses, you need to deal with the landlords. And how do you deal with the landlords? You go downtown to housing court. That's the site where you need to be." It didn't occur to Mullings and her research team to go to housing court, but when they did, who did they see? All the women they had been trying to interview about housing conditions: they had been fighting unfair practices based on their own research in their tenement apartments. Housing court was where women who were protecting their families came into view.

The women were already doing research to figure out who owned the buildings, to document conditions, and to determine what was owed to them. Despite the fact that many didn't have a high school diploma, they were working together to produce research that was actually useful in their fight to change living conditions. This kind of research is going on all the time, but it doesn't count. The most powerful collaborations in resistance research require scholars to know where research is actually happening and to connect with it. Such collaboration leads to not just data but to research with transformational power.

Theories of Change: Breaks and Radical Empathy

When the Labor Community Strategy Center in Los Angeles established a summer school for organizers, they didn't just focus on the most effective tactics, and didn't just go out and organize. The school provided the space for organizers to develop an informed analysis to several questions: How does change actually take place? How has change taken place in the past? How can we do it in the present? And what are the changes that we really want?

After Freedom Summer in 1964, SNCC (the Student Nonviolent Coordinating Committee) founded freedom schools based on similar questions: What is it that we want? How do we get that? What is in society that we want to discard? The SNCC freedom schools provide an important tradition of strategizing how to make change by collectively imagining what it is that we are actually fighting for. Without a theory of change, struggle is going to be an exercise in futility.

Having no theory of change is one problem with some youth resistance literature, in part because it is so locked in the category of youth. Once you fetishize the category of youth as a life stage, it is hard to conceive of a theory of change. By bracketing youth out of social movements, the work can only be about identity formation. Such work relies on a theory of change that denies full personhood to young people, treating them only as those who will be inheriting the future and not as part of the active present. The theory of change is about convincing young people; then, change is what is planned for them, done to them.

But the fact is that young people ought to be, and already are, the ones at the forefront, struggling over the questions of social policy. Ironically, so many of the laws passed in the last 10 or 15 years have directly affected young people, but their rights to weigh in on the political and economic practices of neoliberalism have been denied. At the same time, young people are coming through a system of education that is not designed for freedom. It is designed to take one group and put them away in prison, and take the other group and convince them that neoliberalism is the logic of modern society and there are no viable logics outside of it. It's no accident that so much of neoliberal theory and policy targets our schools, our public spaces, our jobs, prisons—these are the places where young people end up populating.

I have worked from a set of principles of change, many of them informed by Marxism, though I am very critical of Marxism. I don't believe in waiting for a revolution to make change. I believe that change is slow, incremental, that people just sort of get smarter over time. In this way, all change is revolutionary. In my reading of Thomas Kuhn on paradigm shifts, change requires a set of simple breaks in structure—structural power breaks, like breakthroughs in access to power. Perhaps most importantly of all, those breaks are also conceptual because you cannot design a different future, unless you can think through the current one. All of the discussions I ever have about change in my work are about the breaks. *We are* the breaks.

In *Freedom Dreams*, I identify certain breaks in thinking, even if those breaks did not lead to the anticipated outcome. If you only attend to the outcome of breaks in terms of impacting structural change, you can miss how the breaks are actually conceptual shifts. For example, the election of a Black president did not lead to any dramatic structural change, because the Bush administration policies continue. But in President Obama's election there was at least the potential for a conceptual break centered on the notion that organizing and activism can actually produce the desired changes in national leadership. The potential was for people to see that all of the voter registration, the organizing, the activism could make the impossible possible: Getting someone many thought to be a long shot, into office. But it didn't provide the more significant conceptual break, because it reinforced the prior notion that policy change must come from the top, from elected officials. There was a missed opportunity to break from representative democracy to a more participatory democracy.

Another principle of change is that all change, ultimately, is local. Even though almost all of the attention is paid to global and national struggles, significant local changes are always taking place as a result of revolutionary activity or conceptual changes, but they don't become the models of change. For instance, I find it interesting that the local organized struggles and local victories taking place in Palestine don't get proper attention, that the prevailing sense of the story is a young person aiming a rock at the tanks of the Israel Defense Forces. And that's the singular representation that gets circulated outside of Palestine. The radical local transformations that are taking place—the two steps forward and one step back—those stories are not circulated because they don't fit within nation-state-level change narratives that we like to hear. Yet change is local, even global change is local.

A final principle is concerned with challenging the dominant way that we have thought about identity politics. Not to say that identity is unimportant, but change requires a kind of radical empathy that is more than alliances, more than coalitions. What I am talking about is a complete rethinking of who your people are. When Trayvon Martin was killed in February 2012, one of the great outcomes was the identification of young people across racial lines to say, "I am Trayvon Martin," without diminishing the fact that if you're a white girl from Orange County, you're not going to be shot. White girls from Orange County said, "I know I'm not going to be shot, but that act of violence and murder is unacceptable, and it's going to stop here." That's a very powerful position, to say I stand with those who are fighting for justice for Trayvon Martin, not because I feel sorry for the Negros, but because the injustice is unacceptable, period.

I get tired of hearing about workshops in schools that are trying to move white young people towards a kind of empathic position for particular communities. That approach treats all other people as victims. Multiculturalism becomes a kind of zoology: "You're in these cages here," and, "I feel so sorry for these victims." Even Rosa Park's story becomes a victim story in these empathy workshops, "Oh, I bet you Rosa Parks was so sad when she was told to go to the back of the bus." These workshops miss the opportunity to teach our students that injustice is the thing we're fighting against—we're not fighting on *behalf* of victimized people, we are fighting *against* injustice. And once you say that, then your analysis becomes concerned with the specificity of oppression in particular places. The best of the old left said, "We see oppression on very, very different levels. But wherever it is, we're going to be there. We're just going to be there, to witness, to fight. We're going to stand there with the people who are facing injustice. We know racism is a thing. Sexism is a thing. Class oppression is a thing. Anti-disability is a thing. Homophobia is a thing; but we're just going to stay on with these people, period, because we don't like injustice." Radical empathy politics means that injustice anywhere is injustice everywhere. That was Dr. King's position. We need to do the difficult work of building the beloved community. To do that is not to leave our defenses at the door, not to pretend that they don't exist, but to really engage them, embrace them, understand them, and also understand them not as intrinsic or inherent but as products of the exploited and oppressed situations that we live in.

What I am calling a radical empathy is required for change. There's no possible way that the current ways in which we think about identity politics could ever produce this kind of change. You've got to be able to cross those lines of race, gender, sexual identity, sexual orientation—not to erase those lines or pretend they don't exist but, on the contrary, make them hyper-visible. Radical empathy means working across identity lines by making them hyper-visible in order to recognize specific struggles that people on different sides of those lines experience. This recognition is fundamental for any change.

There is no way that we can talk about the future of youth in the United States without a discourse of settler colonialism as part of our framework for history. What we teach young people about existing social movements and our history is such an important element of change. Our history is the most contested narrative. We take for granted that multiculturalism provided the framework to teach young people the right history. The history offered by the narrative of multiculturalism is totally bogus. It is a myth because it doesn't deal with the question of power, even within various groups. Youth need to learn the history of the groupings that we have inherited and how these groupings have actually been reconstructed over time. That dynamism is very important. We live on one earth, and this one earth is characterized by great mobility. But the problem to me is not about mobility and not even about just possession. It's about power because you could occupy an area, but to exploit it and the people raises the stakes. To understand how that happens, why it happens, and why it needs to stop, is essential; because if we don't, then we're going to think of climate change as a mistake to be fixed as opposed to part of a system that produced it.

Resistance Changes the Conditions in which You Resist

Resistance can tighten the noose, if you will—this is the Paul Willis position. Resistance can dislodge certain oppressive and social practices. Resistance can lead to conservative reinforcements of power. Resistance simply is a description, I think, of pushing against social forces. Sometimes, that pushing is very self-centered and narcissistic and egocentric. Sometimes that pushing is collective and visionary. Sometimes, maybe most of the time, that pushing is informed by some portion but not the full understanding of the circumstances in which people live—this can make resistance confused.

But the most important thing about resistance—and this makes me an old-fashioned Marxist—is that resistance always changes the conditions in which you resist. It may make them better, worse, but the conditions are changed. Resistance is a motive of history in some ways, in that when the conditions change, it means that you cannot always use the same strategies to respond to those new changed conditions. As Stuart Hall says, hegemony is hard work.

Resistance is a dialectic. If it were not, then you wouldn't have anything to resist. To organize in that dialectic requires you to think two or three steps ahead of the conditions you're in. It requires imagination to figure out other places, means, strategies to resist.

Sometimes, resistance means to not do anything. To step back—a judo move—and allow the inertia of power to fall on its face. So resistance is a fight. It's a constant fight. It's a constant dialectic, where we ask: What do we want it to do?

I would love for there to be deep revolutionary transformations, plural—because even when you have revolutionary transformation, it's not the end of history. Such transformations produce new conditions constantly. New conditions produce new challenges. New challenges require new modes of resistance.

Resistance will never end, ever. It's just a pertinent part of life. I would love for resistance to produce the conditions for social justice, for ending economic exploitation and social degradation, and for producing the possibility of greater redistribution of power and greater political participation. That's ideally what we want resistance to do. But because resistance is against power and forces that outweigh us, it can only win some and lose some. My goals for resistance involve recognizing that societies all over the globe are unsustainable, and that we need to end injustice. My vision draws on Dr. King's beliefs that our work is to end injustice and end the deepening of inequality in society. I believe we need to dislodge the dominant pillars identified by Dr. King that uphold unjust societies—militarism, materialism, racism—and also other pillars, homophobia, ablism, heterosexism. In dislodging these pillars we need to produce new ways of thinking, not so much to end resistance, but to produce new forms of resistance that could, again, advance us as a society to ending injustice. That's the bottom line. You cannot do it without young people.

Works Referenced

Abu-Lughod, L. (1993, January 1). The romance of resistance: Tracing transformations of power through Bedouin women. *Art in small-scale societies: Contemporary readings,* pp. 203–219.

Alexander, M. (2010). *The new Jim Crow: Mass incarceration in the age of colorblindness.* New York: New Press.

Buras, K.L., Randels, J., & Salaam, K. (2010). *Pedagogy, policy, and the privatized city: Stories of dispossession and defiance from New Orleans.* New York: Teachers' College Press.

Damned (Group). (1973). *Lessons from the damned: Class struggle in the Black community.* Washington, NJ: Times Change Press [distributed by Monthly Review Press, New York].

Hedges, C. (2009). *Empire of illusion: The end of literacy and the triumph of spectacle.* New York: Nation Books.

Kelley, R.D.G. (1994). *Race rebels: Culture, politics, and the Black working class.* New York: Free Press.

Kelley, R.D.G. (1997). *Yo' mama's disfunktional!: Fighting the culture wars in urban America.* Boston, MA: Beacon Press.

Kelley, R.D.G. (2002). *Freedom dreams: The Black radical imagination.* Boston, MA: Beacon Press.

Kelley, R.D.G. (1996, February 5). Freedom riders (the sequel). *Nation, 262,* 5.

Lipsitz, G. (2001). *American studies in a moment of danger.* Minneapolis: University of Minnesota Press.

Mullings, L., & Wali, A. (2001). *Stress and resilience: The social context of reproduction in Central Harlem.* New York: Kluwer Academic / Plenum Publishers.

Rawick, G. (1969). Working class self-activity. *Radical America, 3,* 2, 23–31.

Rawick, G.P., Roediger, D.R., & Smith, M. (2010). *Listening to revolt: The selected writings of George Rawick.* Chicago: Charles H. Kerr Publishing Company.

Scott, J.C. (1990). *Domination and the arts of resistance: Hidden transcripts.* New Haven: Yale University Press.

Williams, R. (1977). *Marxism and literature.* Oxford: Oxford University Press.

Willis, P.E. (1977). *Learning to labour: How working class kids get working class jobs.* Farnborough: Saxon House

7

WHAT DOES AN UMBRELLA DO FOR THE RAIN?

On the Efficacy and Limitations of Resistance

Signithia Fordham with Eve Tuck and Greg Dimitriadis

ROCHESTER, NEW YORK

Signithia Fordham is a public intellectual and cultural anthropologist at the University of Rochester, where she also was the Susan B. Anthony Professor of Gender and Women's Studies (2001–2006) in the Susan B. Anthony Institute for Gender and Women's Studies. She is the author of the ethnographies *Blacked Out: Dilemmas of Race, Identity and Success at Capital High* (1996) and *Downed by Friendly Fire: Black Girls, White Girls and Female Competition at Underground Railroad High* (forthcoming). Her research and essays have appeared in public media, including *Education Week*, the *Chicago Sun-Times*, *The Washington Post*, *The New York Times*, and *The London Times*, and academic journals such as *Transforming Anthropology: The Official Journal of the Association of Black Anthropology*, *Urban Review*, *Anthropology and Education Quarterly*, *Teachers College Record*, and *Harvard Educational Review*. Her current research, and the subject of her forthcoming book, focuses on female competition, bullying, and aggression. Her recent work chronicles the ambiguous, female-specific route to academic achievement at a suburban high school (Fordham, 2013).

Origins of the Acting White Hypothesis

As a graduate student I developed what I came to call the acting white hypothesis mostly by reflecting on my own experiences as a child, my experiences as a then-adjunct instructor, and time that I spent in homes of friends who were teachers, listening to their stories of children in classrooms. I had much of my own experience in classrooms that confirmed the acting white hypothesis. As a child, I loved school and I loved doing the work, pleasing teachers, doing extra activities. There were consequences for me for loving school and being a kind of go-getter as a young person. I never failed to speak my mind when the situation called for it, and I was willing to challenge what I thought was wrong. My sister was very different from me, both in appearance and in temperament, but our parents expected us to do the same activities—I learned something important in seeing how differently she experienced school and teachers than I did, and then how we were treated by our peers because of this. As an adult, my teacher friends wondered if the world had changed because their students did not love school as my friends and I did when we were children. Their students resisted schooling by not doing homework and withholding their engagement. They were protesting, essentially.

Then, when I began doing a study at Capital High—the school featured in my 1996 book *Blacked Out: Dilemmas of Race, Identity, and Success at Capital High*—I saw the students participate in acts of resistance to schooling that were similar to those described by my teacher friends. At first, I didn't know how to name what I was seeing—it was so different from my own way of participating in school, and I worked to really understand all of the ways that these students were refusing what school was trying to offer them. I began to see how these youth saw schooling as deeply associated with whiteness, and to articulate the corollary burden of acting white placed on those who dared to try to do well in school. I used the term "cultural inversion" to describe what I was seeing for the first time in a paper I presented in 1982 at the American Anthropological Association. After that presentation, my advisor John Ogbu suggested the term "oppositional culture," and we wrote about this together using data from Capital High.

What I remained excited about was the possibility of theorizing *the burden of acting white*. Of course, I recognized this burden and its consequences from my own childhood. However, I wanted to understand how classrooms manifest the tension of school success as acting white and what happens to Black youth who want to achieve in school, but don't want to be turned into the Other in doing so. They want to succeed in school, but don't want to do so at the costs of losing membership in an important community. I talk about this as fictive kinship (1987), i.e., the way that the Black community uses family-based language—mothers, brothers, sisters—to understand itself. This family-community is omnipresent in church and home settings, but school settings don't permit collective identities. In school, everyone is individualized; to succeed is to differentiate oneself from the others. Not every child is willing to step outside that collective identity, perhaps at risk of losing it, in order to do the self-promotion and self-individuation that school requires for success.

This is how I came to think about Black children's success in school as conferring the burden of acting white. It is indeed a burden. School success requires that you become unrooted, in a sense. You are not accepted totally in your own community, and you certainly are not totally embraced in the dominant community because you still have dark skin. Yes, I know that times are supposed to have changed, but things have not changed much in this regard for Black children.

The structure of schools still compels them to be lone individuals rather than part of a meaningful self-identified community.

Theorizing the Burden of Acting White

It is important to note that I have theorized school success as it relates to *the burden of acting white*. Everyone talks about this as acting white, which I do not see as the same thing. Part of the complexity is elided in just talking about this as acting white.

One perplexing thing was that after reading my work, colleagues in the academy often wanted to know if youth literally used the words "acting white" to describe the behavior of other students—and if they had not used that exact language, then I had misinterpreted what the students meant. This focus on whether those exact words were uttered by youth strikes me as peculiar in the academy, a space in which analytical and abstracted thinking is supposedly not just invited but compelled to do a command performance in all interactions; as if the only way one speaks is through the actual use of words. Language is much broader than that; much more than what we say. For example, I would say to Black students, "Do you want to go swimming? Go skiing? Visit the Smithsonian?" And they would tell me, "Oh no, Black kids don't do that." They taught me about the burden of acting white through exchanges like this.

In *Blacked Out*, I tell the following story told to me by the principal of Capital High: someone tried to rob a middle-aged woman on a city bus, taking her purse. Capital High students saw what happened, went after the robber, and were able to retrieve the purse for her. The principal learned of this and, thrilled by what they had done, made an announcement on the school's intercom system to recognize what they had done, inviting them to come to his office to be celebrated. Not one of the kids went to his office to be recognized. As he told the story to me, he was extremely frustrated. He couldn't understand why they wouldn't want to be rewarded for their honorable behavior. What I understood, but he did not, was that he was asking them to single themselves out from their peers. He didn't see that Black youth are meaningfully rewarded in Black communities for being part of the collective, being connected to the community. The rewards for being part of the community outweighed the rewards he could offer for singling themselves out. This is not ever said explicitly; learning one's culture is as effortless as breathing. They knew it would not be okay to go down to his office and have him announce their names over the intercom. It would cost them too much. This is what I have focused on in my work, *the burden* of acting white.

There are so many community spaces, public spaces, in which Black youth are very visible. They are front and center. But in the school in which I am now doing research—Underground Railroad High—the Black kids are virtually invisible in the classroom. They aren't called upon very often. They don't talk very much. They are virtually voiceless in the classroom. That's so strikingly different from how they perform in the cafeteria, in the gym, in the auditorium and other public spaces. Young Black men who play basketball in the annual, nationally televised March Madness college tournaments excel in that public arena, because of what they bring to the collective, to the team. They are committed to being a part of the community where they could work to do things well, do things together. But in the classroom, children are pitted against each other, and I believe Black children withdraw because they are reluctant to compete against each other when there is so much to gain from being part of the collective in out-of-school spaces.

Teachers are frustrated because they don't see their Black students individuating themselves by working hard to achieve, to show that they are smart. They don't see that if classrooms were more collaborative, Black children would be more likely to achieve and contribute to the success of the collective. I didn't know this when I was doing research at Capital High, but now at Underground Railroad High, I see that the hierarchical structure of schooling forces people to behave in ways that are profoundly different from how they have learned to behave in their home communities, in which they are rewarded for helping rather than competing against others for success. This doesn't mean that you can't do your own thing, but that you would likely want to find a way to do it in a way that supports the collective.

Competing to Lose

One thing that I know much more about now is the significance of gender as it plays out in rewarded behavior. Recently I have been writing about the ways that women are rewarded for telling stories in which they lose (see Fordham, forthcoming; and Fordham, 2013). I have been working to theorize how women compete to lose, in order to win. For example, if you tell your girlfriend a sad story about something that happened to you, e.g. you survived a hurricane, it is likely she will have an even greater tragic story to share with you about the loss she suffered. This is a way that women compete with one another, through loss stories. Loss is central to the lives of women, and competing through loss stories confirms our female identities. This is not so for men; stories of loss undermine masculinity and achievement.

My current work at Underground Railroad High chronicles the violence allied with young women's aggression and bullying, and the ways in which Black girls in particular are socialized to be competitive, seeking achievement in ways that are often seen as too masculine. While physical fighting is a part of this, what I am especially trying to understand is forms of aggression in which women are complicit in the violence of destroying people's reputations and relationships. At the same time, when I talk with kids at Underground Railroad High, they insist that they don't feel challenged, they don't feel powerful. They say their teachers are boring, and they find it hard to engage.

Resistance Is Part of Life for People on the Margins

Because my early work was shared with my advisor John Ogbu, he often receives credit for our collaborations, even those portions that I contributed. Beyond that, though, there are many men and women who have taken up the hypothesis of acting white, it seems that male scholars are overly cited in the literature. My sense is that my work is still seen as controversial. In part, the work has been taken up by people who are trying to *quantify* the impacts of acting white. What they are overlooking is that this analysis emerges ethnographically. In my work I am looking at the non-quantitative, messy cultural features of the burden of acting white. For example, one recent book (Harris 2011) tries to critique the notion of oppositional culture by insisting that children do not want to fail in school. Of course kids don't want to fail; no human being wants to fail. The Black children I have met in my research have resisted schooling precisely because they were trying to avoid failure. In order not to fail, they resist by not doing anything. This is clearly a double edged-sword, even maybe counterproductive. They knew that in order to succeed, you have to risk failing, and they were unwilling to do that, so they did nothing. They were pushing back against failure, resisting failure.

Resistance is part of life for people who are marginalized. They seek not to fail, but failure is so pervasive, it's so likely. The opposition to what currently exists comes with a cost. It comes with a real possibility that you're going to fail. Human beings calculate *what are the possibilities that I'm going to fail, and if the possibilities are high, I do nothing*. Doing nothing, absolutely guarantees failure; that's the irony. Kids don't want to fail. That's true; but they also want to succeed concurrently. Those things operate at the same time. We navigate how to do both things at the same time: To avoid failure and to succeed.

More than an Umbrella

I am frustrated by the idea of resistance, especially as I now understand it. Historians have argued that revolutions are incredibly rare, almost never occurring. Revolutions require a total wipeout of the current system of what exists. Resistance does not accomplish revolutions. Resistance enables us to vent, to talk about our displeasure. Derrick Bell's *Faces at the Bottom of the Well* (1992) tells a story in which Black people in south Mississippi kept showing up, year after year, to a polling site, knowing they would be denied the opportunity to vote. When he asked one Black woman why she continued to show up, she replied something to the effect of, "My goal in life, and the goal of all people who are subordinate, is to make the lives of people who are in power, hell." She was not letting the powerful forget that denying others the right to vote is not okay, that it was not acceptable. Albert Camus made a similar argument; that we should resist despite knowing that the outcome is going to be a loss. In this way, Camus argues that resistance is essential to human life; we know we will lose, but we make the effort because it is how we are human. So yes, in this sense, I celebrate the humanness of resistance.

But at the same time, I have to say that I am under-impressed with the efficacy of resistance because I don't think that we're going to change the world by not tampering with the whole structure. If you've got an umbrella and it's raining, you put the umbrella up. The rain doesn't fall on you any more, right? But what does it do for the rain? Resistance is similar in effect. The rain is coming, we can put up an umbrella and resist the rain but it does nothing to stop the rain. It doesn't change the rain, it doesn't keep the rain from falling, it does nothing to the rain. The umbrella is just there. It continues to rain but I can walk without getting wet. But everybody else who's outside is experiencing the rain in ways that I'm not experiencing it because I have an umbrella. I'm frustrated with that limited scope of resistance.

Laura Nader has written about the importance of "studying up," studying those who have power rather than the powerless, as anthropology usually does. We study kids in classrooms, for example, but their power is limited by the structure of schooling. Nader argues that we need to pay attention to those who are making the decisions that structure the lives of those with less power, those like Arne Duncan, (the current Secretary of Education). Yet when you say you want to study the powerful, you don't get funding. You can say *I'm going to study these Black children in school*, and you can get funded, because your findings may not matter very much in the bigger scheme of things, in terms of really uncovering where power is located. In contrast, if you were to say *I want to study how education policy is made, I want to study the Educational Testing Service or Princeton*, for example, you are unlikely to get funding for that.

People everywhere are told just put your head down and don't get involved. Don't make waves. Well yes, we could all do that, but that is like being covered by the umbrella. I may not be getting drenched by the rain, but I'm doing that by not upsetting the apple cart, by not engaging in any kind of confrontation. Women are treated like good girls for doing that, and are rewarded for not challenging the system, for not bringing attention to inequities. You don't get any brownie points for pointing out inconsistencies and injustices. Everyone hates your guts. They say, "Oh, she's always got to bring up something else." No one will reward you for challenging injustice.

The Violence of Schooling

To successfully navigate the academy, critical researchers must be soldiers who appear to be harmless. This means that we are complicit in the violences that the academy promotes. It is inevitable. I like the notion of symbolic violence from Pierre Bourdieu's works. It helps me to see how when we seek to embody the norms of a society—I, Signithia Fordham, for example—I am complicit in the violence that I experience. Paul Farmer is an anthropologist that many of my colleagues and I admire. The irony he identifies is that violence is everywhere; we could walk right out the door and face violence, participate in violence, not by hurting or fighting anyone, but by using the norms that are employed to judge and oppress people. For example, to describe a woman's body as too fat is a form of violence.

Nancy Scheper-Hughes and Philippe Bourgois co-edited a volume called *Violence in War and Peace* (2004) that discusses all of these invisible violences. Most of the girls with whom I talked at Underground Railroad High have never hit anyone at the school, have never engaged in a physical altercation; yet they routinely engage in gender appropriate, legitimated violence. In my forthcoming book, I tell the story of one altercation between Nadine, a Black girl, and Kirstin, a white girl, that occurred in the cafeteria when Nadine and her erstwhile girlfriend Keyshia went to lunch to try to reclaim their friendship. Nadine's and Keyshia's friendship had ended the year before my study began when Keyshia secretly began to date Nadine's boyfriend, Kyle. Keyshia and Nadine, the two Black girls who were trying to repair their friendship, arranged to talk about it at lunch in the school cafeteria. They put their bookbags at the end of a long cafeteria table that was not unofficially designated as the Black table. Kirstin, a blonde cheerleader, entered the cafeteria shortly thereafter with a group of other white cheerleaders. When Nadine and Keyshia came back to the table after getting their lunch trays, Kirstin and the other cheerleaders told them they were not allowed to sit at the table they had chosen. Nadine was especially upset, because she had made elaborate arrangements to talk with Keyshia in order to re-establish their broken friendship. Kirstin and Nadine argued, both being very vocal. Suddenly, Kirstin called Nadine the N word and the B word in the same sentence, two labels that you do not impose on Black people or women. Nadine, the shorter of the two Black girls, reached up and slapped Kirstin in the face. School officials immediately came and took Nadine to the office and suspended her for five days. They did nothing to Kirstin, the white girl. The white girl cried and with the help of her all-girl posse went to the principal's office where they called her mother who came to get her and took her away from all the violence. Nadine protested and said, "Well, you know, she did something harmful to me, too. I was hurt and humiliated. She called me two of the most horrible names that one can call a Black woman." However the school administrators could not see what had been said as violence. They saw the physical slap as the only violence in this incident, so Nadine was punished and Kirstin was not.

Violence is so pervasive in our society, and I don't just mean the violence of slapping someone, although our society has more than enough of that kind of violence. A more insidious form is happening every day, so commonplace we don't even see it as violence. Not challenging kids so that they do the best they can in school, or being afraid of challenging students, or not expecting them to do homework, these are all part of the whole spectrum of violence that youth experience in schools. To deny them with a viable reason to be in school is a form of violence. Youth resist schooling because they are unconciously resisting that violence.

Transformation

Resistance does not lead to transformation—just resisting something is not going to transform it. Moone (2004) argues that maintenance and change co-exist, that it is not one or the other, but both, in tandem. Sometimes maintenance is more powerful than change, and other times change is more powerful. But a third prong to this must be transformation. Otherwise, it's just reorganizing the order of the chairs on the *Titanic*. You can get a new Secretary of State because that one wasn't effective, but because it is the same position with the same expectations and limitations, nothing really changes. The desegregation that we fought for in the Civil Rights Movement resulted in integration into the existing frame, not the change we had sought. There is evidence of change, but not to the existing frame. For me, this explains some of what we are seeing in Egypt and other nations: the so-called Arab Spring.

My recent work is more concerned with transformation than resistance, even though I am unsure whether transformation is possible. Transformation would mean working within a new frame, a new way of organizing society, a new language for life. This is so hard to achieve, but transformation is what we need now. We need people who are not just resisting but who are committed to transformation. As painful as that is, we've got to work towards transformation.

Things all around us are changing, and not in the ways that we would necessarily like to see. One of my friends was telling me last night, "Oh, the world is changing so much I can't take it." I tried to comfort her with the idea that even this kind of change is not penetrating—things feel like they are changing, but really it is just moving the chairs around on the *Titanic*. It is funny to take comfort in this thought, but we have to see that the structure is largely not yet being tampered with. And until we do that, we can predict the outcomes of the changes we see in our world.

Apparently, we think that resistance is supposed to transform reality. Yet for all the resistance that we see enacted, it does not transform the existing frame. I don't even think it's capable of doing that. Resistance often entails accepting the legitimacy of the frame, at a very basic level. I think—as I have already noted—we tend to start resisting in a context where we accept the legitimacy of the frame. For example, in the United States, people resist in order to claim a right to democracy, or to self-actualization. Then, a people are disappointed because resistance doesn't do what they want it to do, having never questioned the legitimacy of democracy or self-actualization as the frames that require some to win and others to lose. Resistance itself can be a form of legitimizing problematic existing frames, undermining our ability to transform into a more ideal community.

For most of us Americans, the most compelling feature of democracy is equality and the presumed attendant sameness. However, I believe our desire for sameness has to be undermined or altered. As I see it, equality does not mean sameness; it does not mean that I have to be indistinguishable from you in order to be worthy of whatever it is that is deemed valuable. I want to be the pilot in my life—not the co-pilot—and that means that I can be different. That doesn't mean I don't deserve your help and support or that you don't deserve mine.

Equality does not mean sameness, especially given that we all start at different social and economic points in life. Transformation will require us to embrace difference, but not in the shallow way that we do today. As it is now, a child who has lived in poverty all of his or her life, will never achieve equality with a child who grew up in a privileged neighborhood, even though they are subjected to standards that say they all should be accomplishing the same thing—at the same time. The outcome of such a mandatory social policy is predictable and reflective of what we have today: Social reproduction and permanent inequality, also known as status inequality, or what I am labeling in my forthcoming book "statusitis."

We need to figure out a way to reconcile our professed commitment to equality and our unending quest for status and power—in and out of the classroom, and, by the way, that includes me. When I was a kid, I remember my mother's constant refrain: "You must give your sister the same amount of the candy bar that you have, exactly half." She was teaching me the hegemonic narrative and, secondarily, trying to reign in my tendency to take more than I gave my sister. Doing what my mother suggested is not enough. In addition, we've got to rein in the idea that we must have the exact same things, because if somebody needs more, they probably are deserving of more. If we reduce fairness to mean, *you've got five ounces, I've got five ounces, and that means we've got equality*, then we will never have justice.

I see this phenomenon as growing out of the desire for achievement or, stated differently, a desire to be unlike everybody else, which is hard for me to reconcile sometimes. Like lots of other Americans, I sometimes desire to have more than my share: A bigger office, a better car; a better house; all of those status-conferring things that undermine the idea of equality. Yes, I sometimes desire to impress people that I'll never see again in my life. In these ways we all lust for status and by extension the unacknowledged desire for inequality.

We're not getting closer to justice by doing what we're doing now—and what we have always done—not only in the classroom but in the larger social context as well. As academicians (and Americans in general) who are at least verbally committed to social justice, we really need to think seriously about what it is that we're doing and what it is we're creating in the world. As the historian John Blassingame repeatedly told me: "Little girl, I am giving them a history they can use," and as the historian James Loewen (2004) points out repeatedly in his book, *Lies My Teacher Told Me*, "the truth" is often both not impartial and repeatedly reborn.

As marginalized people, we Black Americans were disappointed with the outcome of the Civil Rights Movement and the implementation of *Brown v. Board of Education*, primarily because the expected change did not happen as fast as we thought it should, or not at all. Moreover, when Black students were in permitted white schools, the schools were structured to ensure segregation, using intra-school rather than official segregation. Tracking, testing and designations ensured that school classrooms are not ever truly integrated, and the racial, gender, and class separations have persisted. These movements and cases were important actions of resistance, which is why I am concerned for the efficacy of resistance. As I have said, I am under-impressed at this point. I don't mean that we should not resist—of course we should—and will. After all, we are human. I just don't think that resistance can live up to all the enormous expectations we have for it. As a metaphor for resistance, an umbrella is essential in protecting an individual in the rain. However, after years of contemplating this social issue, I here concede that I don't think that an umbrella has the potential to alter the rain.

Referenced Works

Bell, D.A. (1992). *Faces at the bottom of the well: The permanence of racism*. New York: Basic Books.

Blassingame, J.W. (1979). *The slave community: Plantation life in the antebellum South*. New York: Oxford University Press.

Bourdieu, P. (2004). Gender and symbolic violence. In N. Scheper-Hughes, & P.I. Bourgois (Eds.). *Violence in war and peace*, pp. 339–342. Malden, MA: Blackwell Publishing.

Camus, A. (1961). *Resistance, rebellion, and death*. New York: Knopf.

Farmer, P. (2004). On suffering and structural violence: A view from below. In N. Scheper-Hughes, & P.I. Bourgois (Eds.). *Violence in war and peace*, pp. 281–289. Malden, MA: Blackwell Publishing.

Fordham, S. (1982). Cultural inversion and Black students' school performance. Unpublished paper. 81st Annual Meeting, American Anthropological Association, Washington, D.C. December 5.

Fordham, S. (1996). *Blacked out: Dilemmas of race, identity, and success at Capital High*. Chicago: University of Chicago Press.

Fordham, S. (2013). Competing to lose: Black female school success as Pyrrhic victory. In N. Long & H. Moore (Eds.). *The Social Life of Achievement*. New York: Berghahn Books.

Fordham, S. (forthcoming). *Downed by friendly fire: Black girls, White girls, female aggression, bullying and competition at Underground Railroad High*. Minneapolis: University of Minnesota Press.

Fordham, S., & Ogbu, J.U. (1986). Black students' school success: Coping with the "Burden of 'Acting White,'" *Urban Review, 18*, 3, 176–206.

Harris, A.L. (2011). *Kids don't want to fail: Oppositional culture and Black students' academic achievement*. Cambridge, MA: Harvard University Press.

Loewen, J.W. (1995). *Lies my teacher told me: Everything your American history textbook got wrong*. New York: New Press.

Moone, J.R. (2004). Persistence without change: A property of sociocultural dynamics. In N. Scheper-Hughes, & P.I. Bourgois (Eds.). *Violence in war and peace*. Malden, MA: Blackwell Publishing.

Nader, L. (1969). Up the anthropologist: Perspectives gained from 'studying up'. In D. Hymes (Ed.). *Reinventing Anthropology*, pp. 284–311. New York: Random House.

Scheper-Hughes, N., & Bourgois, P.I. (Eds.). (2004). *Violence in war and peace*. Malden, MA: Blackwell Publishing.

8

RESISTANCE IN THE BLOOD

Gerald Vizenor with Eve Tuck and K. Wayne Yang

NAPLES, FLORIDA

Gerald Vizenor is Distinguished Professor of American Studies at the University of New Mexico and Professor Emeritus of American Studies at the University of California, Berkeley. He has published more than thirty books. *Native Liberty: Natural Reason and Cultural Survivance, Survivance: Narratives of Native Presence, Native Storiers, Father Meme, Fugitive Poses: Native American Indian Scenes of Absence and Presence, Hiroshima Bugi: Atomu 57, Shrouds of White Earth*, and *Chair of Tears* are his most recent books. Vizenor is a citizen of the White Earth Nation in Minnesota, and has received an American Book Award for *Griever: An American Monkey King in China*, the Western Literature Association Distinguished Achievement Award, and the Lifetime Literary Achievement Award from the Native Writer's Circle of the Americas.

The Centrality of Stories

Survivance is an intergenerational connection to an individual and collective sense of presence and resistance in personal experience and the word, or language, made particularly through stories. Intergenerational communication looks different in other communities, passing on a business, trade, or profession, but in Native communities on this continent the knowledge of survivance is shared through stories. In my own family, I didn't experience this formally, of course, or as a theory of culture. I just understood survivance as a very significant experience, a really exciting kind of variation of stories about people that I had met and knew, and, of course, about my own family. Survivance stories are much richer than mere descriptive or moral stories. They last longer, and are not commercial. My elders, and mostly my grandmother and great uncles told stories, and all of their stories were tricky, elusive, and I'd have to listen to some of them several times. The stories they told were never the same, so I never expect a story to be the same. Because of this I had to imagine how the next story would be told and imagine the scenes. It is easy to romanticize Native stories, but the stories my grandmother told me were elusive, and always invited my interaction or participation. My grandmother was a great storier. She could just walk in and work out a story. She did not permit me to just listen. The stories had a teasing element, and every story had a new meaning.

My grandmother was ditched by her first husband, and after being single for many, many years she married a blind man who was about twenty years younger. When I visited her, I'd ask if she had gone out during the week? Yes, and she told stories about taking the bus to the suburbs. They often took the public bus to the end of the line to the suburbs of Minneapolis so her husband could sell brushes door-to-door. They would never get past the second or third door before some woman invited them for lunch. I'd say who invited you to lunch this time? And my grandmother would always comment that the women were so lonely stranded out in the suburbs. My grandmother gave these lonely women a voice, and told stories of their families. The lonely women always showed family photographs. And then my grandmother would make her part of a family, a new family in photographs and a story. It was remarkable. It was just great.

My grandmother taught me survivance in this way, not the word, of course, and not as a lesson, but through her perceptive stories. Every week, my grandmother and her blind husband would go out to the suburbs. And then I'd hear the stories on the weekend. They never really sold any brushes. They didn't have to because that wasn't really what was going on. They liked what they were doing. It was an adventure, trip, and they always met interesting people. My grandmother never told a bad story.

Maybe there were some bad stories, but she didn't bother to ever share or comment on them. My grandmother was poor. She and her husband lived on the limited income of social security, and yet she was concerned about lonely women in the suburbs. They rented an old, tiny, Murphy pulldown bed apartment near downtown Minneapolis. She was literally going out to the suburbs to do social work, or, in my stories, she was a survivance worker.

Believing what John Squirrel Said

In 1968, I was a journalist for the *Minneapolis Tribune*. I was writing about many subjects and events, politics, corrections, education. I heard there was a federal court hearing about a wild rice issue on the Mille Lacs Lake Reservation in northern Minnesota. I checked with our city editor at the paper, and he said, yeah, we got a notice but we have our assigned court reporters there. I said, "Well, I've got to sit in."

I got there just before the hearing started, and the court reporter was not in the courtroom. I went to look for him because I wanted to let him know that I wasn't encroaching on his journalistic territory. I hadn't been assigned to write

invade

about the case, I was just a spectator. But when I found him, he was sleeping in the reporters' office in the courthouse. I decided to let him sleep. I went into the courtroom, covered the story, and it was published the next morning.

The case was concerned with a legal debate over who has the right to decide when the wild rice was ripe and ready to be picked. Mille Lacs tribal members said they had an inherent right, and the federal attorney said the government had the right to determine when the harvest was ripe. It seems like a mundane issue, but it was a significant issue of sovereignty.

Justice Miles Lord was the presiding federal judge. I knew him from other trials and he was a wonderful judge with a sense of irony, and he often looked favorably on Native issues because he had a deep understanding of the history. It was unlikely that any other federal judge would have agreed to hear the case. One of the first issues of the hearing was about language. Mille Lacs witnesses decided to only speak in Anishinaabe, or Chippewa. Everyone could speak English, of course, but in speaking only in Anishinaabe they were saying that the judge would first hear about the issue in a Native language, not the language of the federal government. The judge agreed to the use of Anishinaabe by witnesses, and informed the federal attorneys, "You're going to have to find a translator." Miles Lord was an exceptional judge. Few other judges would have allowed a Native language in testimony. The federal attorneys complained that they would not be able to find a translator because no one would translate for the government. "Well, you're just going to have to use the translator the Mille Lacs people have provided. You'll have to share the same translator." The federal attorneys had to agree, and did so very reluctantly.

The Mille Lacs attorneys called Charles Aubid, a Native man in his eighties, to start the testimony about the wild rice harvest. Charles was unusually tall and he wore very thick spectacles that magnified his eyes to the effect of having an intensely penetrating gaze. He was asked to explain what he knew about the agreement with the federal government and the reservation elders. Charles said he was there as a boy, some seventy years earlier, when old John Squirrel talked with the federal men about the wild rice harvests. And they told old John Squirrel that the elders of Mille Lacs always had the rights to decide things on their own, when to harvest wild rice, and the seasons of hunting and fishing.

Charles spoke in Anishinaabe and his testimony was translated into English. The federal attorney challenged the testimony as hearsay and not acceptable. The attorney wanted to know what the witness understood, not what somebody else told him about the wild rice harvest.

I had no idea how this was going to play out. Competing versions of what constituted the truth were being confronted in the courtroom, and in the translation of Anishinaabe. There was the story of old John Squirrel, which was true, and the court rules of evidence, which was a different kind of truth. To be there that day in court was very exciting.

The judge turned to the witness Charles Aubid and told him that he could not tell what other people said, just what he knew to be true. Charles nodded, and then started to tell the story again, but this time, a different version in transla-tion from Anishinaabe. That moment in court was almost as if—and I have used this idea in my own critical writing—the testimony or story was a hologram of memory. As if the story was a kind of visual memory that depended on the situ-ation and circumstances—who is listening, whether they are family or not—the story could be told from multiple perspectives, in different contexts. The second story of old John Squirrel was basically the same but the descriptive and visual elements include different parts and even built on previous scenes in the story. The testimony that day in federal court became a great cultural story.

Charles told the story again from a different perspective, but still referred to what John Squirrel had told them about the agreement with the federal agents. Again, the federal attorneys objected. Charles told the story several more times, each time with old John Squirrel and each story prompted an objection from the federal attorney. The judge was irritated and told the translator that the witness must understand that the court cannot accept hearsay.

Charles Aubid stood up and faced Judge Lord. He said loudly in English, You're damn right I understand what you're saying, but if you don't believe what old John Squirrel said, then I don't believe anything in those law books. Charles pointed at a stack of law books. He was referring to bound volumes of legal cases and decisions, the precedent of legal reasoning. Legal cases are also stories, and Charles was saying, If you don't believe my stories, then I don't believe your stories.

Very unlikely that this would have happened in any other courtroom in Minnesota, maybe nowhere in the world. Judge Miles Lord pushed back in his chair, and seemed stunned by the truth of the reference to stories—not necessar-ily the legal truth of it, obviously, but the *truth* of good stories in a culture and in the legal profession. Judge Lord turned toward Charles and declared, You've got me there, and ruled in favor of the Mille Lacs Lake Reservation.

Everyone these days knows about hearsay, but what is interesting is that recently the International Criminal Court, for the first time in history, decided to accept hearsay as evidence in cases of genocide because so few witnesses survive a geno-cide. The court recognized that the testimony of stories from secondary sources must be considered as evidence. Charles Aubid inadvertently anticipated the deci-sion to recognize hearsay as evidence: *There aren't enough survivors left to tell the story; you're going to have to listen to me and what I know about what happened at that time.*

Language as Resistance

My strategies of resistance have always involved transforming language and lan-guage play. Obviously there is a great power in language, and in using it pow-erfully you could pay a real price for it, but also build a sense of presence and confidence. If somebody gets pissed at you for something you said, you know what it's about. It's about language. I am more convinced about the power and resistance of language than I am about the power of mass movements.

作者发明 "postindion" 作为在
natives 的 resistance.
语言的改变是对底不对面(Indians) 的揭示
Resistance in the Blood   **111**

I realized early on that language was my form of resistance, so I needed to work on changing language. I went to work on the word "Indian." I was interested in the excitement around the abusive images of Indians, and I thought that I could get a good discussion going to identify the manifest manners in that debate. I was not particularly interested in confronting images of "Indian," for example baseball teams for using Indian images, because those images were never real images of Native people. They were images of the invented Indian, invented by settlers. My argument about Indians all along has been that we just have to change the name, the actual language of reference. Leave the inventions of the Indian to the people who created it, and then we can easily humiliate them for their silly behavior. They invented an Indian, an image that makes them feel good, or not. The invented name, in my view, has nothing to do with Natives.

But I was not able to convince everyone. In fact, people were kind of angry with me and accused me of taking the issue too lightly. No, I am rather intense about negative images of Natives, but not the inventions of the Indian. I wanted to change the whole language about this and not go on forever policing every use or image of Indians. I had to get back to language, and thought to myself that I would need to write in fiction and nonfiction the irony of this and see if I can find an audience. And I did, but not just by confronting the word "Indian." The mere deconstruction of the word was not enough to change the language. I had to create a new language about Natives.

I created the word *postindian*, a theoretical language and a new idea so that people could say, "No, I'm not Indian, but if you insist, you could say I'm *postindian* because I'm not the Indian that's been invented for popular culture. I came after the invention, and the invention is not me. I'm a young person. I'm not obligated to all that stuff. I didn't participate in it. I'm not an invented Indian, but if you like, you could say I'm *postindian*. I'm a different kind of person imagining myself after the popular cultural indulgence in the invented Indian." The language of resistance and *postindians* seems to have worked pretty well.

Part of the strategy of using *postindian* is that I could connect it directly without a hyphen to the word "Indian" and eliminate the capitalization of the word Indian. There was a lot of teasing from readers and other theorists for going *post*, for making use of French theory and subscribing to the idea that everything's got to be *post* something. But *post* descriptions and nominations are delightful. You can set as a linguistic marker exactly what and who you want to be. I don't want to be an invented Indian. I would rather tease the invention and with the declaration of postindian enter a new conversation. I am present long after that ridiculous word was invented. Postindian is not a culture, but a discussion of identity.

To resist, tease, and change language is a serious responsibility. I doubt, however, that resistance through language provides a pathway to speedy change. The following example took almost forty years to make a change, more than a generation. I published *The Everlasting Sky: New Voices from the People Named the*

Chippewa in 1972. The title of the book alone reveals the problem the book was trying to address. I explained in the introduction that I was going to try to draw readers into the difficulties of the language, and to do so the word *indian* was italicized and in lower case in every instance. Readers were directed to the problem of the invented word *indian* in italics. The word is forever a problem, and should be printed in italics, because the word has no real referent. Indian is used for everything: language, food, culture, you know, everywhere. The word has no discrete meaning. I used the word "Native" to describe specific and distinct and unique cultural practices and stories.

A Play with many Voices

One time, I had an idea to work with young people on what I called a "play of voices." I brought together a group of urban Native teenagers by offering good food at rehearsals and was determined to create something compelling by using the words that white people wrote about Indians. I used documents and quotations from Minnesota historians, politicians, military leaders and put them together in a dialogue.

Of course, like all young people, the Native teenagers who participated were very sensitive about their identity. Rehearsals were a struggle because the young people were so self-conscious about their voices and bodies that they would just mumble and I could barely hear their voices. At the same time, they were really pissed off by what the quotes were saying about Indians. We were all frustrated, and at one point I yelled, "Goddamit, just shout the parts!" One young man shouted the next line—a quote from a governor—with such rage that it fired everyone up. Then, the next person shouted his assigned line, and the next one shouted his line. It was a shouting play of voices, and it was overwhelming.

The thing was, a performance like that can't be done more than once; it was a once in a lifetime performance just for those of us who were there in that rehearsal. The rage of that first rehearsal would have scared an audience anyway. We did put the play on several times, but never like that spontaneous rage and shouting play of voices in rehearsal. What had happened that day was a pretty good way to read, a pretty good way to think about resistance.

Youth resistance has to start in language, and that's not something that most teachers or institutions like. They want the resistance to be culturally determined, definable, categorical, collective, academically productive, and then conclude the resistance and meet with others to reach a consensus. The institutions would have young people create an effective presentation to authority, someone outside the very energy of change and resistance.

There are those good teachers and adults who take the ideas of young people very seriously, and some teachers work behind the scenes to prepare audiences for presentations of resistance. This is a kind of conspiracy, a positive conspiracy, but still a conspiracy to state a confrontation that everybody will feel great about because the work was done behind the scenes. But resistance that is managed, however sympathetically, becomes a mere performance. This sort of resistance is more like entertainment, and amounts to nothing significant or truly memorable as resistance because people feel good about the moment and just go on and do something else. There isn't anything going on, no creative energy of resistance that changes anything. There's no real language confrontation.

Survivance

Of all of the things I have written about, the concept of survivance has been a runaway from the themes of historical absence and victimry. I first raised the idea of survivance in my book *Manifest Manners: Narratives on Postindian Survivance*, first published in 1994. I deliberately did not define the word in my book. I still haven't fully defined survivance in a conventional way. I have talked about its nature, usage, the vital sense of verbal presence and cultural appreciation, but the word is resistance and should be discussed not defined. It is exciting to see how survivance has entered the language of institutions and has created a sense of resistance in literature and art.

There is no way to know the outcome of survivance. It is a spirited resistance, a life force, not just anger, negative or destructive. Survivance is a force of nature, a new totem, and it has to be expressed and imagined to create a sense of presence. Survivance stands in contrast to concepts of absence and victimry that are frequently applied to Native communities.

Victimry is still a powerful literary theme and cultural and political sentiment; it is thought to motivate good citizens and politicians to action because they get a good audience if they're doing good, liberal things to help Indians as victims. I would never make a good fundraiser because I confront those feel good victimry narratives. Victimry leaves people breathless and dispirited because to fulfill this narrative, people must play the part of a victim and believe that they are so lucky that they got this and that because of their status as victims.

Victimry leaves Native young people with nothing to imagine. You look around at almost all popular culture and literature and film and public uses of Native images, and even the so-called positive ones and the romantic ones are nostalgic with absence and victimry. Historical absence and victimry are invested in the manifest manners of cultural dominance. Native young people have been hard pressed to find a referent for themselves, not one referent outside of victimry. Survivance is that new reference of resistance and an active sense of presence.

The language is changing, however, and a new language of survivance confronts absence and victimry everywhere. Yet, it will take a long time to get rid of the victimry images of Indians. I'm not sure what popular culture will come up with next—probably a kind of hip, punk skateboarding Indian as the replacement for the victim—but that's got to be better than an absence. Maybe skateboarding is a resistance to victimry. Anything that suggests a sense of presence and survivance has to be better than the burdens of victimry.

Natives and others have become more sensitive to the notions of cultural victimry and the forceful declarations of a sense of presence in the world. These are complicated ideas but consciousness is growing out of that. Survivance is unmistakably a form of resistance. It is in the blood. Survivance is resistance in the blood. You can find it everywhere. It confronts victimry, but survivance is not a theory. That's why I haven't made a model of it, a definition out of it. Survivance is a metaphor and the meaning must remain open and adaptable in any context.

Listening In on the Extension

One of the first ways that I tried to make a difference was by working as an unpaid advocate for Native people through a settlement house in the early 1960s in Minneapolis. The settlement house provided an office and a phone, and I took to the streets as a kind of roving advocate for Natives. The settlement house was located near the largest Native urban population along Franklin and Chicago Avenue. Most Native people faced health problems, but also finding a job, a place to live, and other problems associated with people arriving in a new place for the first time. There were many, many instances of Native people needing help for their sick children.

Every day was a constant encounter with real and tough human problems, and nothing that I could offer would really correct the situations of poverty. I had good connections with social service programs and with the Salvation Army, so I could arrange for people to get some cash to get them through a few days, or get a few days worth of food or lodging. This relief was needed, of course, but I was frustrated by not being able to inspire more significant changes. I was looking for a way to radically resist the injustices of poverty.

One day a woman who had just arrived from a reservation in North Dakota called me from a phone booth near the Band Box, a fast food restaurant at the time near Chicago Avenue in Minneapolis. I went to meet her here. "They took my children away," she told me. It was winter, and she barely had enough clothes to keep warm. She had nothing with her, no clothes, no money, everything was gone—no family, no connections. The place she had lived as a child was destroyed by the construction of the Garrison Dam on the Missouri River in North Dakota. She had troubles with drinking, with drugs. The depths of her problems were far greater than I could ever help her to change or even balance. As we talked about her situation, I felt a sense of crisis over the paucity of what I could do to help. There was nothing I could do in a day or two, or even a month or two that would relieve the tragic burdens of her worried heart. I could not help her to restore or change anything. I could tease in the Native way, of course, and that is a sense of resistance and survivance. I could be playful, and I was, and that made her laugh, but I could not make a real difference in her life.

Suddenly I was struck with a very risky idea. "I want you to come to the settlement house, and I want to show you something," I told her. I had a directory of social service agencies in the city. I showed her the book, and the way human needs were categorized for service. I said, "Let's choose the categories of your needs," and we did just that: homeless, poverty, drinking problem, children removed by welfare, no winter clothes. She did, however, have a great sense of humor in spite of her trouble. I called several social service agencies and invited her to listen on the telephone extension.

I dialed the numbers, got someone on the phone, introduced myself and presented her as a real person with a real problem, and what could the agency do to help her? I knew from calling these agencies before that they only ever select someone who had been certified through their immediate offices, someone who satisfied a formula, a service model. Agency after agency told me, "Well, yes, but you see, our program only serves specific problems. . . ." I just kept calling and calling. And she listened to the conversations on the extension, just listened and listened.

This was really dangerous, and I doubt that I would do the same thing today. I wouldn't recommend it because it was so risky emotionally for her to hear the way the agency workers talked about her, not knowing she was listening. I didn't know what the outcome might be.

Finally, the woman put the phone down and burst into laughter. I realized I had just been saved from my own risky involvement. The idea had been that I would show her another side of the reality of poverty, but what those agencies offered and how the representatives talked about her wasn't real either. They were hung up on a service model, and there was nothing real about it. As I was making those calls and she was listening on the extension, I got a whole other perspective of the unreality of these services. The formulas and models at the center of those services were fantasies, made up by social theories of what I later wrote about as "manifest manners." The people on the other end of the phone calls were very pleasant and professional. Yes, they had carefully described programs that make it seem like they could benefit people, but the reality that someone could fit the actual definition of specific services was impossible without deliberately misrepresenting the problem. The Native woman broke the service model by laughter, an almost hysterical laughter, and her response saved me that afternoon. She taught me about manifest manners right there, a lesson that has become part of my literature.

Serving people as an advocate on the streets taught me how to think about models, manifest manners, resistance, and survivance. I learned concepts and counter theories as an advocate on the streets. I'm telling you today, the lessons she taught me were better for me than for her. She did not know what a good teacher she was at the time. I think when I started out, I wanted advocacy to work much more neatly. You try to do things to help out, and situations would change, and people would live happily ever after. I'm being ironic, of course, but what I mean is that I never expected significant changes, only an appreciation of resistance and change. Yet, I had much simpler hopes that some sort of change would still be possible in a chance encounter.

And as I talked on the phone with her listening on the extension, I immediately understood the limitations of advocacy. She saved me from that false consciousness. I was only in the position to help her by chance, without a doubt the situations could have been reversed. I bought dinner and we shared family stories at the end of the day at the Band Box, the very place we had first met earlier in the afternoon. When we parted ways, I had arranged for her to have a few nights in a hotel, and some warmer clothes provided by the Salvation Army. She smiled and we said goodbye that winter after dinner. I never saw her again.

Resistance Is in the Blood

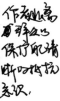

I believe that the strength of resistance is in the blood, and in the blood of every person, but the outcome is never the same because of individuality, family influences, and culture. I am purposefully not saying it is genetic, but saying that it is in the blood, a metaphor of resistance. Resistance is not a gene but a natural force of survivance. Consciousness is formed and changed by resistance, and in incredibly diverse ways. The consciousness of resistance must be individual to have any meaning or significance. It must have individual meaning to appreciate a sense of presence. So, I am troubled, and always have been, by mass movements and collective resistance because people can be drawn into the excitement of a movement without a decision, only by persuasion, emotion, by false consciousness, and the attraction and inspiration of a crowd.

I have been drawn into mass movements several times, but never trusted the energy. I must have developed early in my life a sense of the resistance in my blood to collective resistance movements. I have never trusted mass movements. I don't know how that mistrust was first realized, but as a boy I can remember knowing the difference between the approval and disapproval of my friends, and the need for acceptance, from the frenzy and anonymous excitement of a mass movement. I better understood the general idea of mass movements when I was a college sophomore and read *The True Believer* by Eric Hoffer. I saw that mass movements could be powerfully appealing and exciting and a true or terminal belief.

I remember clearly one meeting on the Pine Ridge Reservation the night before the American Indian Movement occupied Wounded Knee in 1973. We were gathered in Calico Hall, and the leaders of the American Indian Movement were presenting their decision to seize Wounded Knee on behalf of the elders and residents of the reservation.

The room was packed, so packed that I did not have to use my own bones and muscles to stand. No one had to exert any effort to stand because each person was held up with the crowd, by the bodies packed into the room. It was a lovely feeling at first, a rare experience to have that absolute, full, human contact without it being culturally embarrassing or invasive. To have my body completely supported by all the other bodies was an incredible sense of liberty, although it was a false sense of liberty. It was as if I never had to do anything again. I was in a state of beautiful peace for a short time. The elders went downstairs and conferred, and then the music started, a deep and powerful beat of drums. Suddenly I felt overwhelmed by the crowd and the sound of the drums. I could barely hold on to my own sense of presence, barely. And I was certain I was about to lose my sense of presence and connection to the world.

I caught myself and started to push my way through the crowd and out into the open night air. I had separated myself from the power of a mass movement and got outside and looked up at the sky and realized that my identity and independent sense of resistance was more powerful than a mass movement. I have never been a good subject for conversions because of my sense of individual resistance—in other words, I'm not vulnerable in crowds, at rallies and to the demands of inspired movement organizers, or evangelists who wait for the "true believers" to bear witness. I have never been a terminal believer, but, at the same time, I almost had lost my personal sense of resistance at Calico Hall on the Pine Ridge Reservation. I have worked with many people over the years in political and social groups, but I have never found a lasting sense of peace or resistance in a crowd. Looking back, I feel that was one of those great tests of my resistance and sense of liberty.

I write and tell stories about my experiences, and that gives new meaning to my sense of resistance and survivance. I have rushed out into the night to evade a mass movement, but my sense of independent resistance is not separatism, not an escape from people, but rather a way to protect my sense of presence in a real community. Natives have always been inspired by independent visions, and by unique experience as part of families and cultures. Native visions and resistance in the blood are not separations from families or cultures. Resistance in the blood is communal, not separatist, and yet that collective sense of false peace generated by a mass movement is very difficult to resist in the name of survivance, native reason, and personal liberty.

Works Referenced

Hoffer, E. (1951). *The true believer: Thoughts on the nature of mass movements.* New York: Harper and Row.

Vizenor, G.R. (1972). *The everlasting sky: New voices from the people named the Chippewa.* New York: Crowell-Collier.

Vizenor, G.R. (1994). *Manifest manners: Postindian warriors of survivance.* Hanover, CT: Wesleyan University Press.

Vizenor, G.R. (1998). *Fugitive poses: Native American Indian scenes of absence and presence.* Lincoln, NE: University of Nebraska Press.

PART II

The Relationship Between Youth Resistance and Theories of Change

Introduction to Part II

Eve Tuck and K. Wayne Yang

As those who have spent time in and with youth organizations know, there are several goals of youth work—be it advocacy, community education, organizing, development, or research—that can be generalized; these goals take shape as "raising youth voices," "consciousness raising," "increasing visibility," "making safe spaces," and other hopeful outcomes. In this way, in the United States and other neoliberal multicultural states, there seems to be a lot of agreement about what youth work should aspire to do. Of course, such goals are common in part because foundations and funders have determined them to be fundable. But they are also common because they are all related to one another through a shared theory of change in which raising visibility about an issue or community leads to good and just things. A theory of change asks *how* what we do leads to good and just things. This is not to say that raising visibility *does not* lead to good and just things, but that it is profoundly important to think through *how and why* it leads to good and just things, and not just assume that it does. For example: Are there other things that need to be in place for raising visibility to work? Might there be some instances in which visibility does not lead to desired change? The answers are, *of course*, but it is the asking of the questions that matters.

"Theories of change" may be thought of as a shorthand for "theories of the changes we want," as the usage generally implies the conceptualizations/theorizations on how to get the changes we desire. This book as a whole does not promote one theory of change over another, though it is critical of colonial theories of change in which individuals or communities collect evidence of their broken-ness or damage in order to try to convince someone powerful outside of their communities to give up resources (Tuck, 2010). Such a theory of change is flawed for at least three reasons: it requires individuals and communities to depict themselves in a one-dimensional way as damaged; it locates power completely outside of communities; it rarely actually works (Tuck, 2009).

Instead, this book advocates for a pedagogical engagement with change, involving conversations and reflections on how change happens. According to the poststructuralist turn, change is always occurring, and within a more cynical critical approach, change is never happening or if it does occur, it reinscribes relations of power. Within many Indigenous epistemologies, change is always happening (although different from the poststructuralist sense), and it can take on many forms—desirable or otherwise. These varying perspectives on change matter with regard to human agency, and thus matter with regard to resistance. Each perspective is going to have different implications for how humans should spend their time on the planet.

For example, if one subscribes to what Malcolm Gladwell (2000) called a tipping point theory of change, in which societal change occurs when a critical mass of people hold a new view or idea (likened to the spread of a virus), then she would spend time trying to convince as many people as possible of that new idea. Further, she is likely to be better off starting with those on the fence or in the middle rather than those who are diametrically opposed, because what is needed is a critical mass of people who agree, not an argument that could convince even the least convincible. So, she would spend time in conversation with people who are likely to agree with her, then those who are just a little less likely, then those who are a little less likely until she can build a critical mass. In this theory of change, there is little need to be in conversation with those most likely to disagree. An instructive example of how a tipping point theory of change has been retheorized and applied in struggles over school culture is "Gangstas, Wankstas, and Ridas," by Jeff Duncan-Andrade (2007).

In another example of a theory of change, Deleuze and Guattari (1987) write that it was a series of molecular (rather than molar) shifts—those "flows or flees that escape the binary organizations, the resonance apparatus, and the overcoding machine" (p. 216)—that prompted the May 1968 resistance in France. Such molecular flows are imperceptible, creating "zigzag cracks," "tiny trickles," leaks between the segments which escape the centralization of molar segmentarity (*ibid.*). Deleuze and Guattari's theory of change is dependent on molecular flows, those which escape and prevent the totalization of molar segmentarity. In such a framework, change appears as if from nowhere, and mapping it perhaps is only possible in hindsight: "As Gabriel Tarde said [about earlier resistances in France], what one needs to know is which peasants, in which areas of the south of France, stopped greeting the landowners" (*ibid.*, insertion ours). The molar and molecular are simultaneous, so it is altogether likely that molecular flights and flows reinforce molar segmentarity—but there are other, wholly unpredictable flows that manage to escape and in so doing, manage to shift the whole plane of segmentarity. This is to say, molar change happens as a byproduct, not as a direct result of molecular human activity (and this is true at greater and smaller scales, because this is a fractal theory). In this theory of change, it happens whether we take direct action to affect it or not, and in fact, our direct actions to affect it might foreclose the change we seek. So what is there for humans to do inside this theory except for be human?

There are innumerable other theories of change that we could name here—they are at work (or not) everywhere around us: boycotts, psychotherapy, peace (Thich Nhất Hanh, 1989), revenge (Tuck & Ree, 2013), anarchy, prayer, doing nothing.

Not only will a theory of change inform the nature (the "toward what") of change, but also the "for whom" of change. Clearly, when we theorize the change we want and how we get there, the "we" becomes very important to unpack, as the desires of different groups for change radically depart—whether it is the desires of the privileged or powerful to stay in power (or not); the desires of the neoliberal machinery to expand the market; the desires of the dominated to be less violated within nation-state arrangements; or the desires of those whose lives were interrupted by empire for a return/renewal of life after, beyond, and despite the modern arrangement of nation-states.

Theories attempt to answer the questions of change that are already territorialized and temporalized. Theories of change tend to be plural—the same actors often have multiple theories of multiple changes appropriate for their multiple modes of engagement with colonial modernity. They operate exponentially, simultaneously, on different timelines and within different geopolitical frames. Theories of change try to ask and answer questions about the territory or the scale of change: How does change happen within my body, this neighborhood, this school, this school district, this city, this state, this nation-state, this system of nation-states, or outside and between all of these borders? Theories of change also try to ask and answer questions about the temporality of change: What kinds of immediate changes are possible? How can the needed efforts to foment change be sustained? How do immediate changes connect to longer-term political transformation? Finally, there are questions we must ask of theories of change that help us to understand possibilities for transhistorical struggles that exceed even the current political processes, including struggles for Indigenous sovereignty, decolonization, and intergenerational, repatriated life, Indigenous futurity, Black futurity, and the non-permanence of (the) settler colonial nation-state(s).

Chapters in Part II

This section includes chapters in which the significance of theories of change in youth resistance research is foregrounded. These chapters circle back to, extend, amplify the discussions by each of the foundational theorists of youth resistance in the first section, and do the important work of making the argument that is so central to this volume: Youth resistance research requires attention to theories of change. The chapters, representing different locations and modes of youth resistance, examine some of the types of problems in theorizing change.

In *Thinking with Youth about Theories of Change* (Chapter 9), we engage the expertise of many colleagues, teachers, researchers who learn with, think alongside, and work with youth in fomenting change. Although the contributors have worked with youth for years, decades in many instances, the chapter attends to the immediacy of resisting alongside youth, and the thinking/theorizing that unfolds in those particularities, times, and places of struggle. This chapter yields evidence of what is possible in theorizing with youth about theories of change and making discussions about how change happens part of research that happens with young people. It provides a set of diverse learnings, critiques, and hopes about change that are emergent—they are on the ground and happening, becoming, right as we type. This chapter represents a few snapshots of an ongoing conversation that is always being updated at the website for this book, www.youthresistanceresearch.com. We hope that readers will consider contributing their own thinking with youth about change at the site.

In *The Politics of Coming Out Undocumented* (Chapter 10), Lisa (Leigh) Patel and Rocío Sánchez Ares discuss the youth resistance activities of those called the DREAMers, a network of organized youth who have quickly become a new model of youth resistance. DREAMers are a point of inspiration and hope for many on the left precisely for their ability to create and sustain a social movement in the United States. Patel and Sánchez Ares' chapter, informed by the theorizations of DREAMer activists, considers these multiple hopes, disappointments, strategies, and critiques of organizing around DREAM Act immigration reform. They reveal in sharp relief the temporalities of immediate relief, short- and longer-term immigration reform, and the even longer (but hopefully not too long) present of settler colonialism in North America.

In *Rethinking Resistance Theory through STEM Education: How Working Class Kids Get World Class Careers* (Chapter 11), Antwi Akom, Allison Scott, and Aekta Shah challenge the very positioning of "youth resistance" in oppositional relationship to educational institutions. In the complex tradition of Woodson and Cooper (see Introduction, this volume), they do not surrender the role of structures, including American institutions, in the longer-term project of Black (and brown) emancipation. Here, they introduce *structural resistance and agency* (SRA) as a conceptual bridge between youth resistance and structures that resist. This chapter loosens the calcifications of the paradigm that claims its origins in Willis' (1977) *Learning to Labor*, by distinguishing between the specificities of an industrial society with working-class, white, male workers-in-waiting, and of post-industrial, "eco-apartheid" (Akom, 2011) society with Black and brown bodies never meant for employment in the lucrative science, technology, engineering and mathematics (STEM) careers in the San Francisco Bay Area.

In *Hands Clasped Behind Her Back: Palestinian Waiting on Theories of Change* (Chapter 12), J.I. Albahri questions the inscription of resistance on to Palestinian youth bodies, by Western media and as well as Western activists, and how such prescribed resistance can actually deny the changes that indigenous Palestinians desire. She engages the "collusion of multiple theories of change" with respect to the Boycott, Divestment, Sanctions (BDS) Campaign against Israeli settler and apartheid practices. She also unwinds the temporality of change by considering how multiple generations of Palestinian "youth" coexist/haunt/meet in a frozen present of the *Nakba*, the ongoing catastrophe. The chapter reveals the connections and disconnections between actions designed towards immediate policy changes, and the long durée of Palestinian return to their indigenous lands.

As all of the foundational theorists all pointed out in Part I of this book, we have to distinguish between forms of resistance—especially with regard to how they reinforce, subvert, or radically interrupt systems of domination. Likewise, it is important to distinguish between forms of change, with regard to (field[s] of) power—which itself is changing too, is dynamic and shapeshifting. If there is but one central intervention this book makes into youth resistance research, it is concerned with the need to bring conceptualizations of change and agency to the forefront. It is not enough to describe resistance, activism, movements, and other human activities and analyze whether they are successful or not; researchers must also engage the worldviews and perspectives that inform the decisions that resistors and activists make. Thus, the chapters in this section necessarily trouble what we think of as "change," as well as the theories that inform what we think change is and how it occurs.

Works Referenced

Akom, A. (2011, April 1). Eco-Apartheid: Linking environmental health to educational outcomes. *Teachers' College Record, 113*, 4.

Deleuze, G., & Guattari, F. (1983). *Capitalism and schizophrenia*. Minneapolis: University of Minnesota Press.

Duncan-Andrade, J. (2007, November 1). Gangstas, Wankstas, and Ridas: Defining, developing, and supporting effective teachers in urban schools. *International Journal of Qualitative Studies in Education (qse), 20*, 6, 617–638.

Gladwell, M. (2000). *The tipping point: How little things can make a big difference*. Boston, MA: Little, Brown.

Thich, Nhât Hânh. (1989). *The moon bamboo*. Berkeley, CA: Parallax Press.

Tuck, E. (December 07, 2009). Suspending damage: A letter to communities. *Harvard Educational Review, 79*, 3, 409–428.

Tuck, E. (2010, September 1). Breaking up with Deleuze: Desire and valuing the irreconcilable. *International Journal of Qualitative Studies in Education, 23*, 5, 635–650.

Tuck, E. & Ree, C. (2013). A glossary of hauntings. In S. Holman Jones, T. Adams, & C. Ellis (Eds.). *Handbook of autoethnography*, pp. 639–658. Walnut Creek, CA: Left Coast Press, Inc.

Willis, P.E. (1977). *Learning to labor: How working class kids get working class jobs*. New York: Columbia University Press.

9

THINKING WITH YOUTH ABOUT THEORIES OF CHANGE

Edited by Eve Tuck and K. Wayne Yang

With Jennifer Ayala, Kristen Buras, Caitlin Cahill, Justice Castañeda, Jeff Duncan-Andrade, Valerie Futch, Rubén Gaztambide-Fernández, Patricia Krueger-Henney, Django Paris, David Alberto Quijada Cerecer, and Sarah Zeller-Berkman.

Editors' Introduction to the Chapter

When we began envisioning this book, we knew that we wanted to include a discussion about thinking *with* youth about theories of change. In Robin Kelley's words, "All around us, young people are at the forefront of asking how we imagine a different future, but their theorizing goes unnoticed because youth are still seen as the junior partners of the social movement" (Kelley, this volume, p. 88). In this chapter, contributing authors discuss strategies, lessons, and examples from their own participatory action research with youth, experiences in which they have engaged youth as co-researchers and co-theorists on educational injustices. They describe approaches to identifying and analyzing theories of change that root social justice actions.

We use the words "theory of change" to refer to beliefs or assumptions about how social change happens, is prompted, or is influenced. We are aware that in recent years non-profit foundations have expected funded participants to identify "theories of change," "logic models," and other expressions of how certain activities will result in certain outcomes. In these cases, theories of change are used synonymously with "organizational model."

It is clear that what we mean by theories of change is not the same as what those foundations mean, because we do not mean anything certain or linear. We're not ready to cede the term to those other evocations—instead, we want to deepen the notion of *theory* and deepen the notion of *change* in our use of the

term. Reflecting or imagining a theory of change is an ontological and epistemological activity, related to core questions of being and knowing. Much time and
human energy is invested in various political activities—but how is it that change
really happens? This is a question that communities and individuals may never ask
themselves, or may have to ask themselves again and again.

For example, one theory of change that links Otpor in Serbia, Kmara in
Georgia, and Pora in Ukraine—youth resistance movements of the early 2000s
dedicated to overthrowing authoritarian governments—concerned the power
of non-violently targeting and undermining (in their words) the "pillars of the
regimes."

> [The young rebels] believed that authoritarian governments were not
> impregnable monoliths but a series of vulnerable institutions which
> depended on individuals who could be convinced or shamed into defect-
> ing. "Even a dictator can't collect taxes on his own," one of the Serbs told
> me. "He can't deliver the mail, he can't even milk a cow: someone has to
> obey his orders or the whole thing shuts down. The task is to convince
> them to disobey. When they change sides, the government starts to fall."
> (Collin, 2007, p. 5)

In our recent work, we have tried to think through the flawed theories of change
that operate in educational discourse and educational research (Tuck, 2010; Tuck
& Yang, 2013). *All* social science employs some theory of change. Among the
most common theories of change involves documenting an individual or community's (supposed) dysfunction or deprivation in order to convince someone
more powerful, usually the state, to provide additional resources or rights. It is a
theory of change that mimics the legal system. It is a teleological theory of change
that places the Western world and neoliberal ideology at the finish line of societal
evolution. It can also be characterized as a colonial theory of change, because it
locates power and control outside of communities, and requires them to appeal
to the logics of the state to get piecemeal gains (though ironically, as Signithia
Fordham has observed, moral arguments are rarely effective with the neoliberal
state or other authorities [p.c., March 29, 2013]).

There are consequences for engaging in social science research without considering theories of change, but those consequences are just as evident in domains
of education, community organizing, politics, and art. Thus, envisioning theories
of change is important for all of us to do, in work, in life, and in community.

The goal of this chapter is to describe examples and strategies in which researchers have been prompted to rethink the theories of change that undergird their
work with youth co-researchers and co-theorists. We realized that we could not
go to the literature to write this chapter, but instead, must go to our colleagues,
our friends, our teachers, our companions in this work. We found ourselves recalling the many discussions on walks, long car and subway rides, or in other casual

conversations; this is a topic that is infrequently discussed in publications. Thus, our approach to writing this chapter was to crowd-source the discussion points. We wanted to compile the insights and experiences of a variety of people across settings and research topics. We began with a list of questions that we posed to a group of friends and colleagues immersed in collaborative research with youth.

The remainder of this chapter is the assembled words of eleven scholars doing exciting participatory work with youth. Much of what was generated in response to our questions appears in this chapter. We have also created a website where all of the responses are posted in full at www.youthresistanceresearch.com to host an extended conversation about theories of change in youth research and youth participatory action research that expands beyond this book. We hope that readers will come to the site and post their own thoughts and experiences on thinking with youth about theories of change.

Theories of Change/Feelings of Change/ What Change Feels Like

Chispas, Choques, Corrientes—Jennifer Ayala

Change can be an end result, measured in discrete outcomes, and change can be a relational process of continuous becoming. There is change, then there is the work of change, characterized by what some have called "endurance labor," and it is important, I've learned, to attend to both aspects. The work of social change can be disheartening, validating, exhausting, and energizing. It is spirit work (Anzaldúa & Keating, 2002) because we wrap so much of ourselves into the thinking, the doing, the connecting. The change-work itself of a collaborative, the participatory process, is one, perhaps the first, transformative act.

Change can happen in different speeds, through different mechanisms. As *chispas*, the spark of a moment that incites change; as *choques* (Anzaldúa, 1987), the shifts that occur, for good or ill, as a result of clashes; as *corrientes*, slower, but moving currents of change. Sometimes change is a subtle pressure that leaves a fading imprint, like running fingers through wet sand. We have to reach deep, invite many hands, to leave a more lasting impression. Our work together, with youth, adult allies, cushioned by the voices of our intellectual othermothers, has taught me about operating with multiple layers of change. With Pedro Pedraza, I understand meaningful change as systemic change, dismantling structures of oppression and exploitation (p.c. April, 2013). I also understand change as "small wins," local efforts to make the immediate conditions of our communities and ourselves better.

Agency of Hope—Jeff Duncan-Andrade

When I started teaching 21 years ago, I knew that I wanted to be the kind of teacher that provided a classroom experience that mattered for students in their immediate realities, as well as for their long-term goals. *Partnering* with students to identify the most pressing needs in their lives and then develop classroom projects and pedagogy that allowed them to identify and examine those things has led to several profound theories of change. *One* that is heavily influencing my work at the moment is a theory of hope and hopelessness that surfaced in the work of some of my high school students about seven years ago. *They* were conducting sociological inquiry into the material conditions affecting their communities, in a research project we called "Doc Your Block." *One* group found that the popular narrative of their community as one of hopelessness had some merit to it. They coined a term, "habitus of hopelessness," to describe the way that many of their community members found themselves trapped in habits of hopelessness as the result of chronic exposure to toxic stress. *The* presence of hopelessness was not a new discovery, but the lens through which they understood and analyzed the kinds of negative coping mechanisms employed to deal with the hopelessness, and the subsequent habits of mind and body that develop as a result was profoundly insightful. *What* they added to the discussion, though, was a counter-narrative, one that is not often captured in research into urban poverty. *They* identified "agency of hope," an indomitable spirit that transcends the hopelessness. Time and again, they found places and people where hope found its way to the surface in a community wrought with the despair caused by racism, violence, and poverty.

Historical Consciousness, Intergenerational Resistance—Kristen Buras

My collaboration with youth and youth advocates through Urban South Grass-roots Research Collective in New Orleans has reinforced what I learned from my own work as a public high school history teacher: The history of the people is indispensable to their liberation. Youth programs affiliated with Urban South Grassroots Research Collective rely on a critical sense of history, inter-generational exchanges, and place-based pedagogies to foster youth agency. For example, veteran teacher and education activist Cherice Harrison-Nelson builds on the legacy of her father Big Chief Donald Harrison by working with youth through the Guardians Institute; Big Chief Harrison was a well-known Mardi Gras Indian (Kennedy, 2010). The Mardi Gras Indian tradition dates back more than a century in New Orleans, where community groups "mask" or ritually process in handmade suits through Black working-class neighbor-hoods in honor of the historic solidarities between Africans, African Americans, and Native Americans in southern Louisiana. Slave revolts and resistance often were fomented in the backswamps where African Americans escaped and lived alongside Native Americans. Through the Guardians Institute, histories of resistance, stories, songs, sewing techniques, and more are shared by commu-nity elders. Intergenerational exchanges have proved to be a potent strategy for igniting historical consciousness in youth and providing them with an enduring sense of place. They understand their responsibility for sustaining the legacy of racial resistance in the community—they are its guardians.

An Ongoing Collective Conversation—Caitlin Cahill & David Alberto Quijada Cerecer

Seven years ago the Mestizo Arts & Activism Collective came together in Salt Lake City, Utah to do participatory action research with young people. Ever since then we've been thinking through our theories of change with young people. This is an ongoing conversation. Rather than a linear process that we can trace across a page like these words strung together in a sentence, our ongoing dialogue about who we are, what we want to be, become, and do, is a dialogue between all of us involved. Whoever is in the room is shaping it. And because there are many of us, the stories of who we are and want to be are intonated in different voices and given new shapes to fit around our different bodies.

These shapes might take the form of questions such as: What are we trying to accomplish with our research? Who is it for? What matters more—the integrity of the research or the effectiveness of the action? Are we transforming the academy by engaging new questions/reframing theory or by opening up the educational pipeline? Or, how are we transforming ourselves? How might we intervene and challenge xenophobia in a state that recently passed Arizona-like anti-immigrant legislation? How are we contributing to social movements (locally, nationally)? These questions were starting points for conversations that were not resolved in one way or another, but that we spun around and gathered new ways of thinking at each turn. Usually we would be spinning multiple questions at the same time, like plates on sticks, where some would wobble around slowly and others had momentum. Some days we paid more attention to one question then another, depending on what was happening in our collective and also what larger conversations we were contributing to.

There is no one way, one-theory-fits-all, or idea of change that we have slipped into comfortably. Instead perhaps we begin with a commitment to this: An ongoing collective conversation that embraces us all in this very moment with a radical acceptance. While we look backwards with steamy eyes at all that we have accomplished, what and who we have loved and lost, at the same time we look forwards with optimism, anxiety, and a shared sense of possibility. What we are committed to is each other and this very moment. Is this a theory of change? Or is it a commitment to love as a verb, as an ongoing act of commitment? As expressed in the words of Che Guevara, that our co-founder the late great Matt Bradley (RIP, 2012) used to quote, "At the risk of seeming ridiculous, let me say that the true revolutionary is guided by great feelings of love."

Researching with Youth about Change

Happiness Crushes My Radical Illusions—Rubén Gaztambide-Fernández

When some of the Latin@ immigrant youth who participated in our exploratory research into their experiences in Toronto schools asked our research team to return to the school to conduct further research and to support them in finding solutions to the challenges they faced, I immediately thought that yPAR was the only way to go. The youths' desire to conduct their own research challenged my doubts that yPAR could ever be initiated by the youth themselves. Yet, from the beginning, I remained skeptically curious as to whether the kinds of "change" that are typically described in yPAR participants would manifest in our own project. I wanted to believe in—and searched for evidence of—the theory that once given an opportunity to engage critically in an analysis of their social circumstances, the students would become radicalized and start to share *my* thinking of how colonization, racism, and imperialism shaped their schooling experiences. I say this, of course, with a hint of sarcasm, but I do see this as a goal of some who do youth participatory action research.

These "illusions" were crushed when the youth in the project came to the agreement that what they wanted most was to understand how social institutions affected Latin@ immigrants' *happiness* in Canada. How will these students, I wondered, become radicalized in my own image if they wanted to study happiness? I managed to suspend disbelief and continued to support the youth in their research projects, which involved four different approaches for examining Latin@ immigrants' "happiness" in Canada, including Canadian schools. Their findings were not earthshattering, and did not result in any overtaking of school board meetings or marches in city hall. The importance of the work that we did together, however, did manifest in a more subtle and perhaps more profound change, which I was completely unable to see until the students themselves began to point it out: the students were building community and taking initiative to do things that made them—yes—happy. For some of them, this involved developing a youth radio show focusing on youth issues on a local Spanish radio station, which has been going strong now for almost two years. For others it involved returning to work with a second group of youth researchers to work as mentors and share their research skills. Still for others it involved organizing workshops for both teachers and other students, and participating in academic conferences where they traveled to share their research in collaboration with the adult academics.

Counter-Topography and the Lived Character of Space—Patricia Krueger-Henney

Between 2007 and 2009, I was part of a New York City-based youth participatory action research collective whose logics of inquiry and findings filled the pages of my doctoral dissertation. In 2008, after an in-depth discussion about intensified police presence in many public high schools in some of New York City's most economically deprived communities, a youth co-researcher remarked during one of our weekly research meetings: "It is true that there are more people watching us, but it does not necessarily mean that they are paying attention to us." She continued to describe her public high school in Queens to her co-researchers, and how her learning spaces increasingly resembled scenarios of crime control and social containment. Her nine co-researchers agreed and reflected on how throughout the school day armed police officers and school safety agents visibly patrol their hallways and lunch areas; vigilant mobile precincts are parked in front of school buildings; and metal detectors scan their bodies as well as those of staff and visitors.

The next few research meetings were filled with us researching information and learning about criminal justice-based school discipline practices, now commonly referred to as the school to prison pipeline. The systematic removal of poor, non-white, immigrant, and gender non-conforming youth from their schooling spaces and their over-representation in suspension rooms and in juvenile detention facilities had us talking about spaces and places in securitized and surveilled schools. More specifically, co-researchers created lists of specific locations of police officers inside schools, or where exactly surveillance cameras were installed. Topics centered on policed space and place facilitated our comparison-making between schools co-researchers attended.

When another youth co-researcher commented: "We know that all of these officers don't make us feel safer, then what's the purpose of it all?," we realized quickly that our quantifying approach would provide us with a limited response to this question. Instead, we began to question the extent to which safety and security technology were perhaps influencing how young people assigned different use-values to school spaces and their processes of schooling. Our collective curiosity was sparked, and we decided then that we wanted our yPAR project to focus on the securitized (re)production of school space as both a product and informant of students' day-to-day lived experiences.

The findings that our research collective gathered about co-researchers' encounters with intensified criminalizing and punitive school safety measures in New York City public schools were situated within a theoretical framework that examined both deep and across multiple spatial-temporal school-based setting. Co-researchers created cognitive maps which detailed their daily movement and encounters with securitized spaces and places of their schools. We followed and centered our analysis on what Cindi Katz (2001) calls "a counter-topography" to unravel interconnections, interrelations, "tensions, contradictions, and affiliations" (p. 1228) within and across co-researchers' daily trajectories in schools. Thus our analysis was guided by the *lived* characteristic of space. We aimed to show the multi-faceted journeys of young people through the securitized spaces in New York City public schools and how these are increasingly interrupted by an institutionalized relationship between the public schools system and the criminal justice system.

Counter-Storytelling—Kristen Buras

Since Hurricane Katrina, elite reformers in New Orleans claim that charter schools will save the city. In opposition, young *neo-griots* affiliated with Students at the Center, a writing program in New Orleans, decided to share their counterstories or experiential knowledge and testimonials as a way to challenge the dominant narrative. In *Pedagogy, Policy, and the Privatized City: Stories of Dispossession and Defiance from New Orleans* (2010), which I coauthored with Students at the Center, student Maria Hernandez reflects:

> I've lost my home, my friends, and my school. I'm always on the verge of tears. But the worst part of it all is that the public officials—both elected and hired—who were supposed to be looking out for my education have failed me even worse than the ones who abandoned me in the Superdome [after Katrina]. . . . Now I'm fighting to reopen [Frederick] Douglass [High School] and other neighborhood schools in New Orleans and to provide a quality education for people like me. (In Buras et al., 2010, p. 86)

While Maria critiques the closure of open-access neighborhood-based public schools and their replacement by citywide charter schools, Tyeasha Green speaks against the corresponding closure of public housing in New Orleans. Tyeasha speaks out:

> My old neighborhood taught me so much. I would really hate to see it go. That's why I hope that officials from New Orleans, the state, or the federal government do not tear down my old home. . . . [They] should be building up not tearing down. (p. 93)

Ultimately, what emerged was a shared understanding that counterstories were instruments of critical race commentary and community resistance.

Participatory Theory of Change Modeling— Sarah Zeller-Berkman

In 2008–2009 I was working on a PAR project with young women from a New York City organization called Girls for Gender Equity (GGE). We had collected almost 1,200 surveys from young people in middle and high schools all over New York City about sexual harassment in NYC public schools. We had done our analysis and were beginning to develop collective action based on our findings. GGE formed the Coalition for Gender Equity in Schools to help move from research to a more intense focus on activism based on our findings—however, bringing together representatives from seventeen organizations was not without its challenges.

Concurrent to working on this PAR project, I was also working as a consultant for two participatory evaluation organizations, ActKnowledge and Kim Sabo Consultants. I came to value using theory of change modeling in my participatory evaluation work and proposed doing a collective theory of change process to launch our first coalition meeting. Young people and adults from a variety of organizations participated in the process of identifying how to accomplish our long-term outcome of "ending sexual harassment in schools."

The theory of change process provoked critical conversations about our shared definitions of terms like "sexual harassment." We identified five or six larger strategies that the group wanted to move forward in the next year, and we were able to get into the details about which organizations would move forward which part of the work and when. The process allowed for critical conversations to take place, a shared vision to emerge, as well as a concrete work-plan.

Although the integration of theory of change into my PAR work happened in a later phase of my project with GGE, I began to use participatory theory of change modeling as a starting point after this experience. I have since used it as a participatory method of getting adults and youth to collectively envision change they would like to make in their programs in a youth–adult partnership initiative I direct with with six, school-based community centers in New York City.

Shifting the Questions from Individual to Organization—Valerie Futch

Recently I worked with a youth participatory evaluation (YPE) team to develop a logic model for their after-school program. As a research team (four high school members of the program, four undergraduate co-researchers, two staff, and two faculty) we worked together to sketch out our collective ideas of the logic model for the program. This activity came directly from Kim Sabo-Flores' (2008) book. We used large sheets of poster paper to establish our views on "populations served," "program activities," "short-term outcomes," and "long-term outcomes." What we found was that the youth had an entirely different conceptualization than the adults. Whereas we tended to frame the population in terms of demographics—thus over-determining and presuming needs based on demographics—the youth framed the populations based on social and psychological needs that they entered the space with. Rather than "at-risk" or "low SES youth" our poster had "people who want to change the world," "people who want an outlet," and "people who want to perform." Similarly, the other categories included such shifts so that, ultimately, what began as an evaluation that could have focused in on individual outcomes, we were able to shift the focus to organizational functioning.

Then, as a team, we gathered stacks of index cards and wrote down every possible question we wanted to know about the program we were evaluating, as well as questions we thought different people would want to know. We tried to imagine the perspective of funding agencies, parents, board members, staff, youth, potential users, etc. in doing this. We developed over 100 questions and sorted these into themes and "big" and "small" questions in order to develop our overall research questions to guide the evaluation. In the short-term and more practical sense, this meant that everyone's voice was present on those cards, and as we shuffled them around and reorganized them it helped keep everyone's ideas active.

After rereading Sarah Zeller-Berkman's (2010) article on critical youth studies and youth participation in evaluation, I realized that this task helped us accomplish something more important. The result, primarily from the number of questions the youth co-researchers provided, was that all of our final evaluation research questions were framed in terms of the organizational level, not the individual level. While other funding agencies might still be asking that we frame outcomes in terms of the individual, this shift in questions seems significant. The questions could have easily slid right back to the individual level, which can be unfair when evaluating a program, as Zeller-Berkman points out. Instead, we have organization-level questions to guide us into the research. While I think our success in tapping into organizational over individual-level outcomes remains to be seen (we are in the middle of analysis), it definitely made me realize the importance of framing and how the multiplicity of voices in the room can help move the research from the individual to the structural.

Listening to Demographic Change—Django Paris

From 2006 to 2008 I learned about a changing community with Black, Latina/o, and Pacific Islander youth in the California city of South Vista. As we explored the changes in community we came, together to reveal what these changes meant for the ways race and ethnicity were lived through language and cultural engagements. The changes lived by these youth are part a larger story of changing urban schools and communities sweeping California (as well as other Western states and many cities across the nation from the Midwest to the South). Coupled with the continued residential and educational segregation of communities of color, one major effect of these shifts has been that many of California's urban communities that were once predominantly African American are now predominantly Latino/a, with significant populations of Pacific Islanders, Southeast Asians, and other immigrant communities of color.

The youth I learned with lived this change and theorized about what it meant to their own racializations and the ways they lived difference within and across various linguistic and cultural practices. Beginning by learning with youth about their changing community allowed us to ask what these changes meant for them and their families across community and school settings. Questions about linguistic practices in, for instance, African American Language (AAL), Spanish or Samoan or Dominant American English grew out of our shared interest in how the various ethnic communities of South Vista used language within and across groups. And questions about engagements in cultural activities and spaces of, for instance, hip hop, basketball, church, or temple, grew out of our shared interest in these spaces and activities.

We came to know that AAL and Spanish were not only tools of solidarity, but were shared across race and ethnicity in important ways that previous research had not documented or conceptualized. We came to know, as well, about the ways the Church space supported Samoan language learning and maintenance. We also came to know the ways participations in hip hop and basketball provided activities that both reinforced dominant racial division and also to challenged those divisions. In essence, listening to stories of a changing community invited subsequent collaborations on what this change meant for the present and for the future. I believe that any understanding of change begins with listening to youth about the changes they care about, participate in, and live.

Radical Acceptance—Crazy Glue Theory of Change—Caitlin Cahill & David Alberto Quijada Cerecer

Rather than a theory of change, our commitment to this work begins with a commitment to each other. Our starting point for doing collective/collaborative/participatory research and action is taking seriously the *participatoriness* of our collective, the relationships we have with each other and to the work we are in. Here community is strongly felt, strongly grasped, and intimate. People who might not ordinarily know each other or spend time together, come together in a truly intimate way in order to share a commitment to each other. Inspired by our co-founder Matt Bradley, we began to think about what love can really do. If love is showing up and being present, that's what we did. And like love, it can make you feel kooky, happy, brave and fearless. In our collective we needed each other to learn new ways to love, which is where social change emerges in the reminding and knowing that there are others committed to love (or social change)—a type of love to dismantle oppressive conditions that constrain love (or liberation).

Our work is about creating a space of radical acceptance for all parts of ourselves. Our *whole* selves. This feels especially important in a space/state (i.e. Salt Lake City, Utah) where so many are forced to go undercover or not take pride in who they are publically. So another plate to spin, might be how can we create a process for people who are differently positioned/situated to come together with a shared commitment to recognizing our whole selves? Perhaps this is our starting point, a crazy glue theory of needing each other and having each other's backs; honoring each other within a collective where the personal is reframed as social, shared, and political. Here love is a collective embrace and understanding that we have a stake in each other's lives, and that what's happening to you is what's happening to me. Our group hug. Or an analysis that situates one's personal experience of racism within a larger political economic context. The recognition that we are all in this together. And that's why what we need to start with is our commitment to each other.

The theory or rather crazy glue that bonds our collective love is a strategic "we" that places emphasis on our shared standpoint as researchers–compadres–comadres who are working together toward social change. This is not to erase the messiness of our process, which was rich with dissent and negotiation, but instead to highlight our political stance as a collective. A collective that understands that love like social change is collectively produced, evolves, requires guidance and daily reminders that we know how to love like we know how to dismantle oppressive conditions through our shared participation in the world.

Institutions and Change/Uncertainties in Theories of Change/Caveats

Dry Feet to Walk On—Justice Castañeda

For just under a decade I have worked with youth matriculating through the iterative levels of incarcerated communities—meaning both the daily iterations of of carceral institutions: Schools, juvie, schools, jails, schools, prisons, as well as the reiterations of matriculating from one such institution to the next. I've worked as an educator, an advocate, or as a liaison between them and the court system.

I started learning to think about pedagogy in the U.S. Marine Corps, where the voice of the platoon leader guided its direction. The art of pedagogy predates the Marine Corps, which could be seen as much as a violent perversion of the art, as an exemplar of organizational efficiency and efficacy. Yet as an educator, I am forced to examine theories of change in terms of Marine pedagogy and organization, because the classrooms and schools I work in are as morally dichotomous as the Corps. Schooling represents vast contradictions in values and intent. One important distinction is that unlike the classroom, participation in the Marines for poor children and children of color does not increase their likelihood of a life culminating in incarceration, and subsequent political and economic disenfranchisement.

Young people in poverty, in the Marine Corps, in public institutions, and in carceral communities have taught me that the beginnings of change feels like dry feet. At Garfield High School in San Diego, I witnessed students coming to school with soaking shoes, and remembered how the platoon operates by first making sure everyone's feet are dry, bellies full, bodies housed and rested, and medical needs met. The collective provides, and then works to develop the sociality needed to function as an organized body. At this point in my work, I am preoccupied, maybe obsessed, with how personal health, economic self-determination, and ability to meet one's basic needs form thus the material premise to imagine a future that is otherwise. Currently, these options do not exist in any collective sense for poor children outside of the institutions of prison and military.

We Cannot Afford to Be Romantic—Kristen Buras

We cannot afford to be romantic about what will be required to challenge the conditions of our times. Cherice Harrison-Nelson, despite the indispensable contributions of her work with youth through Guardians Institute, was among the 7,500 veteran teachers and school employees who were illegally terminated in 2005 after Hurricane Katrina. All were fired *en masse* while inexperienced college graduates from outside the community were brought in by Teach for America and other alternative teacher recruitment initiatives to "save" the children of New Orleans. Such efforts are guided by a dramatically different theory of change—one rooted in a market-based model of education that says managerial practices, including strict classroom discipline and student socialization into "white" ways of knowing and being, promise academic achievement and upward mobility. Longstanding youth organizations in New Orleans know better and I have learned from their accumulated wisdom.

Conclusion

Much of daily life tries to facilitate change, but opportunities to think together about how change happens are far more rare. Evidence of the need for change or action is immediately available to us, almost bombarding the senses. A perspective on the larger structures of change can be overwhelming, even as it offers critical insights. The pace, time scales, and ends of desired change can confound our urgent desire for it.

This chapter brought together local, immediate efforts at change with youth, often in intergenerational dialogue with their community members. Like points in a constellation, they begin to imply larger silhouettes of shared struggle—in Audre Lorde's words—"and the edge of each other's battles/the war is the same" (1997, p. 380). Each vantage point interprets the shared figure from a unique, local perspective. This situatedness of theories of change, at once local and immediate, at once analyzing the broader scales of social justice brings us into the framings of resistance and change offered by the chapters in this section.

Threads and themes emerge across the accounts above, perhaps most salient are those concerning the need for humility, for earnestness and for listening. We can see the importance of not holding on to preconceived notions too preciously and not taking oneself too seriously, not only to ethically engage with youth co-researchers, but for the sake of the quality of concepts and ideas that flow from those collaborations. What seems to cascade across the accounts is a rendering of collectivity itself as a theory of change.

Indigenous intellectuals and post-structuralists assert, albeit differently, that change is inevitable, constant. In the United States, many people believe that social change is achieved through social movements, but what is it about social movements that yields change? What does it mean that social movements take different shapes in different nation-states, comparing the history of social movements in the United States to Maori movements in New Zealand, for example? Others emphasize the importance of paradigm shifts and breaks, but how does one identify or create these breaks? How does change really happen?

These are pedagogical questions, meaning they are meant to be asked in community, in conversation with lived life. The answers are important, yes, but more important is the opportunity to think and feel through these questions collectively.

Works Referenced

Anzaldúa, G. (1987). *Borderlands/La Frontera: The new mestiza*. San Francisco: Spinsters/ Aunt Lute.

Anzaldúa, G., & Keating, A.L. (2002). *This bridge we call home: Radical visions for transformation*. New York: Routledge.

Buras, K.L., Randels, J., Salaam, K.Y., & Students at the Center. (2010). *Pedagogy, policy, and the privatized city: Stories of dispossession and defiance from New Orleans*. New York: Teachers' College Press.

Collin, M. (2007). *The time of the rebels: Youth resistance movements and 21st century revolutions*. London: Serpent's Tail.

Katz, C. (July 01, 2001). On the grounds of globalization: A topography for feminist political engagement. *Signs, 26*, 4, 1213–1234.

Kennedy, A. (2010). *Big Chief Harrison and the Mardi Gras Indians*. Gretna, LA: Pelican Publishing Company.

Lorde, A. (1997). Age, race, class, and sex: Women redefining difference. In A. McClintock, A. Mufti, E. Shohat, & Social Text Collective (Eds.). *Dangerous liaisons: Gender, nation, and postcolonial perspectives*, pp. 374–380. Minneapolis: University of Minnesota Press.

Sabo-Flores, K. (2008). *Youth participatory evaluation: Strategies for engaging young people*. San Francisco: Jossey-Bass.

Tuck, E. (2010, September 1). Breaking up with Deleuze: Desire and valuing the irreconcilable. *International Journal of Qualitative Studies in Education, 23*, 5, 635–650.

Tuck, E. & Yang, K.W. (2013). R-Words: Refusing research. In D. Paris, & M.T. Winn (2013). *Humanizing research: Decolonizing qualitative inquiry with youth and communities*. Thousand Oaks, CA: Sage Publications.

Zeller-Berkman, S. (2010, August 2). Critical development? Using a critical theory lens to examine the current role of evaluation in the youth-development field. *New Directions for Evaluation, 127*, 35–44.

10

THE POLITICS OF COMING OUT UNDOCUMENTED

Lisa (Leigh) Patel and Rocío Sánchez Ares

> Youth resistance is transformative, and it is still slow, contested, and painful but always moving toward social justice. It is this movement that understands transformative resistance as a de-centered process that communicates deep and layered understandings while it critically and creatively acts to transcend our shared and disparate bodies with oppression. (Quijada-Cerecer, Cahill, & Bradley, 2011, p. 592)

Quijada-Cerecer et al. (2011) provide a familiar affirmation of youth resistance in view of its revolutionary potential. This statement would likely be supported, invoked, and uttered in differing versions across left-leaning, progressive, and liberatory circles. Resistance as a trope of youth is not unique to these circles, nor is it unilaterally seen as a harbinger of social justice across scholarship. The resistant young person is a ubiquitous image in developmental psychology circles, where the stage of youth is verily defined through rebellion and resistance (e.g. Lesko, 2001; Patel Stevens et al., 2007; Willis, 1981). These intonations do not unilaterally see resistance as desirable, or as Quijada-Cerecer et al. put it more hopefully, as inherently moving toward social justice. Resistance, as this volume explores in detail, is never wholesale positive, negative or even merely teleological. It is, instead, a form, location, and permeable container for negotiations of power, identity, and inclusion. In this chapter, we draw upon our work as researcher activists with immigrant youth who have "come out" as undocumented, to discern the underlying theories of change in the undocumented movement. We take resistance as a site of social negotiation, of re-signification. We draw upon frame analysis (Oliver & Johnston, 2000) to analyze the frames through which undocumented youth resistance engages the frames of the white settler colonial state. Through our analysis of undocumented youth-led resistance to anti-immigrant policy, we seek to illuminate the offerings, compromises, and sacrifices made in their framings of undocumented resistance. Of keen interest is what this moment and form of youth resistance can tell us about the boundaries of resistance and change.

Undocumented Youth

For undocumented immigrant youth, the shape, promise, and perils of resistance are complex. Held at bay from inclusion into society across multiple lines of identification, including documentation, life stage, income level, and race, undocumented youth variably seek and reject visibility and inclusion. According to recent estimates, there are more than 2.1 million undocumented young people in the United States (Batalova & McHugh, 2010). Verily barred from access to higher education because they are unable to apply for federal financial aid, undocumented youth are paradoxically entitled to a K-12 public education. Incongruent access to schooling, as one facet of being undocumented and young, demonstrates how existence is marked by severely delimited inclusion in U.S. society.

For undocumented youth, seeking inclusion and the basic human desire to be seen is in direct tension with the need to remain invisible. Undocumented youths' bodies are conjoined with illegality, as their crime is defined as bodily presence in the United States without federal sanction. Although this is technically a civil offense in the U.S., punishable only by fee, it is instructive that being without government papers is criminalized in legal proceedings that include detention and incarceration, as well in the collective imaginary where undocumented is synonymous with "illegal." For many, the process of "learning to be illegal" (Gonzales, 2011) involves identifying the places where visibility is perilous: Filling out paperwork for work, education or social services, being caught in an altercation with law enforcement—such everyday events are eclipsed by the always looming threat of being asked to supply papers.

Undocumented youth also negotiate being a "youth" as temporarily peripheral to the more openly embraced states of romanticized childhood and validated adulthood (Vadeboncoeur & Patel Stevens, 2004). Young peoples' words and actions are always more dismissible, as people regarded as not fully legitimate to act on their own accord and yet less deserving of stewardship than children (Luke & Luke, 2001).

Finally, undocumented youth, now mostly from the Global South (Passel, 2006), are recast as racial minorities in the context of a nation founded on institutionalized racism (Harris, 1995; Jefferson, 1853), where statistics of income disparity, educational outcomes, incarceration, and health fall along disturbingly neat racial lines (Alexander, 2012; Ladson-Billings, 2006).

Cumulatively, the combined identity markers of being undocumented, racially minoritized, and in low-income work overdetermine immigrant youth as exempted from laws, from safety, from projects of self-determination. It is from this location that many undocumented youth activists have rejected invisibility and have instead "come out" as undocumented, voicing a corresponding desire to talk back to this host state.

Context Matters: White Settler Colonialism

Central to our inquiry is who undocumented youth are speaking to and what they hope to say to this interlocutor. The act of "coming out" undocumented is intrinsically connected to larger immigration waves under a white settler colonial power; their interlocutor is the white settler colonial state. Here we define white settler colonialism and fragmented global capital interests, then situate acts of coming out in relative dialogue with these projects, ultimately to better locate the theories of change and resistance in these acts.

The project of white settler colonialism seeks to permanently occupy land, resources, and peoples. Settler colonialism differs from more traditional descriptions of colonialism made in history textbooks—this kind of historicizing itself an act of colonialism—wherein empires took control of nations/states in order to extract peoples and resources. In settler colonialism, the desire of the colonizer is to stay, to make nonexistent and make complicit Indigenous peoples to the settler colonial project of ownership and control (Wolfe, 1991). This project also includes the import of cheap human labor, first slaves and now immigrants, defined in legal code as lacking full personhood. As Tuck and Yang (2012) describe,

> These modes of control, imprisonment, and involuntary transport of the human beings across borders; ghettos, their policing, their economic divestiture, and their dislocatability; are at work to authorize the metropole and conscribe her periphery. (p. 5)

Within this umbrella project of settler colonialism, capitalism, and white supremacy are political strategies that define implicitly and often overtly, the goals of a stratified society based on racial construct and socioeconomic class.

According to Grosfoguel (2002),

> immigrants in the United States experience the effects of racism as hegemonic imaginary of the modern/colonial world-system. Racial/colonial ideologies have not been eradicated from [...] centers which are in grave need of a socio-cultural decolonization. (p. 480)

Because racial/colonial ideologies materially shape social locations, immigrant groups endure the alienating design of racism, whereas whites enjoy racial privilege as property (Harris, 1995). This dynamic was inscribed in the founding of this nation, and its subsequent re-codifications, including the U.S. Constitution, through policies that affirmed land/resources as the domain of white (mostly male) Europeans, that constructed race in ways to erase Native Americans and to remove African Americans outside of the realm of property ownership, and that established the legal associations with whiteness that acted as figurative property (Harris, 1995). The location of low-wage earning immigrants as a criminal threat to American citizenry is a direct extension of these colonizing genealogies that first worked to destroy Indigenous populations and later import African and Asian populations to provide labor (Smith, 2011). White settler colonialism functions to refresh and preserve reputation and rights for "native"-born, Standard English-speaking, and mostly white property owners.

Coloniality is alive in racist capitalist politics, which play out globally to reproduce local stratifications of populations, concentrate wealth in the hands of a few, and prescribe labor and struggle for the most vulnerable. In this way, contemporary societies are aptly understood as conditioned by "fragmented global capitalism" (Katz, 2004), whereby people's lives are constantly shaped by their access to the prosperity, efficiencies, and technologies of globalization. Fragmented globalization produces, on the one hand, structured opportunities for those in power to expand their own interests, and on the other, structured exclusions from the accumulation of capital for those on the outside (Castells et al., 1999). Globalization thus simultaneously generates and is the outcome of uneven material social practices. The interaction between immigrant and the host state is then not just related to past U.S. colonializations, but it is echoed in current colonial thirsts for capitalist accumulation. It is against and within this context of white settler colonialism, fragmented global capital, and youth as resistant liminal subject, that we situate our analysis of coming out as undocumented.

Because coming out is a collective action engaged to effect social change, frame analysis provides an apt analytic tool. Used extensively within the sociology of social movements, frame analysis posits that much broad social interaction, including social movements, is conceptualized and actualized through parameters of desired action, perceptions of interlocutors' stances and priorities, and tactical moves to engage in the "politics of signification" (Hall, 1982). In Benford and Snow's (2000) literature review of collective frame analysis, movement actors are signifying agents actively engaged in the production and maintenance of meaning for constituents, antagonists, and bystanders or observers. Moreover, both frame analysis and studies of settler colonialism remind the reader that interlocutors shift their discourses in relation to others; nothing is fixed and, typically, the shifts reflect a desire to maintain constructed identities and positions. We position these acts of "coming out as undocumented" as framed for a conversation with the white settler colonial state, spoken through a fluid set of settler signifiers.

Talking with the Master: Coming Out to a White Settler Colonial State

Coming out as undocumented is a signifying practice that has gained momentum in some immigrant youth activist circles in the past five to ten years. Through our analysis of media accounts, interviews with undocumented youth activists, and our own work towards equity for dispossessed immigrant and settler youth, we see two primary frames of resistance: Justice and human connection.

The concept of justice is one of the most salient frames through which acts and statements of coming out manifest. Undocubus, a traveling bus of undocumented youth activists, toured across the U.S. in summer 2012, starting in Phoenix, Arizona and ending at the Democratic National Convention in North Carolina, to raise awareness about the policies directed at immigrant populations (nopapersnofear.org, 2012). The starting location of Arizona put the spotlight on what is often seen as ground zero for anti-immigrant sentiment and codes. Phoenix is also within the Maricopa County jurisdiction of Sheriff Joseph Arpaio, who has become synonymous with racial profiling of immigrants by law enforcement (ACLU, 2008). The ending location was chosen to pressure Democrats, the political party most sympathetic to immigrant populations, to stand for justice. The website for the campaign explains:

> Riding the bus alone is a great risk because of the checkpoint and profiling that has become so common. But the ride is also an arena for mobilizing, where we will build with those who have a story to tell, who have realized the community is an organized one. We have overcome our fears and are ready to set a new example of courage. We hope this country and its officials will be brave enough to follow. (http://nopapersnofear.org/index.php#about)

By coming out as undocumented, these immigrant youth challenge a nation whose image is hinged to discourses of bravery and fair play to match their bravery. Their resistance embodies a political re-signification, where immigrant activists confront unequal power structures in part by invoking the nation's own narrative about itself, here in the provocation about bravery and justice. This framing seeks to enter a face-to-face discussion with the white settler nation through settler signifiers of, as the song goes, "the land of the free and the home of the brave."

This framing is also found in the social media messages from and affiliated with the Undocubus tour. For example, one Facebook update from August read, "*Cuando la injusticia se hace ley, la rebeldia se hace obligación*. When injustice becomes law, resistance becomes duty" (https://www.facebook.com/UndocuBus, 2012).

In addition to this tour and its tactics of profiling state-sanctioned acts of exclusion and appeals for justice, the dialogic act of coming out often involves young undocumented immigrants telling their story of migration and living in the United States. A common strategy of circulating their messages and emotions to different audiences lies in sharing their knowledge and stories. Immigrant youth coming out as undocumented relies on epistemological effects of storytelling to re-signify how they are viewed by the white settler colonial state. In other words, they use the affective impact of storytelling to gain sociocultural capital, invoking themselves as relatable people worthy of human kindness. The Student Immigrant Movement (SIM) is a group of undocumented youth organizers with whom we work as activist-researchers. Conrado, a SIM organizer and undocumented college student from Brazil living in Boston, characterizes this form of strategic storytelling in the following way:

> We do not have a lot of allies, but we have our stories, but that means we have to expose ourselves and share them in public. That's scary, especially for those who do not talk, not even at home. People approach me in the street and ask: "what do you do?" I say: "I am undocumented, and an organizer for immigrant youth rights," so they go "oh, ok." People are not safe, but our stories are also our shield, our protection. Now you know who I am and you may be able to help me or join me.

Conrado's words reveal the underlying theory of change in the activist act of coming out as undocumented. By sharing personal stories, the theory is that a process of humanization, hinged to an appeal to the connectedness of living being, will protect undocumented youth from, as they have framed them, unjust practices of the state. This protection comes from not simply sharing the story but telling it in a way to engender others to become allies. This dialogic move of coming out as undocumented envisions change as a process enacted by many, which would otherwise be dangerous when sought by a few, and is thus hinged to human connection.

However, as is the case with all frames of interaction, by putting forward a particular narrative, other stories and protagonists are backstaged, in essence sacrificed from view. This is endemic to framing decisions, but in the analysis of what gathers visibility and what remains in the shadows, we can come closer to a dynamic view of resistance and change as enacted desires. Common to the stories of coming out undocumented are: Trips of being brought to this country as children; holding great promise as intelligent, capable young people; and being held back from their promise by a cruel set of anti-immigrant policies (Kuras, 2012). This narrative of desirable yet unjustly excluded immigrant youth is consistent with the discourse surrounding the DREAM Act, which would provide a potential pathway to citizenship for some undocumented youth. Written into the various incarnations of this federal bill has been a steady suite of eligibility requirements that all work from a view of the United States as a meritocracy, whereby worthy people who play by the rules, who work hard, should be rewarded with safety and status in society (McNamee & Miller, 2004).

By and large, undocumented youth advocacy across the country supports the DREAM Act. In doing so, many activists know they risk a political signification that divides immigrant communities into those more and those less worthy of recognition by the state. SIM stands as a great supporter of the DREAM

Act initiative, which would grant citizenship to some undocumented youth in the U.S. Yet, these youth's advocacy for passing the DREAM Act surrogates the needs of numerous undocumented populations that cannot afford or do not contemplate college as a plausible goal. Such is the case of Julio, an undocumented young activist who left his home in Guatemala and arrived in Boston eight years ago, and who cannot apply for any pathway to citizenship or sanctioned residency.

Julio shared some of his colleagues' enthusiasm saying, "I am sad I do not qualify for it, but I am happy for the students [...] they need hope, and this is a good opportunity." As much as Julio's words echo the solidarity of the SIM collective movement to resist anti-immigrant policies, they also communicate knowing oneself as already excluded from the colonial meritocracy frame. Julio refers to other undocumented "students" in the third person, because he had to drop out of high school to work full time. His words remind us that the terms of inclusion and exclusion are in uneven contention within the frames of undocumented activists (Patel, 2013).

The underlying theories of change in coming out as undocumented are dynamic, influenced by and influencing actions of the nation–state. Here we turn to the framings of immigration and youth that have officially flowed from the federal government.

Call and Answer: The Deferred Action for Children's Arrival

On June 15, 2012, President Barack Obama announced a memo from the Department of Homeland Security outlining leniency for undocumented immigrant youth brought into the country illegally by their parents. Hours before the press conference, social media outlets exploded, not only announcing the press conference, but speculating that the President was about to make a major announcement providing "leniency" and "amnesty" for "DREAMers," as activist undocumented youth fighting for access to higher education are called (Patel, 2012). Only days earlier, *Time Magazine* featured on its cover, a dramatic shot of a group of DREAMers against a black background, with the headline: "We are Americans; just not legally," and the central figure of Jose Antonio Vargas, an undocumented Filipino journalist whose 2011 article, "My life as an undocumented immigrant," brought him to national prominence.

When the President appeared at the designated time to address the press corps at the White House, he painted an empathetic picture of the nation's duties to undocumented youth, who were "Americans in their heart, in their minds, in every single way but one: on paper," echoing the language of the *Time Magazine* cover. He then proceeded to outline a change in deportation practices that would, if followed, provide undocumented youth with relief from immediate deportation and eligibility to apply for two-year, renewable, work visas under the conditions that: They had entered the country before the age of 16 illegally, were currently under the age of 30, had consistently attended and graduated from high school, and had not been convicted of any crimes. Far from a policy change, it expanded prosecutorial discretion for ICE in determining which undocumented youth warranted pursuit for detainment and deportation (Napolitano, 2012). The edict, commonly known as DACA (Deferred Action for Children's Arrival), prompted undocumented youth to identify themselves with little to no assurance that their coming out would not be used to pursue, detain, and deport them.

The DACA announcement primarily used the frame of meritocracy to position the United States as benevolent overseer of opportunity, which it equitably afforded to those who play by the rules. Meritocracy is used unproblematically by the white settler colonial state, allowing the state to re-signify itself not as a genocidal colonial power interested in subjugation, but as the overseer of a benevolent society based on reward for merit. In addition, DACA uses the frame of childhood innocence; its very name, Deferred Action for *Children's* Arrival, signifies children not youth, even though the policy is designed for those under the age of 30. The other crucial bracket to eligibility is that the young person must have entered the country before the age of 16; when still a child. Rhetorically, this frame re-signifies "illegal" immigration as essentially an individual and adult, criminal act, while absolving children as innocent pawns in these migrations.

Call and Answer in Dynamic Relation to Each Other

DACA acts as a double-edged sword that employs a paternalistic rhetoric to "protect" some undocumented youth, while maintaining absolute right to police and thus divide the immigrant community. Here, we examine the material effects of this double-edged sword on the daily practices and events of SIM. As a youth-led immigrant activist group in Boston, prior to the DACA announcement, SIM's leaders engaged audiences of various ethnic, racial, and documentation statuses in dialogic workshops where participants had a chance to share their views, experiences, and concerns regarding their rights as well as SIM's support. These talks took place in cultural centers, public libraries, local churches, and schools. In addition, SIM mobilized different communities through pro-migrant rallies, anti-deportation campaigns, as well as other political actions. A young organization, SIM was nonetheless able to actively and publicly challenge various anti-immigration laws in collaboration with multiple support networks. However, SIM had to change its dialogic space and reformulate its action plans as a result of the DACA announcement.

Following the President's press conference and public dissemination of the memo from the Department of Homeland Security, the vast majority of SIM's activities shifted in focus from political action and cross-community dialogue towards service: Organizing informative clinics with the purpose of explaining the pros and cons of the DACA announcement to large numbers of would-be applicants. Kathy, an undocumented student and SIM leader, commented on the impact of DACA on organizers' material practices:

> Because of DACA we are putting all our focus on application centers. We changed the structure of things. We hired people to come to work in our community and help people to apply. We put other campaigns on hold because of DACA. We had other things to do, and because of that we lost some members. They have not come to our meetings. We did not even have a meeting! We have been so focused on DACA! We are waiting for these months to go by, so we need to get together and re-coordinate, because I feel we have been so much into DACA that we neglected other work, and that is the work we have been building for the past years.

Although Kathy regarded DACA as both a move in the "right" direction, albeit with significant issues, she resisted a singular, celebratory response to the memo. On one hand, she felt a sense of victory over real gains in access. "After all this work," she explained, "I was so happy because I qualify, and I will be able to work legally and drive." On the other hand, she felt the lines drawn across immigrant communities:

> The announcement is so narrow that many people don't qualify. It is very exclusive, and that is not fair. Like parents are not guilty. They want a better life for us, and if Obama is going to do something for the DREAM-ers, he should make something for all students and their parents too. The government is very itchy about immigration and gives a few some benefits and not others, trying to save his [political] butt.

Kathy's critique of DACA reflects an ideological churning for many immigrants, activists, and others involved: Being pushed to negotiate their needs with state power. Although hopeful, she saw how the DACA memo restructured SIM's work into the busyness of compliance, and in that respect, serves as distracting instrument—preventing youth organizers from defining for themselves their goals for and methods of resistance within the U.S. hegemonic political arena.

Resisting Being Co-opted in the Convergence of Colonial Interests

In 1980, legal scholar Derrick Bell indicted the largely celebrated 1954 *Brown v. Board of Education Supreme Court* decision as a tactical move by a racist state to preserve structured inequity. The decision, Bell asserted, was a designed gesture to quell concern nationally and internationally that the United States segregationist policies were diametrically opposed to its constructed identity as land of equality and opportunity. Bell described the convergence of interests: Saving face as a nation that sought to combat Communist governments and win the allegiance of emerging "Third World" nations; reconciling the racism faced by African American GIs returning from World War II with American democratic principles; and economically spurring the South to move from a slave-based agrarian economy to industrialization. Interests had converged that compelled, in Bell's analysis, the racist state to gesture towards equity in order to avoid fundamentally changing an oppressive socioeconomic structure.

The DACA memo, the orchestrated press conference and pre-conference media blitz fit these hallmarks of interest convergence. How could the United States be seen as other than racist and capitalist in the face of the poster youth for the DREAM Act who were romanticized as innocent and desirable? What could a federal incumbent do to reclaim the growing Latino vote after shattering deportation records in the first three years of its administration? How could the image of the United States as a meritocratic country be salvaged against the cases publicized by actions like Undocubus, when merit seemed to be met not with reward but with persecution? In one fell, but highly coordinated, multi-media swoop, the DACA memo and its announcement worked once more to gesture towards equity without changing iniquitous structures. DACA does not provide a pathway to citizenship, does not explain what kinds of proof are necessary to apply, and is not even a law. As a memo from a federal department, it is subject to being ignored or revoked without process of any kind. And yet, it is experienced, perhaps by design, as a "step in the right direction."

Many, if not all, of the undocumented activists we work with recognize that DACA is an obvious election year flirtation by a sitting President. They are fully conscious that this crumb-like inclusion falls significantly short of even their most conservative visions for equitable border and immigration policies. Within this critique, we see great opportunity to forward *more* fundamental articulations of theories of change. Undocumented youth are in a position to ask themselves and others, "A step towards what?"—an essential, although not necessarily common, question for social movements. We don't see many activists imagining that the liminal, temporary, and vague loosening of deportation practices for some undocumented youth will snowball easily into fundamental changes in how borders, inclusion, and personhood are defined and by whom. Rather, we see them struggling to push more on the edges of a frame they've used, meritocracy, and how it works to preserve their lower positions in the white settler hegemony.

Because the state is in calculated conversation with youth resistance, then the very meaning and political possibilities of any particular form of youth resistance are always being changed by the state. Power resistance is a dynamic, asymmetric, and mutually constitutive relationship. According to Foucault, power-driven resistance is never free of its risks. Building from Foucault's argument, Weedon (1997) adds that: "power occurs in relationships [...] Discourses are not constructed in bipolar relations of powerless and powerful" (p. 107). Because power is relational, individuals who challenge these power boundaries rely on complex, often conflicting sets of networks that give these individuals power while at the same time depriving them of some. On the one hand, by coming out, undocumented youth overtly denounce the oppressive power of neocolonial discourses as to build their own support networks; on the other hand, these same activist youth knowingly run the risk of reproducing the same hegemonic discourses that oppress them. These young activists know that they must carefully craft their arguments when in dialogue with the colonial state power.

How Youth Resistance Has Spoken

We do not discount that this cultural construction of life stage, that is, youth, due to its very sidelining, has a view of the system not readily available from the center. It is, in fact, from this view of society, that we posit that these young people have been able to quite easily articulate the complex personhood (Gordon, 1997) they feel in relation to both their frames of advocacy and how it is appropriated by the white settler colonial state. This complexity, which includes excitement, revulsion, resentment, and relief at being marginally seen by the state, is itself an act of resistance worth noting. In this regard, undocumented youth's resistance tries to dialogically weave their multiple needs in a common struggle for control over varied forms of capital and self-definition.

By coming out as undocumented, immigrant youth use visibility to destabilize exclusionary ideologies along the political spectrum. At the core, the act of coming out undocumented is a desire for public recognition without the burden of personal fear. As Hannah Arendt put it:

> There is a deep connection between the public and private selves, between the public and private spaces, here private in the sense of where we have safety, cover and depth, not available to public view. Without this kind of privacy, life "loses the quality of rising into sight from some darker ground which much remain hidden if it is not to lose its depth in a very real, non-subjective sense." (1985, p. 72)

In our work with undocumented activists, we have seen above all else, this desire to be seen as the impetus for symbolically throwing off a signification as victim.

We have also seen this highly personal desire work to connect formerly isolated undocumented youth with social networks of support and care, most often simply other young people. In this sense, the undocumented youth movement lives a collective praxis of living and mitigating a reduction of immigrant as criminal. Anzaldúa (2007) encourages marginalized populations to critically embrace their history as a way of self-empowerment resulting from shared knowledge and cross-community relations. Creating spaces for this knowledge to expand and interconnect with others becomes itself an act of resistance, even if that means, as Anzaldúa puts it, going against one's own cultural beliefs. It is in this complex performance of personhood that the master gaze is subverted and the opportunity may arise to define new social possibilities. These complex performances arise not as a critique of the state but despite the state. So, along with a tightly circumscribed theory of change that celebrates DACA as a "step in the right direction," we also see undocumented youth resistance as more fundamentally concerned with a theory of change that is about care and collectivity.

In order to more deeply resist, we need for a better toolkit of language to frame our practices. Most activists' work in the United States and other white settler colonial nations employs standardized European-derived academic English as a way of communication. Counteractively, Grosfoguel (2002) argues for a revolutionary language as the means to foment the development of transformative epistemological insights among different groups. He explains: "changing meanings of racist discourses implies creating new language and concepts that account for the complex processes of the colonial world-system" (p. 492). Grosfoguel urges different parties not to simplistically debunk the neocolonial paradigm, but to critically and creatively re-define the liberal one. Using a language that breaks with the liberal paradigm represents a first step towards positive social change—a step in which those in the subordinate angle can engage others in disentangling the rhetoric of oppression, while developing new critical insights and revolutionary political alliances. As scholar Andrea Smith put it in her 2010 keynote address to the Critical Ethnic Studies Conference,

> What settler colonialism does is that it sets a ceiling on what the future can be such that we cannot even imagine a future without genocide. This tendency then leaves us to develop critical visions only within the constraints of the possible and that then infects all the work that we do.

Instead, we hope that youth resistance and all forms of resistance learn to see, as the undocumented youth activists we've quoted here can see, the state working its power within its calculated conversations with resistance.

Works Referenced

Alexander, M. (2012). *The new Jim Crow: Mass incarceration in the era of colorblindness*. New York: The New Press.
American Civil Liberties Union (2008). Sheriff Joe Arpaio sued over racial profiling of Latinos in Maricopa County. Available: http://www.aclu.org/immigrants-rights/sheriff-arpaio-sued-over-racial-profiling-latinos-maricopa-county
Anzaldúa, G. (2007). *Borderlands / La Frontera: The new mestiza*. San Francisco: Aunt Lute Books.
Arendt, H. (1985). *The human condition*. Chicago: University of Chicago University Press.
Batalova, J. & McHugh, M. (2010). *DREAM vs. reality: An analysis of potential DREAM Act beneficiaries*. Washington, D.C.: Migration Policy Institute. Available: http://www.migrationpolicy.org/pubs/DREAM-Insight-July2010.pdf

Bell, D. (1980). *Brown v. Board of Education* and the interest convergence dilemma, *93 Harvard Law Review*, 518.

Benford, R.D., & Snow, D.A. (2000). Framing processes and social movements: An overview and assessment. *Annual Review of Sociology, 261*, 611–639.

Bonilla-Silva, E. (2001). "What is racism?" and "Conclusion: New racism, new theory, and new struggle," Chapter 7 in *White supremacy and racism in the post-Civil Rights era*, pp. 193–207. Boulder, CO: Lynne Rienner Publishers.

Castells, M., et al. (1999) *Critical education in the new information age*. Lanham, MD: Rowman & Littlefield Publishers.

Chavez, L.R. (2008). *The Latino threat: Constructing immigrants, citizens, and the nation*. Stanford, CA: Stanford University Press.

Diamond, I. & Quinby, L. (1988). *Feminism and Foucault: Reflections on Resistance*. Boston, MA: Northeastern University Press.

Gonzales, R.G. (2011). Learning to be illegal: Undocumented youth and shifting legal contexts in the transition to adulthood. *American Sociological Review, 76*, 4, 602–619.

Gordon, A.F. (1997). *Ghostly matters: Haunting and the sociological imagination*. Minneapolis: University of Minnesota Press.

Grosfoguel, R. (2002). Colonial difference, geopolitics of knowledge and global coloniality in the modern/colonial capitalist world-system. *Research Foundation of SUNY, 25*, 3, 203–224.

Hall, S. (1982). The rediscovery of ideology: Return of the repressed in media studies. In J. Storey (Ed.). *Cultural theory and popular culture: A reader*, pp. 111–141. London: Longman.

Harris, C. (1997). Whiteness as property. In K. Crenshaw, N. Gotanda, G. Peller, & K. Thomas (Eds.). *Critical race theory: The key writings that formed the movement*. New York: The New Press.

Jefferson, T. (1785). *Notes on the state of Virginia*.

Katz, C. (2004). *Growing up global: Economic restructuring and children's everyday lives*. Minneapolis: University of Minnesota Press.

Ladson-Billings, G. (2006). From the Achievement gap to the Education Debt: Understanding achievement in U.S. school. *Educational Researcher, 35*, 7, 3–12.

Lemert, C. (2010). *Social theory: The multicultural and classic readings*, 4th ed. Philadelphia, PA: Westview Press.

Lesko, N. (2001). *Act your age! A cultural construction of adolescence*. New York: Routledge.

Luke, A., & Luke, C. (2001). Adolescence lost / childhood regained: On early intervention and the emergence of the techno-subject. *Journal of Early Childhood Literacy, 1*, 1, 91–120.

McNamee, S.J., & Miller, R.K. (2004). *The meritocracy myth*. London: Rowman & Littlefield.

Napolitano, J. (2012, June 15). *Exercising prosecutorial discretion with respect to individuals who came to the United States as children*. Retrieved from http://www.dhs.gov/xlibrary/assets/s1-exercising-prosecutorial-discretion-individuals-who-came-to-us-as-children.pdf

Oliver, P.E., & Johnston, H. (2000). What a good idea! Ideologies and frames in social movement research. *Mobilization, 5*, 1, 37–54.

Passel, J.S. (2006). The size and characteristics of the unauthorized migrant population in the U.S.: Estimates based on the March 2005 Current Population Survey. Washington, DC: Pew Hispanic Center. Available: http://pewhispanic.org/files/reports/61.pdf

Patel, L. (2012). What does it feel like to be a pawn? Decolonizingresearch.wordpress. com. Accessed June 25, 2012.

Patel, L. (2013). *Youth held at the border: Immigration, education and the politics of inclusion.* New York: Teachers' College Press.

Patel Stevens, L., Hunter, L., Pendergast, D., Carrington, V., Bahr, N., and Mitchell, J. (2007). ReConcepualizing the possible narratives of adolescence. *Australian Educational Researcher, 34,* 1, 107–127.

Preston, J. (2011, November 12). Deportations under new U.S. policy are inconsistent. *New York Times.* Retrieved December 22, 2011: http://www.nytimes.com/2011/11/13/us/politics/president-obamas-policy-on-deportation-is-unevenly-applied.html

Quijada-Cerecer, D.A., Cahill, C., Bradley, M. (2011). Resist this! Embodying the contradictory positions and collective possibilities of transformative action. *International Journal of Qualitative Studies in Education, 24,* 5, 587–593.

Smith, A. (2011). Plenary addressed delivered to Critical Ethnic Studies and the Future of Genocide. San Diego, CA, March 12, 2011.

Suárez-Orozco, C., et al. (2011). Growing up in the shadows: The developmental implications of unauthorized status. *Harvard Educational Review, 81,* 3, 437–472.

Tuck, E., & Yang, K.W. (2012). Decolonization is not a metaphor. *Decolonization: Indigeneity, Education, & Society, 1,* 1, 1–40.

Vadeboncoeur, J.V., & Patel Stevens, L. (2004). *Re/Constructing the adolescent: Sign, symbol & body.* New York: Peter Lang.

Vargas, J.A. (June 22, 2011). My life as an undocumented immigrant. *New York Times Magazine.*

Weedon, C. (1997). Discourse, power and resistance. In *Feminist Practice and Poststructuralist Theory,* pp. 104–131. Cambridge, MA: Blackwell.

Willis, P. (1977). *Learning to labor: How working class kids get working class jobs.* New York: Columbia University Press.

Wolfe, P. (1991). On being woken up: The dreamtime in anthropology and in Australian settler culture. *Comparative Studies in Society and History, 33,* 2, 197–224.

11

RETHINKING RESISTANCE THEORY THROUGH STEM EDUCATION

How Working-Class Kids Get World-Class Careers

Antwi A. Akom, Allison Scott, and Aekta Shah

Many of us in the environmental justice movement have wanted to create green collar jobs, and not just jobs but world-class careers that are actually promoting environmental protection, jobs that are actually reducing pollution, and have that happen in our communities. We're bringing in people who are from here, from our own communities. People who want to create their own businesses together and do it green. And so those are the members of the cooperatives that we will be starting and that we're starting now. We saw it too often . . . we saw companies come in all the time promising jobs and at the end of the day what we get is a fraction of what was promised. And what we get are the dirtiest jobs and the most dangerous jobs. And what we get more than anything is really pollution, dirty air, dirty water, dirty soil. We think it's important to fight back. To resist this stuff. So we're fighting for the planet and jobs that create opportunities for all. We think this is the most important kind of resistance. We want world-class green collar careers for our communities and a lot of those require training in Science, Tech, Engineering and Math. We get it. You ain't really free unless you own your community and we want to be free. (Educational leader, Oakland, CA)

Living in areas of concentrated ghetto poverty and toxic waste, burdened by the legacy of slavery, servitude, and second-class citizenship, too many Black and brown youth are dying of unnatural causes (Akom, 2011). They are vanishing, or in the classic metaphor of Ralph Ellison, being rendered invisible to such an extent that dysfunctional schools, dilapidated housing, food deserts, brown fields, unemployment, prison, violence, pollution, disease, and early death have now become part of the expected social trajectory for many of youth of color from low-income communities. When youth of color, particularly Black and brown youth resist, when they speak out and make their insightful institutional and social critique through mechanisms including being identified with disruptive behavior, adopting a nonconformist style of dress, talking back, and devaluing educational achievement, they are labeled as social problems by the police, schools, and employers (Dance, 2002; Majors & Billson, 1992). Further, some research suggests that many contemporary youth of color are caught between the natural affinity for their home culture, language, social networks, families, friends, and community and conforming to mainstream culture, or the "white washing" required to complete formal education and assume professional occupations. The resistance to being "white washed" has led many youth of color to adopt what some have called oppositional behavior against "the burden of acting white," thought to result in decreased identification with formal schooling (Akom, 2003; Fordham, 1996; Fordham & Ogbu, 1986; Ogbu, 1978; Ogbu & Simons, 1998). While these examples of oppositional resistance are prevalent, there are also examples of more proactive forms of resistance which demonstrate resiliency within societal structures and are associated with positive individual or community outcomes.

Early resistance theorists such as Willis (1977), MacLeod (1987) and McLaren (1993) examined working-class students' oppositional behavior during a time when manufacturing jobs were readily available. They argued that oppositional behavior constituted a rejection of middle-class culture motivated by an implicit understanding of the myth of meritocracy, and also an explicit expectation that a working-class job awaited them. However, significant changes in our economy have occurred. Working-class manufacturing jobs available to those with limited formal education have drastically declined. Instead, jobs within STEM-related fields are projected to continue growing rapidly (17% between 2008 and 2018) and outpace the supply of skilled workers produced to fill the job openings.

Drawing on sociology, critical race theory, social epidemiology, and critical education, we explore the possibilities and limitations of theories of youth resistance in relationship to Black working-class youth and present a new and expanded theory of youth resistance (within the current economic and educational context) that we refer to as *structural resistance and agency* (SRA). This chapter theorizes about resistance among Black and brown working-class students' oppositional behavior in the context of eco-apartheid on one hand, and the growth in demand for a highly skilled workforce in Science, Technology, Engineering, and Math (STEM) fields on the other. This chapter presents an analysis of youth resistance that requires both structural transformation and individual agency that updates, confounds, and potentially undoes current conceptualizations of youth resistance theory. We offer our theorizings in contrast to works which have focused on the self-defeating resistance of working-class students without acknowledging and studying other forms of resistance that could lead to structural and individual transformation.

By shifting our focus to examining "structures that resist domination" while simultaneously studying what motivates Black working-class youth to struggle and the strategies they develop, we present a way to build transformative structures that can help Black working-class youth move from surviving to thriving in terms of economic wellbeing, safety, health, and sexuality (Ginwright 2011; Kelley 1994). In other words, we reject the tendency to dichotomize people's lives into structure versus agency. Structures are not separate from lived experience or the imagination of what is possible. In fact, structures that resist domination along with individual self-determination and agency are about these things.

As update to Willis' landmark study on how working-class youth end up getting working-class jobs (Willis, 1977), the transformative questions of our study are: How can working-class kids get *world-class* careers while maintaining their racial/ethnic and social identities? While healing from physical and emotional trauma? While exercising self-efficacy and self-determination, and remaining connected to their community cultural wealth (Yosso, 2005)?

These questions get at the centrality of structural racism in the life and everyday experiences of Black working-class youth. Willis and other resistance and reproduction researchers are barely audible when it comes to the race—particularly the structural dimensions of race. Yet, structural racialization, particularly cumulative causation (Akom, 2011), not only figures prominently in the collective identities of Black working-class youth culture, but substantially shapes the entire opportunity structure in terms of access to institutional resources and privileges.

As early as elementary school, the impact of STEM disparities within the K-12 pipeline is readily apparent. Black working-class students demonstrate much lower levels of proficiency in math and science when compared to their white and Asian peers (Scott, 2012). By eighth grade, math and science proficiency levels decrease, achievement gaps widen, and disparities in rigorous course-taking between groups result in Black working-class students and other students of color being less likely to enroll Algebra I in eighth grade, more likely to take lower-level math courses, and less likely to reach proficiency across math and science courses than their peers.

In this chapter we view the emerging opportunities for utilizing STEM knowledge, experience, and occupations to transform individual lives, address social and equity issues within communities of color, and provide proactive resistance to formal and traditional schooling opportunities experienced by Black youth. We theorize that structural resistance places young peoples' experiences squarely within the struggle for self-determination in the context of growing global capitalism and innovative and contextually disruptive technologies. Youth are creating new identities, cultures, strategies of resistance, and generating a wide range of challenges and opportunities for school authorities and adults who often feel it is their job to keep youth in check and reproduce the social order. Nevertheless, we see global restructuring of the economy as important and marking a significant moment in the history of youth resistance theory in general and Black working-class youth culture in particular.

This chapter is less concerned with giving readers heroic best practices than with reimagining and retheorizing youth resistance theory for Black working-class youth in the context of high availability of jobs in STEM-related fields. In the first section, we define structural resistance and agency as a theoretical construct and introduce the six themes that form its core principles, perspectives, and pedagogy. We discuss the availability of high-paying, family-supporting, world-class STEM jobs and some of the structural and behavioral reasons why there is a lack of youth of color prepared to take them. In the second section, we examine some of the challenges of building STEM pathways and schooling outcomes for Black working-class youth not as issues of failure or victimhood. Instead we show how Black youth are rejected by the system and reject the system simultaneously. In the third section, we identify the ways in which structures can be created that lead to greater self-determination, self-efficacy, and self-preservation for working-class youth of color.

The overall goal of this chapter is to try to make sense of how things are as well as how they could be. It is just a small and very incomplete step towards connecting everyday struggles to formal institutional processes, to break free from patterns of structural racialization and historical trauma, and to reject formulaic interpretations in favor of lived experience.

Rethinking Resistance Theory: Introducing Structural Resistance and Agency (SRA)

To advance our understanding of the concept of resistance we present the theoretical construct of *structural resistance and agency* (SRA) and the six basic elements that form its core. Although none of these core principles are new in and of themselves, collectively they represent a new theory and challenge existing modes of resistance scholarship (Yosso & Solórzano, 2002). SRA puts forth the view that individual youth agents and social structure are formed and reformed through the action of each upon the other. The structures of society are its rules, resources, ideologies, and institutions. A SRA framework argues that individual resistance to oppressive structures is not enough, if we want to create sustainable forms of resistance we need to create structures that resist domination, communities that resist domination, cultures that resist domination. Simultaneously, the SRA framework pays equal attention to forms of youth agency that may serve the function of resistance, but were not created with resistance in mind, nor with the idea that its participants understand it as such (Duncombe 2002).

Structural Racialization and Intersectionality with Other Forms of Subordination

The backbone of SRA is a structural racialization and critical race theory (CRT) framework that challenges researchers to extend traditional understandings of racism in which individuals intentionally or unintentionally target others for negative treatment because of their skin color or other cultural characteristics. We argue that this individualistic conceptualization is too limited. Instead we shift our attention from the "single, intra-institutional setting to inter-institutional arrangements and interactions" (Powell, 2008, p. 796).

Willis and other resistance and reproduction researchers are often silent when it comes to the race—particularly the structural dimensions of race (Akom, 2011; Akom, 2009; Massey & Denton, 1993; Powell, 2008). Additionally, although structural racialization is at the center of an SRA analysis, we also view it at the intersection with other forms of subordination such as gender, sexuality, immigration status, language, class, and STEM literacy (Akom, 2011; Collins, 1999; Crenshaw, 1989). SRA theory suggests that, "it is at the intersection of race, class, gender, language, and immigration status that some answers to theoretical, conceptual, and methodological questions related to Black working-class youth might be discovered" (Solórzano & Bernal, 2001, p. 313).

Challenging Dominant Ideology

An SRA framework in STEM education challenges traditional claims that institutions make towards objectivity, meritocracy, color-blindness, race neutrality, and equity while also offering a liberatory or transformative response to racial, gender, sexuality, and class oppression (Yosso & Solórzano, 2002, p. 26). Structural racialization theorists also challenge deficit frameworks used to explain Black STEM educational underachievement (Solórzano & Bernal, 2001). SRA theory, in particular argues that deficit paradigms function through "hidden transcripts" (Scott, 1990) which serve to make invisible the power, privilege, and self-interest of dominant groups. In the next section we demonstrate that youth and adults who operationalize SRA using culturally and community responsive STEM pedagogy, challenge this invisibility and push institutions to seriously address issues of access and equity for Black working-class youth and other youth of color.

Building Sustainable Environments and Commitment to Social Justice

An SRA framework is committed to environmental justice and offers both an individual and a structurally transformative response to race, gender, sexuality, or class oppression beyond human liberation. According to Grande (2004),

> the failure of radical scholars to consider that even in the socialist-democratic imaginary, the end game remains human liberation: a profoundly anthropocentric notion, rooted in a humanist tradition that presumes the superiority of human beings over the rest of nature. (2004, p. 27)

We envision a social justice and environmental justice research agenda that leads toward (1) the elimination of racism, sexism, poverty; (2) the empowering of low-income communities and communities of color; (3) the creation of "green" STEM college and career pathways; and (4) a commitment to environmental justice and building sustainable communities for all. An SRA framework recognizes that multiple layers of oppression and domination must be met with multiple forms of resistance, including caring for mother earth.

Building a Strong Local Economy Rooted in Community, Democracy, and Equity

An SRA framework aims to create communities of opportunity and build strong local economies that offer good jobs, family supporting wages, career ladders, community and culturally responsive STEM training opportunities, cooperative economic models that interrupt traditional notions of global capitalism and transform them into community-based opportunities which redistribute wealth and opportunity to the most disenfranchised and most marginalized; as well as sustainable development solutions that enable people to easily travel between their homes and jobs, school, and day-to-day services. The focus is on educational, economic, and environmental systems that support development and investment in community cultural wealth through local STEM enterprise and community-based capital creation. Mentorships and role models in STEM fields are key to ensuring that these processes are engaged in with a commitment to social justice, and alleviate poverty, racism, sexism, and other dimensions of social oppression. In the context of this study,

> transformational role models are visible members of one's own racial/ ethnic and/or gender group who actively demonstrate a commitment to social justice, whereas transformational mentors use the aforementioned traits and their own experiences and expertise to help guide the development of others. (Solórzano & Bernal, 2001, p. 322)

The Centrality of Local Knowledge and Personal Experience

A SRA framework recognizes that the local knowledge and personal experiences of youth of color are critical to understanding, analyzing, and teaching about structural racialization in the field of STEM education and beyond (Corburn, 2002). An SRA approach seeks to expose deficit informed research methods that silence and distort youth of color, and instead focus on an asset-building approach that views the racialized, gendered, and classed experiences of youth of color as a source of strength (Akom, 2009; Yosso & Solórzano, 2002, Ginwright, Cammarota, & Noguera, 2006). In an effort to accomplish this goal an SRA approach applies a variety of research methodologies including (but not limited to) participatory action research (Akom, 2008; Minkler & Wallerstein, 2011; Torres & Fine, 2006), biographies, auto-ethnographies, digital storytelling, music, video ethnography (Twine & Steinbugler, 2006; Hoachlander & Yanofsky, 2011), and STEM culturally and community responsive pedagogy.

A Transdisciplinary Perspective

A SRA framework challenges one-dimensional approaches to studying educational inequality and insists on analyzing the structural and psychological dimensions to racism by using interdisciplinary methods (Solórzano & Bernal, 2001). In our study of SRA within the context of STEM fields, we draw from sociology, critical race theory, social epidemiology, ethnic studies, psychology, and critical education in our analysis of Black working-class students.

Barriers to STEM Education for Black Working-Class Youth

To reimagine and retheorize youth resistance theory for Black working-class youth in the context of emerging and expanding opportunities within STEM fields of study, this section will explore the barriers facing Black youth in pursuing STEM by analyzing publically available data (e.g. NAEP, BLS, NSF) and synthesizing first-hand narratives from Black students themselves, teachers, and professionals who work closely with them. The narratives have been obtained from several studies examining STEM programs in-school and out-of-school settings.

Projections for the next ten years and beyond indicate that the fastest-growing jobs in urban areas and beyond are in STEM-related fields; seven of the ten fastest-growing occupations over the next ten years are in STEM (Bureau of Labor Statistics, 2011). Nationwide, there are 2.4 million job vacancies for STEM workers projected between the years 2008 and 2018, and in addition to increased opportunities for employment, STEM occupations are also among the highest-paying. Sixteen of the 25 highest-paying jobs in the U.S. in 2010 required STEM preparation, and STEM workers earn 70 percent more on average than their non-STEM peers (Bureau of Labor Statistics, 2011). In addition to the economic growth and health of the economy within STEM fields, these fields offer unique opportunities for innovation to solve some of the most intractable social problems of our time.

However, despite the economic and social opportunities presented by participation within STEM fields, African Americans (as well as Latinos and Native Americans) continue to be excluded from access and opportunities critical to pursuing STEM studies and are thus vastly underrepresented in STEM professions, relative to their overall population. In comparison to their white and Asian peers, Black students demonstrate lower levels of math and science achievement, Advanced Placement STEM course-taking rates, dismal high school graduation rates (some estimates are 50 percent; NAEP, 2011, College Board, 2013). Upon entering higher education, they declare STEM majors at much lower rates than their white and Asian peers; those who do, persist to earn Bachelor's degrees in STEM at rates much lower than their white and Asian peers. In fact, only 2.7 percent of African Americans, 3.3 percent of Native Americans, and 2.2 percent of Latinos have earned a Bachelor's degree in science or engineering. In 2009, African Americans earned just 9.3 percent of all science and engineering degrees and Latinos earned only 8.8 percent (NSF, 2012).

These numbers represent both significant opportunities for structural resistance and transformation and also a crisis in the vast amount of untapped talent that has been excluded from opportunities to pursue occupations in STEM due to pervasive inequalities throughout the STEM pipeline. Interviews with Black working-class students reveal that both structural inequities and psychological barriers impact the STEM outcomes for this group. The most prominent barriers include inadequate access, opportunity, and preparation in K–12, and psychological barriers that limit success and persistence in STEM fields (Scott, 2012).

The following interview with a 20-year-old African American female who is now in college and majoring in engineering serves to illustrate this point:

> It's hard; it's really, really hard. The high school I went to—we didn't even have a science lab, most of the "science" we learned was out of a book, and the books were even 20 years old!

Without access to adequate computer facilities, funding, quality teaching, course offerings, technology, and other resources at the K–12 level, many Black working-class students and other students of color are negatively impacted as they prepare to enter and achieve success in STEM fields. The following interview with a white female science teacher at a public school in Oakland, California demonstrates some of the inadequate access and opportunity issues that Black working-class students face in STEM disciplines:

> Our school doesn't even have a computer lab. So when I think about issues of access and equity, it's a joke. The whole idea of meritocracy is a joke. Every school should have a computer lab. But ours doesn't. It's absolutely unfair that schools in white communities have computer labs, and schools in Black communities don't. How can we expect our students to succeed in the 21st century if they are still writing all their papers by hand?

Black working-class youth are also more likely to be formally or informally tracked into lower-level math and science courses despite ability and are subsequently less likely to be enrolled in advance-level math and science courses. A Black male high school student had the following to say about his experience being tracked out of Algebra in eighth grade:

> I remember eighth grade, all my friends were selected to go into Algebra, and I wasn't. I remember feeling humiliated, dumb, not smart enough, but at that age I didn't know how to put it into words, and I didn't know what it would mean later. . . . If it wasn't for my mom dragging me every summer to the Science Summer Program—I would have never ended up wanting to become a doctor.

Contrary to Ogbu's (1978) findings that Black middle-income parents do not care about their children's education, we found that many Black working-class parents do care and take action to ensure that their children have opportunities to succeed in STEM disciplines. A Black working-class mother of four discussed her daily struggle to help her children succeed, particularly within science and math:

> What gets me up every day is to make sure that my children have a better life than me. For a while I'd take the bus, work multiple jobs, I do whatever it took. I didn't graduate from high school so I know how important getting an education is. So I tell them, "You should go to the math program and go to this science program and try to make something out of yourself." And my children, they like it. They want to do it. They like making things with their hands and seeing other Black folks who made something out of themselves. They like it and my youngest is only in third grade. It makes him feel good about who he is.

What this suggests is that values of social justice, environmental justice, experiential knowledge, and building local economies have motivated the students and adults in these interviews to activate pieces of SRA in their local schools and communities. The final section explores how educators, researchers, organizations, and local leaders can operationalize the totality of SRA in order to build STEM pathways for Black youth.

Revolutionizing STEM Education: Structural Resistance and Agency in Action

Building collective structures of resistance requires coordinated and systematic efforts across sectors, particularly for Black working-class youth and other students of color. To address inequities in STEM education and increase the STEM outcomes of students of color, organizations like the National Society for Black Engineers' SEEK program, Level Playing Field Institute's (LPFI) SMASH and

SMASH Prep, the Institute for Economic, Educational, and Environmental Design (I-SEEED), SFSU, and UC Berkeley's Mapping to Mobilize Program, and Robert Moses' Algebra Project aim to increase the number of Black students entering into STEM fields and disciplines by using culturally and community responsive STEM pedagogy. Such approaches include: Project-based learning, racially and gender diverse mentors and role models, inquiry-based learning tools which are centered upon principles of social justice, and projects examining issues of relevance to communities of color. By employing these practices, these programs aim to alleviate the burdens of the conformity/oppositional resistance binary; and instead promote proactive resistance with implications for both individual and community transformation.

The following quotation provides a practical demonstration of the ways in which organizations employ SRA and consciously build structures with the intent of resisting racial domination to promote outcomes of Black youth:

> We saw a need, a critical need. Given the projections in STEM Fields and the global effect on the economy, we saw a critical need to build pathways and pipelines into STEM-careers for Black-working class youth. The future of Black communities and the whole future of this country was in jeopardy if we didn't do something to change STEM educational outcomes from a structural perspective; and change how Black youth felt about themselves from a cultural perspective. That's why we created the Summer Science program. Our program combines early education STEM skills, with cultural affirmation, and culturally committed mentors and role models. We put together a program that would help our students recover from racism, sexism, and any other "ism" you can think of.

The values of social justice, environmental justice, experiential knowledge, and building local economies has motivated the students and adults in these interviews to operationalize SRA in their local schools and communities, and within a STEM framework. What this data makes clear is that in order for working-class kids to get world-class STEM careers the following recommendations need to happen: (1) increase culturally and community responsive training and professional development opportunities for educators and employers within STEM disciplines; (2) expand programs that develop early interest and counteract psychological barriers to STEM among Black working-class youth and other youth of color; (3) increase access to rigorous courses and level the playing field in terms of who has access to the exposure, extracurricular, and coursework opportunities needed to succeed; (4) expand STEM acceleration and pre-college bridge programs; (5) expand higher education programs that recruit and retain scholars of color in STEM fields and ensure persistence to the completion of STEM degrees; (6) build sustainable environments through the development of strong local economies grounded in community, equity, and social justice.

Conclusion

In sum, SRA frameworks are useful when theorizing about the role of youth agency and structures in educational, employment, and environmental domination or emancipation and empowerment. We are aware that our theory can operate in contradictory ways and that the dominant system is one of such complete ideological and material hegemony that some will attempt to use forms of SRA to be repackaged and transformed into components of the status quo. In response to hegemonic domination, forms of SRA must continually create "safe sanctuaries," "free spaces," and "Youthtopias," in which freed from the limits and constraints of the dominant culture, young people (with or without adults) can experiment with new ways of seeing, being, and developing tools and resources for resistance.

Overall a SRA framework is different from other resistance frameworks in that it (1) challenges discourses on race, power, and the *environment* across race, class, gender, language, sexuality, and immigration status—most school resistance theories are silent when it comes to recognizing forms of eco-apartheid and other environmental impact on educational achievement (Akom, 2011); (2) focuses on the intersectionality of educational, employment, and environmental structures while offering a liberatory response to racial, gender, sexuality, environmental, and class oppression; (3) utilizes a transdisciplinary framework based in critical education, ethnic studies, science, technology, engineering, math, environmental studies, sociology, history, law, and public policy—to better understand the social and material conditions impacting Black working-class youth in STEM fields and how to transform these conditions.

The theory and data presented in this chapter open new possibilities for researchers hoping for more nuanced and complex understandings of resistance, particularly for those researchers looking for ways to examine how both structure and agency can play a role in eliminating racial domination and other forms of social oppression. Structural Resistance and Agency (SRA) offers insight into how societal and individual resistance give shape to one another. SRA extends the resistance literature by departing from an examination of self-defeating resistance in which students implicate themselves in their own domination. SRA acknowledges different types of resistance all of which are fluid and multi-faceted, yet distinguishes itself by adding critical structural and individual dimensions that were previously missing or under-theorized in resistance literature. In order to illustrate SRA in action we have grounded our work in empirical data that emerged from students and adults. Our goal was not to romanticize or give heroic best practices but to rethink and retheorize youth resistance theory for Black working-class youth in the context of high availability of jobs in STEM-related fields.

Early resistance theorists were concerned with how working-class kids can get working class jobs. They argued that oppositional behavior constituted a rejection of middle-class culture motivated by an implicit understanding of the myth of meritocracy. We have shown that a more contemporary and transformative question is: How do working-class kids get world-class careers, while maintaining their racial/ethnic and social identities, healing from physical and emotional trauma, exercising self-efficacy and self-determination, and remaining connected to their community cultural wealth (Yosso, 2002). We hope that through the lens of the SRA framework, our recommendations, and student voices that researchers and educators can deepen the possibilities for resistance that lead to both individual and structural transformation.

Works Referenced

Akom, A.A. (2003). Reexamining resistance as oppositional behavior: The Nation of Islam and the creation of a Black achievement ideology. *Sociology of Education, 76,* 305–325.

Akom, A.A. (2008). Ameritocracy and infra-racial racism: Racializing social and cultural reproduction theory in the 21st century. *Race and Ethnicity in Education, 11*, 205–230.

Akom, A.A. (2009). Critical race theory meets participatory action research: Creating a community of youth as public intellectuals. In W. Ayers, T. Quinn, & D. Stovall (Eds.). *Social Justice in Education Handbook*, pp. 508–521. New York: Erlbaum Press.

Akom, A.A. (2011). Eco-Apartheid: Linking environmental health to educational outcomes. *Teachers' College Record, 113,* 4.

Collins, P.H. (1999). Moving beyond gender: Intersectionality and scientific knowledge. In J. Lorber, B.B. Hess, & M.M. Ferree (Eds.). *Revisioning Gender*, pp. 261–284. Walnut Creek, CA: AltaMira Press.

Corburn, J. (2002). Environmental justice, local knowledge and risk: The discourse of a community-based cumulative exposure assessment. *Environmental Management, 29,* 4, 451–466.

Crenshaw, K. (1991). Mapping the margins: Intersectionality, identity politics, and violence against women of color. *Stanford Law Review, 43,* 6, 1241–1299

Dance, J.L. (2002). *Tough fronts: The impact of street culture on schooling,* New York: Routledge-Falmer.

Duncombe, S. (2002). *Cultural resistance reader.* New York: Verso.

Fordham, S. (1996). *Blacked out: Dilemmas of race, identity, and success at Capital High.* Chicago: University of Chicago Press.

Fordham, S., & Ogbu, J.U. (1986). Black students' school success: Coping with the "burden of acting white". *The Urban Review, 18,* 3, 176–206.

Ginwright, S. (2011). Hope, healing, and care: Pushing the boundaries of civic engagement for African American youth. *Liberal Education, 97,* 2.

Ginwright, S., Noguera, P., & Cammarota, J. (2006). *Beyond resistance! Youth activism and community change: New democratic possibilities for practice and policy for America's youth.* New York: Taylor & Francis Group.

Grande, S. (2004). *Red pedagogy: Native American social and political thought.* Lanham, MD: Rowman & Littlefield.

Hoachlander, G., & Yanofsky, D. (2011). Making STEM real. *Educational leadership, 68,* 6.

Kelley, R.D.G. (1994). *Race rebels: Culture, politics, and the Black working class.* New York: The Free Press.

MacLeod, J. (1987). *Ain't no makin' it: Aspirations and attainment in a low-income neighborhoods.* Boulder, CO: Westview Press.

Majors, R., & Billson, J.M. (1992). *Cool pose: The dilemmas of Black manhood in America.* New York: Lexington.

Massey, D., & Denton, N. (1993). *American Apartheid: Segregation and the making of the underclass.* Cambridge, MA: Harvard University Press.

McLaren, P. (1993). Multiculturalism and the postmodern critique: Towards a pedagogy of resistance and transformation. *Cultural Studies, 7.*

Minkler, M., & Wallerstein, N. (2011). *Community-based participatory research for health: From process to outcomes.* San Francisco: Jossey-Bass.

Ogbu, J.U. (1978). *Minority education and caste: The American system in cross-cultural perspective.* San Diego, CA: Academic Press.

Ogbu, J.U., & Simons, H.D. (1998). Voluntary and involuntary minorities: A cultural-ecological theory of school performance with some implications for education. *Anthropology and Education Quarterly, 29,* 2, 155–188.

Powell, J.A. (2008). Structural racism: Building upon the insights of John Calmore. *Berkeley Law Scholarship Repository,* Rev. 791.

Scott, J. (1990). *Domination and the arts of resistance: Hidden transcripts.* New Haven: Yale University Press.

Scott, A. (2012). *Dissecting the Data.* San Francisco: The Level Playing Field Institute.

Solórzano, D.G., & Bernal, D.D. (2001). Examining transformational resistance through a critical race and Latcrit theory framework: Chicana and Chicano students in an urban context. *Urban Education, 36,* 3, 308–342.

Torre, M., & Fine, M. (2006). Researching and resisting: Democratic policy research by and for youth. In S. Ginwright, P. Noguera, & J. Cammarota (Eds.). *Beyond resistance: Youth activism and community change: New democratic possibilities for practice and policy for American youth,* pp. 81–92. New York: Routledge.

Twine, F.W., & Steinbugler, A.C. (2006). The gap between whites and whiteness: Interracial intimacy and racial literacy. *Du Bois Review, 3,* 341–363.

Willis, P.E. (1977). *Learning to labor: How working class kids get working class jobs.* New York: Columbia University Press.

Yosso, T.J. (2005). Whose culture has capital? A critical race theory discussion of community cultural wealth. *Race Ethnicity and Education, 8,* 1, 69–91.

Yosso, T.J., & Solórzano, D.G. (2002). Critical race methodology: Counter-storytelling as an analytical framework for education research. *Qualitative Inquiry, 8,* 23–44.

12

HANDS CLASPED BEHIND HER BACK

Palestinian Waiting on Theories of Change

J.I. Albahri with K. Wayne Yang

> He is a simple yet tough child, and this is why people adopted him and felt
> that he represents their consciousness.
>
> > Palestinian cartoonist Naji al-Ali, on the
> > character "Handala" (Handala.org, n.d.)

There are snapshots often in the form of images of young brown boys, fists
clenched around the rubble of demolished homes, bodies too small to withstand
the crush of an army jeep or tank bearing down upon them; or YouTube vid-
eos of young women marching in protests, black and white *kūfiyyāt* concealing
grim, half-faces that might meet the next rubber bullet or teargas canister fired
at them; these coalesce to narrate a particular type of Palestinian youth existence
that is inextricably linked to resistance. *Those* resistance narratives are deployed
in a political climate in which Palestinian existence and humanity can be openly
debated and negotiated by any citizen of the West. And yet *our* resistance stories
as Palestinian youth testify a hope, a patience, a yearning for life and land that
refuses to be extinguished or disappeared.

However, we must ask critical questions about these tropes or categories of
Palestinian youth resistance and the theories of change that are applied to them.
In this chapter, I will analyze the Western gaze on Palestinian youth resistance,
and theorize aspects of Palestinian youth resistance that pose a challenge to or
refuse this gaze. I will contrast the theories of change between what the Western
gaze expects of Palestinian resistance, and what Palestinian resistance wants and
rather doesn't want—why she has her hands clasped behind her back.

This chapter is a meditation on portrayals and practices of Palestinian youth
resistance and the theories of change imposed on, implied by, and imagined
through them. I narrate some of my own resistance stories from the perspective

of a diasporic Palestinian youth and scholar-activist, as a way of undrawing the Western portrait of Palestinian resistance and redrawing the attention of the Western gaze to colonialism. *Our* narratives of resistance refuse the change that the West believes we "need," and further, present alternative theories of change that are grounded in desires for decolonization, repatriation, and unsettlement. I surround these stories with discussions of Palestinian youth resistance within Palestinian histories of settler colonialism and dispossession, and the current settler colonial realities that radiate from these histories.

This chapter is in conversation with other recent discussions of settler colonialism, especially Eve Tuck and C. Ree's recent "Glossary of haunting" (2013). There they invoke the notion of haunting to understand the routes for justice for those destroyed, made ghosts, made monsters in the violence of settler colonialism:

> Settler colonialism is the management of those who have been made killable, once and future ghosts—those that had been destroyed, but also those that are generated in every generation. (p. 642)

In this sense, Palestinian youth killed in invasions, those not (yet) killed, those passing through workcamps in the Gulf, those held in ghettos in the Occupied Territories and neighboring Arab states, those Palestinians dislocated in Israel (on Palestinian land), and those in the diaspora who have been erased as "no longer Palestinian," are ghosts. In short, all Palestinians are ghosts. This chapter is concerned with what the ghosts desire, what *our* resistance stories say about Western theories of change, Palestinian strategies to make change possible within Western frameworks, and the gap between strategy and the change we desire.

Renderings of Palestine

In contemporary Palestine, settler colonialism does not function with the sophisticated invisibility that it has achieved in North America. For us Palestinians, it is explicit rhetorically, and undisguised legally, militarily, and economically. One of the clearest manifestations of settler colonialism is Israel's investment in settlement building, in which Jews are incentivized to settle on Palestinian land in both what is commonly referred to as the "Palestinian territories" (Gaza and the West Bank) as well as the areas claimed by the state in 1948. The state's appropriation and redistribution of indigenous Palestinian land it categorizes as "abandoned" or "undeveloped" is a bureaucratized form of ongoing invasion. The ethnic scour(g) ing of indigenous Palestinian Arabs, and the incessant construction of elaborate walls as militarized, moving borders, aims to extinguish or make Palestinian life impossible while expanding settler comfort, privilege, and hegemony.

The dispossession of Palestinians from our homeland is a historical process with firm roots in nineteenth-century European settler colonial discourse saturated by

Zionist aspirations. These settler colonial designs were brought to fruition by a massive ethnic cleansing in 1947–48 executed by Zionist Jewish paramilitary forces that expelled roughly 750,000 Palestinians and destroyed hundreds of villages in historic Palestine. Many Palestinians sought what we believed was temporary refuge in neighboring Arab states such as Egypt, Lebanon, Jordan, Iraq, and Syria. Others of us experienced internal displacement, forced into refugee camps in Gaza and the West Bank. Despite the efforts of Zionist militias, some of us survived and remained in the lands claimed by Israel in 1948. We and our descendants comprise roughly 20 percent of the current Israeli population. Our experiences of dispossession, known in the lexicon of Palestinian collective memory as the *Nakba* (Catastrophe) and the following *Naksa* (Setback), represent not only the violence of expulsions in 1948 and 1967, but the trauma of a loss and the pain of an exile that has yet to find an endpoint. The *Nakba* is not over (Sa'di & Abu-Lughod, 2007).

Like many diasporic Palestinian and Muslim youth in my community, I turned to progressive organizing in my undergraduate years as a way of effecting positive change centered on principles of social justice. I became a board member of Students for Justice in Palestine (SJP) at UC San Diego in 2012, joining some of my closest friends and co-organizers in working for divestment. The SJP board had presented resolutions to the undergraduate-elected student government (the Associated Students) calling on UC San Diego to divest[1] from corporations that profited from the occupation and blockade of Palestine in 2010, 2011, and 2012, and was finally successful in 2013. In recent years, there has been a swell of student groups pushing for a similar divestment of university pensions, endowment funds, and tuition dollars from U.S. corporations that profit from Israel's occupation of Palestine. Divestment is an international effort spurred by the 2005 Palestinian Civil Society[2] call for Boycott, Divestment, and Sanctions (BDS Campaign) to pressure Israel into compliance with international law around three specific demands:

1.   Ending [Israel's] occupation and colonization of all Arab lands and dismantling the Wall;
2.   Recognizing the fundamental rights of the Arab-Palestinian citizens of Israel to full equality; and
3.   Respecting, protecting and promoting the rights of Palestinian refugees to return to their homes and properties as stipulated in UN resolution 194. (BDS, 2005)

These three demands are specifically tailored to stop the particular strategies of settler colonialism used by Israel to suppress Palestinian sovereignty and life.

Material realities for Palestinian youth within Palestine and the diaspora are often bleak. A subordinate Palestinian economy, labor rich and capital poor, is tightly maintained through spatial, economic, criminal, and military policies by Israel, effectively entrapping Palestinians into a cycle of aid dependency and poverty. Foreign aid ensures that the national Palestinian government, the Palestinian Authority, will act in ways favorable to Israel, via the West. (The non-governmental organizations fueled by foreign aid are particularly relevant in the upcoming discussion.) Vestiges of these colonial policies often follow Palestinian bodies in exile. Following expulsion, Palestinian populations were shunted into ghettoes known as *mukhayyamat* (camps)—formerly spaces allotted for temporary shacks and tents—these markers of transient Palestinian life have crystallized into solid concrete structures, and dot the landscape in Arab countries, the West Bank, and Gaza. The *mukkhayam*, conceptualized as exile's waiting room, often operating in contexts in which Palestinians are legally and economically excluded, embodies a similar cycle of dependency and poverty for Palestinian refugee youth. Escape from this cycle often takes the form of undocumented and/or migrant labor in the Levant and the Gulf for many (male) Palestinian youth whose mobility is severely restricted because of their statelessness, embodied in Palestinian nationality (the *Hawiyeh*). This spatialization of "youth" and its temporalization as permanently transient life, is particularly relevant to the upcoming discussion on Palestinian illegibility and distemporality.

The three demands of the 2005 Palestinian Civil Society Call for Boycott, Divestment, and Sanctions represent a plan for change that is designed to intervene on the specific settler colonial practices of Israel. For the call for divestment to work, Western audiences who know little about the occupation must be convinced to think differently about Israel, and think differently or maybe think at all about Palestine. For this reason, mapping the logics for divestment in 2010–12, and understanding what was rendered (in)visible in the final version of the 2013 bill is incredibly important.

Versions of the bill presented to UCSD council in 2010, 2011, and 2012 argued for divestment within legible frames of neo-Orientalist discourse. By this, I am describing how Palestine is rendered visible in the Western gaze as a symbol of the suffering of the world, begging for western intervention. Edward Said opens his foundational text, *Orientalism*, with a quote by Benjamin Disraeli, "The East is a career." Neo-Orientalism seems an apt description for Western activist discourse, in that it constitutes a broader "business" of Palestine from mainstream Middle East newscasters to reality tourists to international NGOs. "The sheer amount of foreign activists who come into the country," enter through the NGO economy, according to Ruba, a Palestinian youth NGO worker (p.c., May 16, 2013):

> In a lot of cases, they aren't even activists at all. Just foreigners who choose to come into the UN/NGO system here and get paid a lot to do it. In a sense the entire Palestinian cause is being turned into a business.

In the earlier versions of the bill, divestment was posed as an affirmation of UCSD neutrality. International law, and Israel's systematic violation of these laws, provided the moral case for a divestment backed by facts collected by U.N. commissions and Western human rights NGOs such as Human Rights Watch and Amnesty International. In this narrative, "Palestinians" are victims in need of rescue by a benevolent, neutral, and peace-seeking West. In order for this framing of the issue to compel divestment, the child-like, resisting Palestinian (the image favored by the Western activist) and the monstrous/Muslim Palestinian terrorist (the image favored by Zionists) must compete over their humanity on the council floor. Thus possibilities for destabilizing or unsettling settler colonial realities in divestment are disappeared discursively.

In 2010, the bill was tabled and sent to a committee of pro-Palestinian activists, Zionists, and council members in a compromise initiative engineered by "progressive" council members. In 2011, the resolution did not even reach the council floor after a last-minute forced "collaboration" between members of SJP and Zionist students fell through. In 2012, the resolution was voted down 13–20–0, after eight hours of public input and council deliberation.

We adopted a different approach in the 2013 bill, which caused greater commotion—if that was even possible—on the campus. In this version we asserted Palestinian indigeneity and directly confronted U.S. settler colonial amnesias by analogizing Israel's occupation of Palestinian land to the United States' occupation of Indigenous land, specifically the position of our university as an occupier on sacred Kumeyaay burial grounds. We were explicit in our naming of colonial occupation as the context for human rights; that is, human rights that began with indigenous peoples' rights in and to indigenous lands.[3]

The council passed a heavily amended version of the 2013 bill. Struck from the "Resolution in Support of University of California San Diego Corporate Accountability through Divestment from Corporations Profiting from the Illegal Occupation, Siege, and Blockade of Palestine" were the following lines:

> WHEREAS, UC San Diego is built upon indigenous Kumeyaay land just as Israel is built upon indigenous Palestinian land; and,

> BE IT FURTHER RESOLVED, that the ASUCSD supports the indigenous Palestinian people in their struggle against a colonial occupier.

These two clauses were struck from the final resolution because they were perceived as undermining the "neutrality" of the council and the university. The UCSD council was able to acquiesce to divestment, but not (yet) to the decolonization of Palestine; although the divestment movement thus far has made strides in facilitating the beginnings of these conversations. The BDS Campaign actually differs from "solutions-based" efforts in that it forefronts Palestinian self-determination, rather than state-negotiated compromises, but nonetheless offers mechanisms (boycott, divestment, and sanctions) to engage the state(s).

The immediate politics of this divestment at UCSD 2013 were the collusion of multiple theories of change—socially responsible capitalism as a motor of change, statist theories of compromise, and sympathies that motivate charity as change. Divestment, as is rendered legible by the Western gaze, can be seen as separate from Indigeneity—from rights of return, repatriation, and self-determination. Decolonization requires a long-term theory of change, that understands the short-term goal of divestment as a way of inviting people to participate in the protracted struggle through their university dollars, but also understands that divestment is an opportunity to encode the larger goals of decolonization/indigenous sovereignties beyond state-centered politics in ways that may or may not be legible to settlers or non-natives. These clauses were included in the divestment resolution because they represented the desire of a ghost (the dispossessed Palestinian), and for that same reason they were stricken.

Renderings of Palestinian Youth Resistance

Youth comprise roughly one-third of the Palestinian population, and thus threaten the settler state with their sheer numbers—a veritable legion of dispossession. Their presence means that new generations, their children and their children's children, will only continue to expand on land that is supposed to be emptied of Palestinians. Occupation produces youth resistance; whether youth are cognizant of their resistance or not, they are interpellated as a breeding generation of disenfranchised, disillusioned, disturbed—indeed resistant—monsters in Zionist discourse.

Although these are the more obvious forms of colonialism that produce Palestinian resistance, I would like to draw attention to a "counter-gaze" through which left-leaning Westerners project their desires for resistance upon the Palestinian youth body. The activist gaze fetishizes the Palestinian cause—celebrating resistance, but condemning resistances that are not strictly secular and/or do not subscribe to Western political discourses of "morality" and "human rights." The activist gaze prefers palatable images that victimize the subject, for example: the iconic 2000 Associated Press photograph of Faris Odeh, a young Gazan who was killed by the Israeli army during the Second Intifada. In it, Odeh is frozen in time, forever throwing a rock at an Israeli tank bearing down upon him. In the Western imagination, such child-like resistance is as inspiring as it is ineffective, generating a whole lexicon of bare-fisted resistance, including "Palestinian rock children" in the *Washington Report* and in the *New York Times*, "sneakers and slingshots."

Not long ago, I had a conversation with my father, who was born in a refugee camp in northern Lebanon, about the 2000 photograph of Faris Odeh.

Yaba. Tizakar as9oora ma3al walad kan birmi i7jar 3ala adababa al-israeliya? Kan bilbis 2amee9 banafsaji?

Ah

Fakarati shu 7asal ma3u?

3asha[4]

In the conversation, neither my father nor myself know his name and we provide only a cursory, and deceptively simple description—the boy in the purple sweater—in fact, his sweater is not purple, only the edges of the sleeves are.

Under the activist gaze, Faris Odeh is frozen in time, ethereal relative to the mass of the tank. Often compared to the Tiananmen Square protester, "The Everyman," this literal poster boy of resistance is framed in a valiant portrait of (secular and) desperate defiance. Outside of that frame lies a radical elsewhere, where other resistances are not only possible but happening in ways that may not be legible to the Western activist gaze. The state of Israel is not only terrified of the image, but all of the radical possibilities that lie outside of its frame.

But in the (Western) activist imagination, Palestinian existence is strictly political—thus "youth" cannot exist outside of its framing gaze, and Palestinian personhood cannot exist at all. It excludes an existence for Faris Odeh in which he is a beloved son, brother, nephew, or cousin or maybe when he is grown, a loving husband or father. The "authentic" Palestinian youth is the voiceless subaltern—whose hands are not behind her back, but are outstretched and forward seeking alms or throwing a stone at a tank—a trope that excludes and erases Palestinian (youth) bodies in the Diaspora, such as my own, or Palestinian youth bodies that embody alternative resistances. When anyone who believes in the Palestinian cause can assume Palestinian-by-ideology, and can thus speak for the changes they believe are needed by the Palestinian (irrespective of Palestinian opinion on the matter), Palestinian youth resistance undertakes meanings that undermine these very categories of needed change in the form of unsettlement and return. They limit ways of thinking about change in relation to indigeneity and decolonization.

Refusing the Gaze

My grandfather was 16 years old when he and his family were expelled from their home in Haifa in April 1948. Unable to find work in Lebanon, where he and his family were "settled" in the refugee camps, he emigrated to Qatar during the oil boom to work as a wage laborer. As a child, I would often ask him to tell me stories from his youth. One of his favorite stories, and one of my few memories of him is his animated narration of the following:

Once ya jiddo, when I was a young man in Qatar I was working for the Shell company laying the asphalt, bta3rafiha, the black tar on the road we lived in a camp, and worked all day in the heat like maybe 120 degrees anyway one day we noticed that rats were eating our food we tried everything traps, poison, everything but one night your jiddo stayed up, and watched the fence where the rats would come in to the camp. Shufthum sliding down a wooden stick on the side so you know what your jiddo did I put razor blades all down the stick the next night as the rats slid down the plank the razors—schhhhhhkkk!—cut their bellies open they didn't even notice and all their guts fell out when they reached the bottom dead. Hahahahahaha. What you don't like the story? Hahahaha.

He told me this story from his youth in English, with a few smatterings of Arabic here and there. His story is seemingly apolitical, making but a passing reference to the *Nakba* and his experience of (continued) violent displacement. He does not re-live the torment of exodus, but focuses on a rather banal if not morbid vignette. Yet, it narrates a Palestinian youth existence that occurs outside of the political realm, a possible radical elsewhere. Politics makes the Palestinian legible, and a refusal of the political is a blinding mechanism to the gaze.

When asked about the boy in his comics, Palestinian cartoonist Naji al-Ali writes,

His name is Handala and he has promised the people that he will remain true to himself. I drew him as a child who is not beautiful; his hair is like the hair of a hedgehog who uses his thorns as a weapon. Handala is not a fat, happy, relaxed, or pampered child. He is barefooted like the refugee camp children, and he is an icon that protects me from making mistakes. Even though he is rough, he smells of amber. His hands are clasped behind his back as a sign of rejection at a time when solutions are presented to us the American way.[5] Handala was born ten years old, and he will always be ten years old. At that age, I left my homeland, and when he returns, Handala will still be ten, and then he will start growing up. The laws of nature do not apply to him. He is unique. Things will become normal again when the homeland returns. (al-Ali, quoted in Handala.org, n.d.)

From a diasporic Palestinian perspective, a lot of change has been imposed (*Nakba* and *Naksa*) and denied (the return). The opportunities for social and cultural reproduction or continuity, too often viewed as the opposites of change, are taken for granted in the West. Survival in exile, or the goal of not being too changed, is intimately linked to questions of how to reproduce one's community, one's memories, and one's hope. The change that preoccupies the West is an advancement of Western democratic faith in Arab countries—the "Arab Spring"—which Palestine is part of and yet separated[6] from. This is because these theories of change, originating from a Western context in which indigeneity is rendered invisible, are antithetical to Palestinian desires for sovereignty, return, unsettlement, repatriation, for a future that unfreezes the present and restores its connections with the past.

The stories I write here, of the divestment bill at UCSD, of Faris Odeh's reasons for throwing rocks at tanks and soldiers, of rats at a desert camp, of Handala's clasped hands, are subsistence for a ghostlife that lives off of memories. They refuse to disappear. They insist on Palestinian life and land. These stories belong together because they already exist in the same distemporality—a Palestinian time that takes place both at some time in the past and now. This distemporality is the radical elsewhere that lies outside of the Western frame of Palestinian boys slinging rocks, and Arabs moving too slowly towards Democracy. But it is a distemporality where we don't wish to wait forever.

Caught between terror and resistance as bodily realities, caught between terror(ist) and resistance as political identities, "Palestinian youth" has already overdetermined meanings not of our own making. Arab Spring is good resistance, Arab-fall is bad resistance. There is nothing outside of resistance.

The life that lives between resistance and terror, on that cracked line where the frontiers of masterstory and counterstory meet, is where my youth story meets her grandfather's youth story. This meeting produces a kaleidoscope of Palestinian youth hauntings. My grandfather tells the story from the perspective of a young man, at my beckoning as a young woman. A story takes place at some time in both the past and the present. Neither of our ghosts are fully present, but exist at, as Audre Lorde says: "the sharpened edge/where day and night shall meet/and not be/one" (1977, p. 35).

Notes

1 Divestment is the disinvesting of assets for political or ethical reasons. The most commonly referenced ethical divestment effort spearheaded by students was the movement to end Apartheid in South Africa that gained momentum during the 1980s (see Noguera, this volume).
2 "the three integral parts of the people of Palestine: Palestinian refugees, Palestinians under occupation and Palestinian citizens of Israel" (BDS, 2005).
3 UC Santa Barbara SJP incorporated a derivative clause in their resolution, pointing out that their university was on Chumash land. Their 2013 resolution failed.
4 I wrote this narrative in colloquial Palestinian Arabic using Latin characters. This orthography is accessible for many Arab youth in the Diaspora who do not feel confident in using, do not have access to, or are simply unable to read Arabic characters. But it is illegible to most people. I have refused to translate it. The reader, unless they are familiar with the strange combination of letters and numbers and vocabulary of colloquial Palestinian Arabic, should be aware that they have been excluded from this conversation and of whatever secret meaning it may have. This unknowability, however, does not alter the story in any way.

5 People are literally trying to put things in Handala's hands, including Israeli flags, rocks, scales of justice, etc. He is holding his own hands. He won't let his hands turn into some other form of resistance.

6 During the Arab Spring, there were Western anxieties that these movements would spread to Palestine. The importance for the West to separate Palestine from Egypt (or Tunisia, or Libya) is that Palestinian claims are about Indigeneity and not only a national struggle against an oppressive regime.

Works Referenced

BDS. (2005, July 9). Palestinian civil society call for BDS. Retrieved May 24, 2013 from http://www.bdsmovement.net/call

Handala.org. (n.d.). Who is Handala? Retrieved May 24, 2013 from www.handala.org/handala/index.html

Hanley, D.C. (2001). Israel's spin-doctors wage war of images and words against Palestinian rock children. *Washington Report on Middle East Affairs, 20,* 1.

Lorde, A. (1977). From the house of Yemanjá. *The American Poetry Review, 6,* 6, 35.

Sa'di, A.H., & Abu-Lughod, L. (Eds.). (2007). *Nakba: Palestine, 1948, and the claims of memory.* New York: Columbia University Press.

Said, E.W. (1978). *Orientalism.* New York: Pantheon Books.

Sontag, D. (2001, February 21). Ramallah journal; bitter, stark souvenirs: Sneakers and slingshots. *New York Times.* A4.

Tuck, E., & Ree, C. (2013). A glossary of hauntings. In S. Holman Jones, T. Adams, & C. Ellis (Eds.). *Handbook of autoethnography,* pp. 639–658. Walnut Creek, CA: Left Coast Press, Inc.

PART III

New Studies in Youth Resistance

Introduction to Part III

Eve Tuck and K. Wayne Yang

This section features new studies in youth resistance—that is, methodologically and epistemologically new approaches to learning from and with youth about resistance and about theories of change. In designating works by authors in this section as new, we do not conscribe those works by authors in Part I as old—indeed, as this volume makes clear, those prior works are timeless in a way that makes each reading new in new times. Thus, in marking works in this section as new, we are referring to a turn away from the trend toward calcification in youth resistance research that Greg Dimitriadis so aptly describes in Chapter 2 of this volume, and the rigidity of expectations for youth resistance that has typified the field in more recent years.

In choosing the contributions for this section, we encouraged chapters that represent different "conceptual breaks" (using Robin Kelley's term from Chapter 6 of this volume) which extend methodologies and epistemologies of resistance, namely: (1) the unique ethical considerations of researching youth resistance; (2) the question of Indigenous resistance, particularly the role of urban Native youth as a continuum in Indigenous resistance to settler expansion, appropriation, and violent erasures of Indigenous people/epistemologies/land; (3) the particularities of queer of color resistance in the tight intersections of race, citizenship, family, poverty, and homelessness; (4) the biopolitics of youth resistance to schools that increasingly criminalize, disable, and negatively impact student health; and (5) the social movement of undocumented students (and their dual-status communities) that include the DREAMers, in considering the work of resistance at the day-to-day level of resisting illegality of one's very presence, and at the larger scales of the U.S. nation-state.

As discussed in the introduction to this book, "youth," is a diaphanous category, both contingent and reductive. There isn't a good reason to consider youth resistance as altogether that distinct from adult resistance; it goes without saying that people who are under age 18 (the legal age ascribed to adulthood in the Unites States, although some rights are withheld until age 21) are whole thinking, feeling, and being people. There is nothing less complete about being a young person in comparison to someone who is in adulthood. However, one unifying experience of young people in many parts of the world, and in North America, where most of the chapters are placed, is that young people are required by law to attend school. Thus, the category of youth is salient insofar as it corresponds to compulsory schooling.

The studies in this section rely upon a range of methods and methodologies, including critical ethnography, participant observation, participatory action research, and narrative analysis. However, as exemplars of new studies in youth resistance research, the chapters do not only revisit resistance, but also make methodological and conceptual strides to deepen the larger empirical repertoire of the field.

The first chapter in the section, *Youth Resistance Research Methods and Ethical Challenges* (Chapter 13), by Monique Guishard and Eve Tuck provides an analysis of the methods that have been employed to document and understand youth resistance over the past 35 years, and points to new and emerging methodologies for learning from/with youth resistance to educational injustices. The authors highlight some of the methodological and ethical challenges of youth resistance research, and discuss the significance of stances of refusal for both research participants and researchers. This chapter is especially tailored for readers who are embarking on their own studies of youth resistance, and consolidates lessons learned from prior studies.

Tracy Friedel's *Outdoor Education as a Site of Epistemological Persistence: Unsettling an Understanding of Urban Indigenous Youth Resistance* (Chapter 14) analyzes the efficacy of an outdoor education program organized by white settlers for Native youth living on the urban prairie, and details the ways in which those youth resisted the curriculum, but more the framings offered by the program. Though many observe (bemoan?) the increased urbanization of the globe, they ignore the *a priori* relationships that Indigenous people have with land stolen to comprise the settler colonial nation-state. Just as frequently ignored are the experiences of urban Native youth who live on the traditional homelands of their people; if they are on the register at all, it is as being deprived of their own land and culture, which programs such as the one described in the chapter try to help fix. Friedel's theorization (and the youth participants in the study) refuses the narrative of urban Native youth needing fixing, and the narrative of the white settler as in any position to offer help.

In *LGBTQ Street Youth Doing Resistance in Infrapolitical Worlds* (Chapter 15), Cindy Cruz describes the ways in which queer street youth who live at the intersection of dislocation from "home" and ethnic communities, homelessness, poverty, and in many cases non-citizenship, must resist in ways that challenge both dominant and minoritarian discourses about community. The chapter defines motility as small acts of resistance which allow education researchers to recognize how LGBTQ youth talk back using bodily gestures and maneuvers. Learning from such "resistance in tight spaces," Cruz also reimagines the role of researchers away from investments in problematizing pathologizing—the tropes of contamination and irresponsibility that are often inscribed onto queer street youth bodies—toward a way of listening differently to narratives that refuse pathology. Thus Cruz gains insights into not just the risks, but also the reasons for such narratives.

In *Out for Immigration Justice: Thinking through Social and Political Change* (Chapter 16), Daysi Diaz-Strong, Christina Gómez, Maria Luna-Duarte, and Erica Meiners write about "coming out" as a practice of resistance among the 1.8 million undocumented youth that currently reside in the United States. Building from activist fieldwork, including the collection of forty interviews with undocumented and formerly undocumented youth in the Chicago area, this chapter examines the role of society in portraying undocumented youth as "a problem people," people whose very existence in the U.S. is considered a violation of immigration and nationality law. The students who participated in the research described in this chapter are enrolled in colleges and universities, apply for scholarships that they have access to, organize in supporting their communities, and work towards providing a future for themselves and their families. Although they have not yet been incarcerated because of their status, youth research participants have no access to vote and are denied access to most avenues of post-secondary education, social assistance benefits, legal employment, and many fear public spaces. Yet, in interviews with undocumented youth and formerly undocumented youth, in their desires for access to higher education and for citizenship, they identify themselves in opposition to the figure of criminality, resisting the image that society is placing upon them. This chapter explores how the youth resist these labels and reinvent their image to challenge their hostile environment that places obstacles in their everyday lives.

This sampling of new studies of youth resistance engages many of the themes, concerns, and hopes of the foundational thinkers in youth resistance research in Part I of this volume. The chapters also resonate meaningfully with chapters in Part II of this volume, on the relationships between youth resistance research and theories of change. Reading across the book, it is possible to see complementary and competing visions for economic change, for environmental justice, for political and education sovereignty, for freedom from violence and persecution, for home.

The chapters in this section detail particularities of youth resistance with attention to complexity and acute attention to youths' lived lives. They embody an active respect for young people not as future-adults, but as now-agents of change, as making the wisest possible decisions for themselves, as theorists on their lives and the world around them. Across the chapters, youth resistance is engaged as a set of dynamic and strategic engagements with and/or refusals of the state. The chapters respond to Michelle Fine's (Chapter 3, this volume) call for youth resistance research that is vigilant in terms of critique while also provoking radical re-imagination for educational justice. They are unafraid to offer "radical imaginaries for what might be" (Fine, this volume, p. 56).

13

YOUTH RESISTANCE RESEARCH METHODS AND ETHICAL CHALLENGES

Monique Guishard and Eve Tuck

What follows is a series of reflections on the pastimes, crossroads, crises, decisions, and resolutions that have comprised our experiences as youth resistance researchers over the past fifteen years. We try to pass along some of the lessons learned from our prior studies in youth resistance, and point to some of the important considerations of this complex work. We write as a brown feminist critical social psychologist and as an Alaska Native de-colonial education theorist; we write as friends, as colleagues, as collaborators. We offer you our insights to swap and share, neon lights that say look this way, earnest re-tellings of the experiences that have informed our work most radically. This chapter is crafted especially for readers who are embarking on their own studies of youth resistance, perhaps for the first time. The first section provides an overview of the methods that have been employed to document and understand youth resistance, with an emphasis on new and emerging methods. The remaining discussions are concerned with the methodological and ethical challenges of youth resistance research, with the hope to help to generate conversation with mentors, colleagues, students, research collectives, and in other spaces in which you make sense of your own work.

Methods for Researching Youth Resistance

Between 2006 and 2008, Eve worked with a group of out-of-school youth, the Collective of Researchers on Educational Disappointment and Desire (CREDD), to understand young people's use of the General Education Development tests, or GED® as a gateway to higher education and employment and also as a get-away from schools typified by injustice. In that work, Eve and her youth co-researchers likened research methods to a box of watercolors:

We try to use the best color to paint the picture we are trying to see, and use the colors in harmony, rather than muddying the image or weakening the paper by using too many colors at once. In this [study on the GED and school pushout], our primary colors are individual interviews and group interviews and focus groups. These are the foundations of our research, and our painting would be incomplete without them.

Our secondary colors have been surveys, opinion polls, cold calls, memoirs, archival research, and mapping. These colors can be blended with one another, but especially the primary colors to create light and shadow, depth and complexity in our work.

We have also mixed colors to create new colors, or new methods such as borrowing activities from Augusto Boal's Theater of the Oppressed, popular education's problem tree, and school yard games such as the slam book and board games. These hybrid colors come alive in participatory action research, are indeed some of the most radical and compelling examples of the possibilities of participatory action research.

A final extension to the metaphor, water, participation, is the stuff that moves the pigment from box to brush to page, that makes the stroke translucent or opaque. (Tuck et al., 2008a, p. 55)

Here, we dust off that watercolor paint box simile to organize some effective methods of studying youth resistance in order to point you to some other readings and other examples (in addition to the others in Part III of this volume) that can inform your design. Some of the methods are participatory, meaning youth help to create and implement the methods, analyze the data and communicate about the findings. Others are not necessarily participatory, but still engage youth as complex theorists of their own lives and worlds. Our hope is to encourage you to look more closely at the studies described below as resources for both thinking about method and what reflexive research design can look like in practice and in writing.

Some of the most widely used methods in youth resistance research include critical ethnography, individual interviews and focus groups, and surveys. We might consider these the primary colors of youth resistance research—methods that can be combined with one another and with other pigments effectively to create a lush depiction.

Critical Ethnography

As noted in the introduction to this book, Paul Willis' *Learning to Labor: How working class kids get working class jobs* (1977) was a lightning rod for the emergence of youth resistance research, critical ethnography, and lived post-structural analyses. Since publication of that foundational book, Willis has been an important advocate of critical ethnography, detailing the significance of what he calls the ethnographic imagination approach. This approach is one that acknowledges the "art" of everyday life, that understands that people make sense out of their lives in creative ways and that there are moments of penetrating insight worth exploring and documenting. (Dolby & Dimitriadis, 2004, p. 5)

Remarkable examples of critical ethnography on youth resistance published in the last few years include Kathleen Nolan's *Police in the Hallways: Discipline in an Urban High School* (2011), Sharam Khosravi's *Young and Defiant in Tehran* (2009), David Kirkland's *A Search Past Silence: The Literacy of Young Black Men* (2013), and work describing activist research with Indigenous youth by Teresa McCarty, Leisy Wyman, and Sheilah Nicholas (2013).

Innovations in Interviews

Innovations in interviews and focus groups in youth resistance research are varied, from participants generating questions for other participants, to digital formats; from art shares, to collaborative storytelling.

Surveys as Public Science

One inspiring new approach comes from Brett Stoudt's (Stoudt & Torre, in press) work as statistical consultant in two recent projects, Polling for Justice, and the Morris Justice Project (both affiliated with the Public Science Project[1] (PSP) at The Graduate Center of The City University of New York). In the latter, Stoudt, Maria Torre, and others worked with an intergenerational team of researchers from the Bronx, the PSP, and Pace University Law Center to survey more than 1,000 residents of the Morris Avenue section of the South Bronx. They used "the Illuminator," a van with a projector that was used in Occupy Wall Street demonstrations to project findings from the survey (think of the bat signal) to "discuss what it means to live, work, raise kids, shop, go to school, play, and pray in a community that experienced nearly 4,000 police stops in 2011" (http://www.publicscienceproject.org/research/projects/the-morris-justice-project/). The Public Science Project, of which Stoudt is a co-founder, has also provided "Stats for the People" workshops to support other participatory research collectives in collecting and interpreting their own quantitative data.

Recent studies have featured methods that attend to complexity and depth of youth resistance. We might think of these as secondary and tertiary colors, not because they are less valued or effective than primary methods, but because their role is to elicit narratives of complex personhood, counter-stories, and dialectical relationships between ideas/experiences. Broad categories of these methods include embodied methods, mapping, and methods derived from school yard games.

Embodied Methods

In Polling for Justice (PFJ) directors Madeline Fox, Brett Stoudt, and Michelle Fine (Fox & Fine, 2012) organized a Participatory Action Research (PAR) collective who designed and dispatched a survey on youth experiences of education, health, criminal justice, and policing in their schools. Fox and Fine (2012) made use of embodied methodologies to tell the stories of their survey results, which were intimately linked to young people's bodies, stories of complex personhood and hybrid consciousness. Youth researchers performed the data, and required that audiences respond to performances in order to incite recognition of the collective responsibility to address the study's findings.

Jessica Ruglis worked with a collective of youth researchers in Project DISH (Disparities in Schooling and Health) to examine, among other topics related to school dropout, the health consequences of *staying in* schools that prompted more to dropout than graduate. They developed an innovative method called "x-ray" maps in which youth used markers and paper to draw their bodies, and locate internal and external impacts of their school day on their bodies (Ruglis, 2011).

Mapping Methods

Patricia Krueger-Henney worked with a Youth Participatory Action Research (yPAR) collective to document criminalizing and punitive school safety measures in New York City public high schools. To do this, they created spatial-temporal maps of the school safety and security mechanisms, their daily trajectories through school spaces, their evaluations of the safety of different spaces inside the school, along with locations that are most trafficked and avoided. These "mini-geographies" of youths' cognitive maps of their schools comprised what Cindi Katz has called "counter-topographies," of the school to prison pipeline (Krueger, 2011).

Eve used a Freirian problem tree-based method as part of a study with the Youth Researchers for a New Education System (YRNES). In this method, youth mapped the symptoms (leaves), supporting attitudes (trunk), and ideological roots of a problem, "the current school system is not working." The resulting map was published and widely distributed as part of an e-report, and was used to develop the design for the study which focused on the lived experience for students attending schools under mayoral control (Tuck et al., 2008b). Tuck and her colleagues in CREDD also used the problem tree method as part of a focus group with youth GED earners and seekers about the problem of school pushout.

Remaking School Yard Games

Sarah Zeller-Berkman and others at the Public Science Project have created new versions of board games to play with youth in focus group settings to initiate discussions about social injustice. Zeller-Berkman and the Participatory Action Team (2007) used their Chutes and Ladders-like board game to present their findings on the everyday struggles and boundaries faced by children of incarcerated parents. CREDD used a board game (a remake of Pop-o-matic Trouble) to initiate focus group conversations about meritocracy, the American Dream, and poverty. In the game, players try to reach all the way around the board to their "American Dreams" without getting tripped up by health, housing, education, policing or social issues, or without getting squeezed out or gentrified by opponents. This game was followed by a facilitated discussion on the myths and realities of meritocracy and implications on schooling.

Finally, following the analogy drawn about a watercolor paintbox, we may think of participation as water, which helps to blend, texturize, saturate, and complete a work. As posed in Chapter 9 of this volume, "Thinking with Youth about Theories of Change," youth resistance research may be most compelling when it is designed to think *with* youth about injustice and resistance. The differences between thinking *with* youth, and simply paying attention to youth voices may appear subtle at first. But we have found that thinking *with* youth is a stance of collaboration that generates new methods all the time. For example, Eve reflects below about how this stance generated a slambook method for youth to think *with other* youth.

> *Eve: In CREDD's Gateways and Get-aways Project, we carefully designed each of our methods to be deeply participatory, interactive and pedagogical. In the slambook method, participants completed questions similar to those that would appear on a survey, but were able to see the responses of all of the respondents before them. We thought this helped to enrich not invalidate the responses of later respondents. In our interviews, survey, and focus groups with high-school aged youth, we made sure that they would feel like experts and collaborators in our analysis and theorizing on the GED and pushout experiences. These methods invited participants to recollect and rethink, to try ideas on and set forth new ideas, to imagine, and to advise.*

Indeed, meaningful elements of participation can be built-in to study designs even outside of participatory methodologies. Some researchers have created youth advisory boards to inform design and analysis, others have asked youth to work with them to develop interview questions or survey items.

Youth resistance researchers have opportunities to create methods in which youth are engaged as experts in their own lives, as complex persons, as co-theorists, as having perspectives worth sharing. However, there are many ethical, political, and epistemological dilemmas when engaging youth as participatory researchers, the topic of the second half of this chapter.

Competing Visions of Youth Participatory Research

In 2008, Monique was asked to serve as Principal Investigator on an oral history project with middle-schoolers at a public school in a small urban center.

Monique and the school leaders signed a memorandum of agreement about the activities that she and a co-facilitator would complete in an after-school setting to develop a yPAR project on the history of their city and school.

> *Monique: Two months into the project the students watched a televised interview of the superintendent of schools discussing a recent recession and its effect on the local economy, foreclosure rates, the school district's funding, and delayed plans to move into a new school building. Watching the video was a pivotal moment for this project. After viewing it, the kids felt depressed, angry, and slighted. They were unsure of their town's future, of their own futures, and were frustrated that decisions were being made about their school without their input. The students asked me to assist them in refocusing the project to gathering data on what their peers thought of these issues. I remember thinking of this time as what Torre and Ayala (2009) would call "a participatory entremundo," when we ceased to exist as individual adult and youth bodies in the same room and became a research team; the moment when we became mutually implicated in each others' lives and organized around action. I decided it was important to assist their growing sociological imagination and sustain their energy. I taught them survey methods and they constructed a questionnaire which they administered (with permission and cooperation from the principal) to 220 of their peers.*
>
> *At the end of the school year our research team was asked to present the project's findings as part of the after-school programs showcase for parents, teachers, and administrators. We created a rich presentation with survey findings, and clips of interviews with teachers and community elders. A few days before the showcase, we were told we needed to reduce the presentation to 10 minutes, so we focused our slide presentation on the findings from their survey. The young people wrote each slide together and thought the final version was a scaled down but adequate representation of our work. Because we were a shy bunch, we recorded the youth researchers' voices to narrate the slides rather than have them present in front of the audience. It was to be the first time anyone outside our research team would see our findings, which included: students felt welcomed in their school, felt that their culture was respected, and that they could confide in at least one teacher at their school. They also found that 86% of the students were dissatisfied with school lunch, and while many students felt safe on school grounds, they also worried about violence after school. The curtains opened, the spotlight shone on our PowerPoint, and our findings were released to the world.*
>
> *On my way out the door that day, I stopped to chat with the principal about his thoughts on the presentation. He told me the presentation was good but he wished he would have previewed the content. I was dismayed by this, because no one had asked to preview our findings before the showcase. He said that we needed to edit/ remove the school violence and safety slides and stick to highlighting the process of developing a research team for the next presentation, this one in front of the Board of Regents. He didn't like the initial parent reaction he was getting. The principal wanted to know why we did the survey in the first place.*

I know that the school leaders were vulnerable in important ways. Yet the admin-istration didn't want the full story of what they had found, only the parts which put their school in a positive light. I was stunned and disappointed by this turn of events.

It is not uncommon for youth research to take shape in ways unanticipated and unwanted by the adults who thought they wanted to hear from youth. Youth research, especially around schools, often summons a clash of divergent ethos, commitments, and ethical positions between youth research and the hidden curriculum of schools. Youth theorizations, politics, and critique can be stifled by school leaders, parents, and other adults who want something more staged, unthreatening, maybe even cute. When schools or adult-led projects commis-sion youth research, they are not always prepared to listen to young people, not ready to take their research seriously. Youth critique is transformative because it unleashes new methods, new theoretical frameworks, new ways of seeing things, and new ethical positions that make returning and reverting to old ways impossible.

Youth participation, in too many studies, is staged and superficial. We have been frequently called upon to serve as consultants to people who are interested in gathering a youth perspective on a particular issue, who think they are inter-ested in Youth Participatory Action Research (yPAR). From these encounters, we have learned that there is a common misconception that yPAR is merely another method of research. This perspective misinterprets the "P" in yPAR as "part"; it assumes that participation is about including more people in research, particularly people who are usually researched. yPAR aims to establish and nour-ish transparent research partnerships between young people and adults that are ideally jointly designed, conducted, analyzed, and distributed, while acknowl-edging the epistemological challenge of "yP," why *participation* in research at all? Participation refers to a set of beliefs about knowing and knowledge wherein youth bodies are not haphazardly inserted or attached to research. In yPAR and ideally other youth resistance methodologies, young people's viewpoints, their critique, their ideas about possible actions are respected and change the very methods and directions of research, throughout the life of a research project.

Participation implies an ethics about researching *with* and theorizing *with* peo-ple. Ironically, in the research experience that Monique shared, the principal's request does not violate institution-driven codes of conduct for research even as it clearly violates the ethics of research itself. In this section, we examine what falls outside of institutional ethics, what about research must be challenged, what must be refused, and what must be re(en)visioned.

Re(en)visioning Human Research Ethics

Our understanding of and practice of what we now consider appropriate ethi-cal conduct in research, what we have framed as decolonial participatory action research (DPAR) ethics (Tuck & Guishard, 2013), has been deeply influenced by our experiences with youth resistance research. In this section we offer a few challenges for future youth scholars to ponder and perhaps resolve for themselves. We end by with an attempt to stretch our collective ethical imagination by weaving in alternate perspectives of what ethical youth research could look like.

Conversations about ethics are usually contained in graduate research ethics courses, modular trainings, and the Institutional Review Board (IRB) submission process. Each of these spaces introduces and reinforces federally mandated rules based on normative ethical principles while highlighting the historical context of ethical abuses which necessitated their articulation. Institutional Review Boards (and their international counterparts) are important regulatory structures that strive to safeguard the wellbeing of young people and secure the confidentiality of the data gathered from research. However, there is much more to consider in developing ethical youth resistance research than what is addressed in an IRB application and approval process (Swauger, 2009, te Riele & Brooks, 2013; see also Guishard, forthcoming and Tuck & Guishard, 2013 for more on this point).

> IRB ethics are fixed at submission, and once a researcher passes through the IRB, it is assumed they are carrying out an ethical project. But feminist qualitative researchers are concerned with deeper ethical standards throughout all stages of the research process. For feminist qualitative researchers, ethics are never fixed but reflected upon continuously. (Swauger, 2009, p. 66)

Writing from a feminist perspective, Swauger points out that ethical commitments must be deeper than a one-time stamp of approval for a research proposal, and must be dynamic across all stages of the research.

As an example, in *Negotiating Ethical Challenges in Youth Research*, te Riele and Brooks (2013) engage international youth resistance researchers to discuss three overarching areas of concern: Youth power and agency, protecting rights and averting harm, and developing trust and respecting youth. These areas of concern drive our discussion about ethical considerations beyond the IRB.

Youth are considered a vulnerable population in scientific research because they are under the age of legal consent (18 years old in the U.S.), are viewed as lacking the decision-making capacity of adults, and are susceptible to coercion and manipulation by adult researchers. Federal guidelines stipulate that children are permitted to participate in research that involves minimal risk, and studies that involve greater than minimal risk if they directly benefit from their participation. The consent and assent process in youth research can be complicated. In general researchers must negotiate permission to approach young people from adults: Administrators, teachers, and organizational staff, and seek parental consent before obtaining youth assent. We have some qualms with how IRB-centered ethics assume diminished capacity and homogeneity among young people and with how the dance of interaction/recruitment is choreographed, constructing youth as vulnerable, IRBs inadvertently disempower them and take away their decision-making abilities. By associating the ability to consent with age and assuming developmental appropriateness automatically occurs when a specified age is reached, IRBs homogenize youth and treat them under the same rules—that adults can and must speak for them. (Swauger, 2009, p. 79)

Young people are a complex, heterogeneous group. Very young children may indeed have underdeveloped abilities, and thus obtaining consent and assent to solicit their participation in research makes sense. This may not be the case for tweens and young adults in the twenty-first century. Youth today are much more technologically savvy and have greater access to information than previous generations. If we acknowledge that young people are a diverse group, if we stray away from deficit analyses of their abilities—then respecting youth power and agency becomes an ethical obligation. There are times when obtaining adult assent and consent is unethical; when following institutional ethical prescriptions may violate youth privacy and put them at risk for harm from the very adults presumably empowered to protect them (Chabot, Shoveller, Spencer et al., 2012).

While analyzing the ethical issues that arose from her study of youth in residential schools, Nancy Bell (2008) distinguished between youth rights as defined by institutional ethics and from a children's rights perspective. Drawing from the United Nations High Commission on Human Rights, Bell suggests that children's rights are "those rights which cannot be waived or denied; impose obligations; are universal; and 'focus on the inherent dignity and equal worth of all human beings'" (Bell, 2008, p. 8). Bell found, after examining the histories of both discourses, ethics, and human rights, that ethical regulations subtly refer to human rights, and yet rights are not explicitly defined, nor is the relationship between human rights and research ethics definitively detailed.

Earlier in this chapter, Monique reflected on the clash of competing views of youth research in the context of a participatory oral history project with middle-school students. Whereas this example highlighted the ethical dilemmas of respecting the dignity of young people, and trusting the importance of their theorizing in the face of adult refusals to do the same, there are more examples of times that researcher refusal is critical—to say "stop" even when institutional ethics say "go."

The Role of Refusal in Youth Resistance Research

In this section, we discuss the significance of refusal (Simpson, 2007; Tuck & Yang, 2014) in youth resistance research. Generally, social science research is extremely interested in documenting and circulating stories about the damage and pain of oppressed communities; this reflects a theory of change that under-girds much of social science, that evidence of oppression is needed for advocates to convince those in power to give up power or resources. This is a colonial theory of change that locates power outside of communities and presumes that it is a lack of evidence of oppression that keeps justice away.

In her examination of the symbolic violence of the academy, bell hooks (1990) consolidates the core message from academic researchers to oppressed communities thus:

> No need to hear your voice when I can talk about you better than you can speak about yourself. No need to hear your voice. Only tell me about your pain. (p. 343)

hooks' words get right to the heart of our reservations about the aims of social science research, and youth resistance research specifically. Taking this further:

> In part, we are trying to help readers think through what there is instead of pain for social science research to look at, and also provide some ways of theorizing the political and sovereign advantages of ascribing limits to settler colonial social science research. (Tuck & Yang, 2014, p. 238)

Thus, we must consider the valuable role of refusal in youth resistance research. Considering the long, problematic history of unethical research in non-white communities, refusals in youth resistance research are needed to mark forms of knowledge that the academy does not deserve. Refusals are further needed to assert that research may not be the intervention that is needed in a given injustice situation:

> Refusal is not just a no, but a redirection to ideas otherwise unacknowl-edged or unquestioned. Unlike a settler colonial configuration of knowl-edge that is petulantly exasperated and resentful of limits, a methodology of refusal regards limits on knowledge as productive, as indeed a good thing. (Tuck & Yang, 2014, p. 239)

Youth resistance researchers especially need to be ready to make refusals in our work. This is not to wring our hands about how vulnerable youth are, but to mark that youth are targets of commercialism and violence in pervasive ways. Youth in the U.S. are encouraged to serve up their stories and put themselves on display in ways that are not comparable to prior generations, with few spaces to consider the costs. As youth resistance researchers, we must consider the reach of media, market, and police surveillance on youth lives, and think about our work in that context.

At the same time that stories of damage are coveted, especially from youth resistance research, we observe that the actual "theorizing back" that resistance does is disparaged or subordinated.

Conclusion: Theorizing Resistance by Theorizing Back

Youth resistance research has "calcified" in recent years (Dimitradis, this volume) in part because it has claimed a genealogy, a self-historicism that become a kind of concrete in which to plant any new resistance research. Theorizing back confronts the proposition that theory flows down the royal lineage of grand narratives and (ag)grand(ized) theory. Monique has framed her confrontations with theory as challenging the bleach of the academy:

> I started out this journey confident and insurgent, passionately enthusiastic at the prospect of conducting research. . . . Later I felt overwhelmingly oppressed by the literature on oppression. I'm not quite sure what happened . . . the best that I can convey is the bleach almost got me (Fine et al., 2003a, b) . . . the bleach is the pungent detergent of the academy. . . . It legitimizes and authenticates knowledge by dictating which bodies can conduct research and posit theory and which bodies get to be researched and theorized about. . . . The bleach thrives on homogeneity and depersonalization . . . demands that you must keep the intellectual, the personal, and the political sharply compartmentalized. . . . It says that knowledge emanating from marginalized standpoints is unworthy and deficient and it consequently inculcates uncertainty, suspicion, and fear. (Guishard, 2009, p. 95)

Feeling free to theorize counter-stories to widely accepted ideas did not come easy for us because much of academic research is based on the supposition that in order to critique theory one needs to possess comprehensive knowledge of a theorist's work and his/her historical influences. Monique's frustrations in re-theorizing Freirian critical consciousness through grassroots parent organizing and youth participatory action research (Guishard, Fine, Doyle et al., 2005; Guishard, 2009), and Eve's disenchantment with Deleuzian conceptualizations of desire after working on two yPAR projects, have made us wonder about the political role grand theories play in knowledge production. We wonder whether future youth resistance scholars really need to read Francis Galton to make critiques of eugenics, or whether they must read Nietzsche to appreciate and evaluate Freire.

We heed those who insist that we know our history, however, and we share the position that histories of ideas do not necessarily need to be taught/learned as a grand narrative of lineal descent to engage with or understand theory. Perhaps genealogical approaches to theory might be more useful, in which the most contemporary is read first, and prior generations that inform that theory are subsequently read. Conflating the history of theory with the authority to theorize devalues emerging youth resistance scholarship and simultaneously devalues youth work and youth critique. If beginning youth resistance researchers are impeded in their attempts to theorize back and if young people are not permitted to speak to the conditions, policies, and ideologies that shape their lives until they perform an understanding everything that everyone has said before them, "knowing the history" becomes a mechanism of keeping youth and youth researchers from ever speaking.

Eve has similarly written about theorizing back which,

> contains a critique of the ways in which whitestream voices are constructed as rigorous, logical, reasoned, and valid while voices outside of the whitestream are considered experiential and emotional, representing devalued ways of knowing . . . it involves a demystifying and de-deifying of grand theory in order to revise, resist and refuse stereotypical or erroneous analyses of us and our communities. (Tuck, 2009, p. 112)

When we write about theorizing back, we are not talking about rejecting theories but of critically assessing ideas in order to discern and articulate what aspects do and do not mesh/resonate with our current work. The goal of theorizing back is not resolving the sour notes or mending the divergence between what parts of an idea survive reflective analyses and resonate in particular contexts. Theorizing back is about naming and articulating the unlike parts, and placing value in the in-commensurabilities. Theorizing back/confronting theory is messy, complicated, onerous work but it also rewarding:

> It does not suffice to use theory and append a list of caveats. The caveats must be practiced, explored, and teased toward entering a conversation that has not included us, has silenced us, or has previously happened with indigenous people, people of color, and poor people as the objects. Theorizing back requires that we shift the language/narrative of theory and policy so that they do not speak against us and so that we in using them do not speak or act against ourselves. (Tuck, 2009, p. 128)

Theorizing back is resisting research, and can be a mode of theorizing resistance. It is consistent with the epistemological stance that youth resistance research, especially when conducted *with and by* youth, generates new methodologies, new ethics, and new theory.

Note

1   Co-founders of the Public Science Project include Maria Torre, Michelle Fine, Jennifer Ayala, Caitlin Cahill, Maddy Fox, Anne Galletta, Monique Guishard, Brett Stoudt, Eve Tuck, and Sarah Zeller-Berkman.

Works Referenced

Bell, N. (2008). Ethics in child research: Rights, reason and responsibilities. *Children's Geographies, 6*, 1, 7–20.

Chabot, C., Shoveller, J.A., Spencer, G., & Johnson, J.L. (2012). Ethical and epistemological insights: A case study of participatory action research with young people. *Journal of Empirical Research on Human Ethics, 7*, 2, 20–33.

Dolby, N., Dimitriadis, G., & Willis, P.E. (2004). *Learning to labor in new times.* New York: RoutledgeFalmer.

Fine, M. (2008). An epilogue, of sorts. In J. Cammarota & M. Fine (Eds.). *Revolutionizing education: Youth participatory action research in motion*, pp. 213–234 New York: Routledge.

Fine, M., Anand, B., Jordan, C., & Sherman, D. (2003a). Before the bleach gets us all. In M. Fine & L. Weiss (Eds.). *Silenced voices and extraordinary conversations*, pp. 113–132. New York: Teachers' College Press.

Fine, M., Bloom, J., Burns, A., Chajet, L., Guishard, M., Torre, M.E., & Payne, Y.A. (2003b). Dear Zora: A letter to Zora Neale Hurston fifty years after Brown. In L. Weis and M. Fine (Eds.). *Working method.* New York: Routledge.

Fox, M., & Fine, M. (2012). Circulating critical research: Reflections on performance and moving inquiry into action. In G. Cannella & S. Steinberg (Eds.). *Critical qualitative research reader*, pp. 153–165. New York: Peter Lang Publishing.

Guishard, M. (2009). "The false paths, the endless labors, the turns now this way and now that": Participatory action research, mutual vulnerability, and the politics of inquiry. *Urban Review, 41*, 1, 85–105.

Guishard, M. (forthcoming) Nepantla and nepantlera ethics para nosotros: Threshold perspectives on ethics for us all. Unpublished Doctoral Dissertation. CUNY Graduate Center.

Guishard, M., Fine, M., Doyle, C., Jackson, J., Singleton, S., Staten, T., & Webb, A. (2005). The Bronx on the move: Participatory consultation with mothers and youth. *Journal of Educational and Psychological Consultation, 16*, 35–54.

hooks, b. (1990). Marginality as a site of resistance. In R. Ferguson et al. (Eds.). *Out there: Marginalization and contemporary cultures*, pp. 241–243. Cambridge, MA: MIT Press.

Katz, C. (2001). On the grounds of globalization: A topography for feminist political engagement. *Signs: Journal of Women in Culture and Society, 24*, 4, 1213–1234.

Khosravi, S. (2008). *Young and defiant in Tehran.* Philadelphia, PA: University of Pennsylvania Press.

Kirkland, D. (2013). *A search past silence: The literacy of young men.* New York: Teachers' College Press.

Krueger, P. (2011). Navigating the gaze: Young people's intimate knowledge with surveilled spaces at school. Ph.D. Thesis, Graduate Center, The City University of New York.

McCarty, T., Wyman, L.T., & Nicholas, S.E. (2014). Activist ethnography with Indigenous youth: Lessons from humanizing research on language and education. In D. Paris, & M.T. Winn (eds.). *Humanizing research: Decolonizing qualitative inquiry with youth and communities.* Thousand Oaks, CA: Sage Publications, Inc.

Nolan, K. (2011). *Police in the hallways: Discipline in an urban high school.* Minneapolis: University of Minnesota Press.

Ruglis, J. (2011). Mapping the biopolitics of school dropout and youth resistance. *International Journal of Qualitative Studies in Education, 24*, 5, 627–637.

Simpson, A. (2007). On ethnographic refusal: Indigeneity, "voice," and colonial citizenship. *Junctures, 9,* 67–80.

Stoudt, B., & Torre, M. (in press). Action research in the criminal justice systems. In D. Coghlan & M. Brydon-Miller (Eds.). *Encyclopedia of Action Research.* Thousand Oaks, CA: Sage Publications.

Swauger, M. (2009). No kids allowed!!! How IRB ethics undermine qualitative researchers from achieving socially responsible ethical standards. *Race, Gender & Class, 16,* 1, 63–68.

te Riele, K., & Brooks, R. (2013). *Negotiating ethical challenges in youth research.* New York: Routledge.

Torre, M.E., & Ayala, J. (2009). Envisioning participatory action entremundos. *Feminism and Psychology, 19,* 3, 387–393.

Tuck, E. (2009). Theorizing back: An approach to participatory policy analysis. In J. Anyon, with M. Dumas, D. Linville, K. Nolan, M. Perez, E. Tuck, & J. Weiss, *Theory and educational research: Toward critical social explanation,* pp. 111–130. New York: Routledge.

Tuck, E., & Guishard, M. (2013). Scientifically based research and settler coloniality: An ethical framework of decolonial participatory action research. In T.M. Kress, C. Malott, & B. Porfilio (Eds.). *Challenging status quo retrenchment: New directions in critical qualitative research,* pp. 3–27. Charlotte, NC: Information Age Publishing.

Tuck, E., & Yang, K.W. (2014). R-words: Refusing research. In D. Paris & M.T. Winn (Eds.). *Humanizing research: Decolonizing qualitative inquiry with youth and communities,* pp. 223–248. Thousand Oaks, CA: Sage Publications.

Tuck, E., & Youth Researchers for a New Education System (2008b). *The YRNES Report 2008.* http://www.ncscatfordham.org/binarydata/files/YRNES_Report_Updated.pdf

Tuck, E., Allen, J., Bacha, M., Morales, A., Quinter, S., Thompson, J., & Tuck, M. (2008a). PAR praxes for now and future change: The collective of researchers on educational disappointment and desire. In J. Cammarota & M. Fine (Eds.). *Revolutionizing education: Youth participatory action research in motion,* pp. 49–83. New York: Routledge.

Willis, P.E. (1981). *Learning to labor: How working class kids get working class jobs.* New York: RoutledgeFalmer.

Zeller-Berkman, S. (2007). Peering in: A look into reflective practices in youth participatory action research. *Children, Youth and Environments, 17,* 2, 315–328.

14

OUTDOOR EDUCATION AS A SITE OF EPISTEMOLOGICAL PERSISTENCE

Unsettling an Understanding of Urban Indigenous Youth Resistance

Tracy Friedel

Here we are, at an outdoor education camp in the Canadian Rockies, 10 urban Native youth, two Indigenous aides, and myself (the researcher).

The person running the camp, a middle-aged non-Native fellow, is teaching fire starting using a knife and flint. "This is the old fashioned way to start a fire," he proclaims to our group, "A skill you'll need to survive."

Upon leaving the city, my aides and I had asked the group not to bring along any lighters or matches, but the weather has been cool and damp so it will be good to get a fire going.

The outdoor educator begins, scraping the flint harshly across the face of the steel, demonstrating to youth how to produce a flood of sparks that will fall on a precarious pile of kindling . . .

[Fast forward . . . to the next morning]

I am standing under the cabin overhang; yet another cool morning. From the corner of my eye I notice a brightly colored object at the edge of the camp yard, next to last night's campfire.

"What's that?" I ask an aide.

"I'm not sure," he says.

We walk over for a better look.

Turns out it's an empty lighter fluid container, bright yellow in color.

Just then a youth walks by, so I ask, "Do you know where this came from?"

"Oh yeah," she explains of her colleagues. "That was Eli's. Ali used it to start the fire last night."

The aide and I turn and look at one other. A short silence and then we begin laughing, recalling yesterday's four-hour fire starting lesson, the painstaking efforts of the outdoor educator to teach our group the "old" way to start a fire.

[Fast forward again . . . two weeks later]

We've arrived to the river flats just outside of the city for a sweat lodge ceremony.

The Cree host is providing some traditional teachings beforehand; he explains the symbolism associated with fire as he strikes up a wooden match to light a small bit of sweet grass at the bottom of a well-worn seashell.

After all have smudged, I notice him disappear into a nearby storage shed. A minute or so later he exits carrying a large tiger torch hooked to a seven-gallon propane cylinder.

He begins setting ablaze the neatly stacked fire logs located at the center of the fire pit. "This is where the ceremonial rocks will be heated," he explains. I can't help but think once more about that empty lighter fluid container . . . (Compiled from reflective field notes, previously cited in Friedel, 2011, pp. 531–2)

This chapter offers an examination of the nuanced response of nine youth of Nêhiyawi (Cree) and Âpihtawikosisân-Nêhiyawi (Métis-Cree) ancestry, plus one youth descended from Assiniboine (Nakota) peoples, to whitestream (Denis, 1997) outdoor education programming on the Canadian prairies. I argue that whitestream outdoor education that constructs urban Indigenous youth as noble savages, as displaced from nature, says much more about static colonial theories of change (Tuck, 2009) than it does about Indigenous youth themselves. While continuing to be conceived of in pathological, anti-modern and inauthentic ways (Battiste, 2002), the reality is that Indigenous youth are at the center of the powerful cultural resurgence now under way across the Canadian landscape.

Historically, Euro-Western schooling has been a major context for the enactment of a complex range of racist, colonial policies targeting Indigenous peoples in Canada. Recent efforts to make schooling more aligned with the desires of Indigenous parents, families and communities are ongoing, and increasingly pursued through the vehicle of outdoor education (Tarrant & Green, 1999). The matter of whether these programs address Eurocentric forms of knowing is of major consequence, as is the issue of whether and how outdoor education may serve to reinvigorate colonial archetypes of Indian resistance. The answers to these questions should be of major consequence to all outdoor educators.

Were we to place youths' response to the lesson on fire-making within the major thrust of Indigenous educational research, concerned primarily with the fruitfulness of educational innovations, particularly curricular ones, that are meant to improve academic achievement (e.g. Ignas, 2004; Richards & Vining, 2004;

Friesen & Friesen, 2002), youths' actions would undoubtedly be interpreted as overt resistance. Such has tended to be the dichotomous trajectory along which Indigenous education research has progressed, with a major focus on curricular innovations to improve achievement levels, and a lesser focus on Native youth resistance as a response to these efforts. In the case of the latter, when the actions of Indigenous students are studied, very often these are interpreted in direct relation to power, viewed as comparatively minor with respect to the effects on altering the status quo. While not necessarily oppositional in a philosophical sense, what is unintentionally set up in this polarity is a tendency for the authoritative or controlling pole, that is, the focus on achievement (or keeping youth in school), to dominate the way we think about issues in Indigenous education, thereby relegating the nature of Indigenous youth resistance to scholarship's outer reaches. In this, a privileged area of inquiry is created; namely, research focused on the achievement gap and how this can be ameliorated. This parallel but uneven trajectory of research (academic achievement/youth resistance to such efforts) constrains our ability to see Indigenous youth resistance in the way that Deloria (2001) might describe it, as associated with Indigenous thought and cultural traditions such as orality.

The intention of undertaking a qualitative study focused on the educational experience of urban Indigenous youth was to, at least in part, learn more about the efficacy of outdoor education for fostering a sense of cultural identity and place-based belonging among young people living in an urban prairie context. In this case, however, the curriculum served to re-power colonial icons, such as 'the ecologically noble savage,' a deliberate mischaracterization originally framed by early European explorers of America (Berkhofer, 1978; Redford, 1990). In considering youths' response to this learning, and to their experience of racialization more generally, challenged are conventional understandings of how Indigenous youth resist, and unsettled are the assumptions that often underpin Euro-Western forms of outdoor education (Friedel, 2011). In place of this outmoded theorizing, urban Indigenous youth's own talk emphasizes their eagerness to participate in the process of restoring Nêhiyawi (Cree) and Âpihtawikosisân-Nêhiyawi (Métis-Cree) principles and practices. The chapter concludes with a call for increased control by Indigenous groups over informal and non-formal outdoor educational initiatives, particularly given the important place these programs have in restoring cultural traditions concerning kinship (relationality) and mutual support (solidarity), and in view of the significant role of out-of-school efforts in continuing a long history of resistance to colonial invasion.

Imperialist Nostalgia and Outdoor Education

As Mohawk scholar Taiaiake Alfred (2010) observes, it is the hanging on by settler societies to the visions of their predecessors that pose the largest challenge for advancing radical, life-affirming theories of change across Turtle Island. At the heart of a colonial vision of North American society is the concept of "imperialist nostalgia" (Rosaldo, 1989), in particular, romanticized notions of an idealized indigene such as the "ecologically noble savage." As Rosaldo (1989) describes, imperialist nostalgia is paradoxical in its manner of making racial domination appear inevitable, at the same time as settler society mourns the loss of what is now gone, for example, the ecologically noble savage.

Since the early seventeenth century, Europe and the modern state have been contradictory in their relationship with nature. The construction of nature as an overabundant availability of resources to be used to increase state power and wealth in the seventeenth century coincided with the taxonomic categorization of Native people as non-human varieties (Anderson, 1998). Deemed as less than human, Indigenous peoples were inscribed within models of species fixity, meaning that in the classification system of the day, Europeans were situated on top while Native people were "rendered coterminous with the diverse life forms that were thought of as comprising 'the natural world'" (p. 126). This Eurocentric view of the world, combined with epidemics and an array of colonial strategies (Harris, 2004), spawned the beginnings of what would become the overt removal of Indigenous peoples from their territories (Henderson, 2000). This history and practice has been upheld to the present day by means of state laws and repressive policies (Alfred, 1999).

This notion of lesser species continues to be employed as vindication for the destruction of the environment (Smith, 2005). As development wages on across North America, heightening destruction across the spectrum of life, the ecologically noble savage gains prominence as a key feature of settler societies response. The dual aim is to absolve settler guilt for the way things are, while at the same time masking a brutish history of racially organized colonial domination. As Indigenous peoples in Canada become increasingly urbanized, the seemingly innocent yearning of imperialist nostalgia shows up in a complex of places, including in the purview of outdoor education. In this context, Indigenous youth are expected to live up to pernicious stereotypes in educational programming that comes replete with human-centric notions of ecology and ethnographic ideas pertaining to a 'bygone' past. In total, this proves just as harmful as the racialized violence and assimilationist tactics of past colonial schooling efforts.

Outdoor education activities geared towards First Nation and Métis youth in this study, offered by a settler organization, and befitting of 'good intentions' (a reference to Canadian residential school policy as described by Chrisjohn, Young, & Maraun, 2006), proved to be a mismatch between what youth had thought they signed up for, and the aims of the outdoor education program itself. Throughout, engaging with whitestream perspectives of nature appeared to be of little interest to youth. What captured their attention from the start was the opportunity the program gave them to connect in kinship ways, to strengthen their sense of Indigenous identity through strengthened relationships with peers, a broader community of people they had not previously met. To engage with one another, in the manner and places of their ancestors, took precedence over efforts by outdoor educators to deliver a more formal curriculum.

Disavowing the "Savage" in the City

Representations of Native youth in twenty-first-century Canada remain closely tied to a construction originating in the nineteenth century. The myth of the noble and ignoble savage (the latter closely linked to ideas about primitivism (Berkhofer, 1978; Francis, 1992) depict Native youth as, on the one hand, victims of cultural discontinuity, highly suicidal, academically and otherwise "at-risk" amidst the chaos that is Western progress, a romanticized representation closely aligned with the work of salvage ethnography, and an imagining that enshrines "noble Indian" status. On the other hand, a persistent pathology encases Native youth in the imagination of many practitioners and policymakers, evident in discourse that portrays youth as antisocial, deviant, criminal, with a propensity for violence and gang involvement, a conjuring of Native youth as ignoble beings deserving of little empathy, but in need of much surveillance from settler colonial society.

The persistence of these dehumanizing stereotypes, overloaded and over-determined signs, are constructions of the "Indian" as primitive, situated at "a stage in a social evolutionary ladder, the embodiment of a genetic wholism or degeneracy, a psychological archetype or a shadow projection of an entire continent" (Duran, 1996, p. 111). In explaining his experience with such entrenched stereotypes, one young man in the study states: "I can tell by just the way people look at me and look at the other kids in the group, sometimes I'd get a long stare or glare or, by occasional people, a tilt of the hat, by the people that [others] would call gangsters" (ELI, research interview). For Indigenous youth in Canada, the ignoble savage continues to act as Furniss (1999) describes it, as "a physical burden, as something that Aboriginal people have to 'pack' around, as an image that precedes them in their interactions with non-Aboriginal people" (p. 130). The perpetuation of the "ignoble savage" also can be seen as providing the necessary justification for the continued theft and occupancy of Indigenous lands, and ongoing attempts to subjugate whole pre-existing societies.

A growing number of Native people in Western Canada now live in urban areas (Statistics Canada, 2008), at times the result of voluntary decisions by themselves or their ancestors, and at other times the result of involuntary relocation away from their traditional territories. Discounted in this story of urbanization is that Native people may well be residing in the very place that their ancestors have inhabited for thousands of years. As Newhouse and Peters (2003) point out, the idea of an urban Aboriginal person became incompatible with the construction of Aboriginal peoples that had developed over the last century; consequently, Indigenous people who chose to live in cities were seen as an anomaly, or as people who had turned their backs on their culture.

In response to a perceived loss of culture, schools in the 1970s began to incorporate traditional activities into the curriculum. However, Mary Hermes (2005) makes the point that teaching cultural activities devoid of a deep cultural context "can intersect with mainstream stereotypes and students' notions of equating a Native identity with these traditions" (p. 10). For the ever-increasing numbers of Native youth growing up in urban areas, it is not only neoliberal strategies (Altamirano-Jiménez, 2004) that result in ever lessening opportunities to engage with Indigenous cultural frameworks. The "colonial cosmology" (Raibmon, 2005, p. 3) that produces a rural/urban binary, through the historical cataloguing, categorizing, and displaying of a Native Other (Edwards, 1992), reverberates in Canada's liberal multicultural discourse generally, and specifically in contexts such as outdoor education.

The Eurocentrism inherent in this study's outdoor education programming was an obvious problem, causing a shift in the focus of the research that would better enable an understanding of the underlying issues, articulated succinctly by one of the young ladies in the study: "I'd like to learn how to be Aboriginal without living in the woods" (FAY, research interview). Also revealed through making urban Indigenous youths' voices more prominent was its revealing of a deep-seated commitment by youth to take responsibility for furthering cultural teachings and practices, as described by one youth: "You can always find out more about yourself no matter how old you are; you can *look back on* your own culture and learn all the different things and help with your identity" (JAE, research interview).

Even in instances where meaningful forms of cultural learning are integrated within a school-based or non-formal outdoor education curriculum, frequently hidden from view is the fact that undermining Indigenous languages and cultural practices has been the target of decades of federal policy, and that Indigenous claims to resources, land, and sovereignty are continually being usurped in favor of colonial capital interests. Indigenous youth constructed as "at-risk," both culturally and morally, a notion prevalent in a wide swath of research, leads to pedagogical interventions that rarely honor youths' actual lives. In this particular context of non-formal outdoor education, youths' collective response is a rejoinder to the colonial curriculum that they encountered, and a reason to shift attention to the important pathways for restoring Nêhiyawi (Cree) and Âpihtawikosisân-Nêhiyawi (Métis-Cree) cultural practices.

In Canada, burgeoning growth rates in rural and urban First Nation, Métis, and Inuit communities have seemed to fuel the discourse framing Native youth as dispersed from nature, and/or within a pathology that defines their failure as measured against colonial notions of economic progress. In other words, it is the noble or ignoble savage (or sometimes both) that often mark how Indigenous youth are understood today. Wishing to challenge these notions is what brought us together as researcher and researched in the first place. Youths' spatialized talk, for example, "the [land] got stolen from us" (ELI, research interview), is a powerful counter-narrative that speaks back to Canada's own nation-building fantasy (King, 2003), at the same time as it connects with historical expressions of Indigenous resistance. Youths' active refusal of stereotypical sentiments—for example, their use of lighter fluid to start a campfire in damp conditions (as described in the opening vignette), juxtaposed by the story of the Elder's use of a propane torch to heat the sweat lodge rocks, serves to disrupt notions of the "noble savage," thereby contributing something valuable to our understanding of how Indigenous youth negotiate whitestream curricula.

It is on the ground, in educational practice, that we can see disruptions to the dichotomy in current academic achievement/youth resistance to these efforts now underpinning the vast majority of Indigenous educational research. This is only possible if we acknowledge up front the dearth of interest paid by these young people to Eurocentric ideas about nature, and if we refrain from immediately inferring that this disinterest represents youth turning their back on an opportunity to learn more about who they are as Indigenous peoples. Conversely, analyzing in cross-temporal ways, across time and space, reveals something important about the persistence of nostalgic ideas about Indigenous peoples, including how these frame current theorizing regarding youth resistance (and in relation to colonial theories of change). The extent to which imperialist nostalgia and associated stereotypical imagery concerning Indigenous peoples has remained static is noteworthy. A more reflective examination also indicates something important about where youth actually are with respect to preparing to take responsibility for perpetuating cultural practices and collective wisdom. Their eagerness to join the summer program in the first place, and their perfect attendance throughout the summer and fall, belie an interpretation of disinterest in both schooling and cultural values and norms.

Youth actions in education are often misconstrued (Giroux 1994; Hebdige 1979). For this research, a turn to ancestral ways of knowing helps to elucidate that youths' behaviors are in fact highly consistent with a culture of orality. We can consider their actions as not only a push back to imperialist nostalgia in education, but also a pull forward along the pathway of cultural restoration. Urban Indigenous youths' active sense of social presence in geographic place serves to reject the historical construction of "the Indian" as uprooted, or as displaced from nature, highly reminiscent of Anishinaabe scholar Gerald Vizenor's notion of survivance (1994).

Avowing Indigeneity

Playing an outdoor game on the study's first day, a chase game involving blindfolds, I heard one youth shout excitedly to another, a male participant who was struggling to catch anyone: "Aren't you a Native? Just listen!" Another youth made note specifically of the prevalence of Nêhiyaw (Cree) ancestry among her peers: "We have the same culture. Most of us are all (in the group) are Cree, and

I'm Cree" (HEB, research interview). The emphasis placed on a tribal sense of belonging is a consistent feature of Indigeneity, and central to processes of learning in First Nation, Métis, and Inuit education:

> Aboriginal learning is a highly social process that serves to nurture relationships in the family and throughout the community. Social relationships are a cornerstone for learning about ancestral language, culture, and history. (CCL, 2009, p. 10)

Leslie Marmon Silko (1977), in the context of Pueblo peoples, also explains the importance of tribal relationships further: "in ancient times cohesiveness was all that stood between extinction and survival" (pp. 38–9).

Elders and cultural teachers regularly tell of how, in times past, Native peoples paid special attention to the weather, the sky, and the earth, an important aspect of a larger system of local monitoring based on personal life histories and experiences. These living memories are then extended through storytelling and information sharing. This oral tradition applies to both the family and community setting, vertically expanding the time period of individual expertise and observations. Indigenous scholar Fixico (2003) explains further:

> Dedication to the "good" life of following cultural norms even during hardship corroborated that the ancestors were right and that traditions should not be questioned. This inertia of continuity provided security between the people, compelling them to depend on maintaining traditions. (p. 53)

The growing wave of informal and non-formal educational initiatives now under way in Canada (CCL, 2009) can be understood as integral to an Indigenous resurgence, underlain by a peoples' desire to pursue the good life, in Nêhiyawi (Cree), miyo-pimâtisiwin (Hart, 2002), in contexts that are less volatile, hostile, or structured than public schooling settings.

The overly deterministic environmentalism that continues to mark a great many outdoor education programs runs squarely up against Indigenous traditions of knowing, for example, founded in Cree notions of orality (Weber-Pillwax, 2001). The expanding presence of out-of-school learning opportunities across Canada is testament to the profound disconnection between oral traditions and public education settings. An altogether different systemization, philosophy, and practices associated with Indigenous orality can prohibit purposeful collation with Western notions of knowledge. Or, as late Lakota scholar Vine Deloria, Jr. (1999) writes,

> The real interest of the old Indians was not to find the abstract structure of physical reality but rather to find the proper road along which, for the duration of a person's life, individuals were supposed to walk. (p. 46)

Indigenous youths' resistance to whitestream conceptualizations of outdoor education is not only resistance to imperialist nostalgia, and the settler desire to emplace Native youth back in nature as part of assuaging the psychological effects of colonial destruction. Youths' actions also reflect what can be termed *epistemological persistence*, a nuanced negotiation of the learning context in ways that disrupt repressive ideas about Indigenous peoples, such as noble savagery, tragedy, and displacement. Youth actions resonate deeply with the longstanding, fluid, sovereign Indigenous pathways of their Ancestors. The desire of young people to gather and collectively share their personal experience, even if it means withstanding a whitestream outdoor education curriculum, perpetuates a long history of transmitting proven strategies for social and cultural survival in the face of colonial capitalism.

Jeannette Armstrong (1996), in the case of Okanagan peoples, explains the importance of a merging of social, cultural, spiritual and physical realities in a particular geography: "We are tied together by those who brought us here and gave us blood and gave us place" (p. 465). The youth in this study were keenly aware of the importance of such interrelationships in a Nêhiyawi (Cree) and Âpihtawikosisân-Nêhiyawi (Métis-Cree) landscape, evident in comments concerning their preference for Native teachers in the summer program: "[Native kids] just see the value in it . . . on a more spiritual level" (FAY, research interview), or their descriptions of place-meaning, "A place is where you belong" (JAE, research interview).

The thrusts of whitestream environmental education curriculum, increasingly evident in public education, should be reviewed carefully for its potentiality to enact *oralcide*, an idea closely connected to the linguicide described by Tove Skutnabb-Kangas (2000), recognition of the fact that the processes of modern schooling continue to actively work to kill orality, and with it, "the Indian in the child." Moreover, as Indigenous education researchers, it is perhaps time to focus our attention more closely on how youth resist assimilation and become propagators of culture, for example, through employing Nêhiyawi (Cree) and Âpihtawikosisân-Nêhiyawi (Métis-Cree) epistemologies.

Historian Julie Cruikshank (2005) states in the context of her work with Athapaskan and Tlingit Elders, "local knowledge is never crudely encapsulated in closed traditions, but is produced during human encounters" (p. 4). The notion of learning as embedded in everyday life, and cultural practices as dynamic extensions across generations, provides the lens through which to regard urban Indigenous youth as co-constructers of culture. The young people in this study have relationships with relatives urban and rural, near and far, and through these important ties strong connections to ancestrally important places are maintained. Youth actions in this study often countered how they were perceived by the study's outdoor educators, assertions that youth were "lost," "disinterested," and "without identity." Such persistent longing for the "real" or "authentic" Indian, recouped by White environmentalists beginning in the 1970s (Bird, 1996), and lingering today in the minds of too many educators, contributes to the misinterpreting of youth resistance, and does nothing to address the ongoing failure of schools to update cultural traditions of learning. This makes abundantly clear that colonial theories of change are in desperate need of reform.

Elizabeth Bird (1996) states that Native people are "loved" when they fit the mold of the picturesque that has been constructed for them, and not when they act outside of these roles (p. 4). Moving within and across their traditional territories in the manner that they do, the young people in this study disrupt primitivist ideas and racial classifications (Li, 2006; LaRocque, 2004) as imposed on them through whitestream curricular discourses, including in the area of outdoor education.

While Indigenous youth in urban and rural areas continue to struggle against a racialized identity (Friedel, 2010), also emphasized is their deeply felt affiliation with their parents and grandparents, individuals who in many cases may also have been urban Native youth. Viewing youth actions through the lens of tribal and intertribal relations helps to move theorizing beyond colonial binaries, and makes it clear that rather than it being Indigenous youth who are culturally deficient; it is an overly deterministic outdoor and environmental education that falls short in endeavoring to recoup genuine cultural traditions. Building and maintaining a variety of relationships is important in urban contexts (for instance, see Belanger, Barron & McKay-Turnbull, 2003), expressed in this case by the eagerness of youth to sign up for this study. The nature of such topics is important for future Indigenous educational research.

Implications for Indigenous Education and Educational Research

> We live stories that either give our lives meaning or negate it with meaninglessness. If we change the stories we live by, quite possibly we change ourselves. (Ben Okri (1997), as cited in King, 2003, p. 153)

Our duty as Indigenous scholars to undertake resistance research involves enhancing the empirical breadth and theoretical sophistication of our work, in the process ensuring that the knowledge that is produced is useful beyond institutions of higher education. The research described here provides insights for formal, informal, and non-formal educational contexts, focusing on the response of urban Native youth to whitestream outdoor education programming. By analyzing their actions through the lens of ancestral cultural practices associated with orality, it is possible to recast notions of resistance to hegemonic curricula as more than that, as serving also to highlight epistemic persistence over time. The places where this study took place are embodied locations, documented through archeological finds and Indigenous oral histories. As Jojola (2004) points out, even in urban milieus, historic places persist and historic patterns of settlement have helped to mold the shape of newer settlements. Understanding urban Indigenous identity not as 'disconnected' but as defined by the interpretive manner in which place continues to be lived is useful for understanding the resistance of Indigenous youth today.

In keeping with Vizenor's (1994) notion of survivance, Indigenous groups may wish to exercise increased control over the content and process of outdoor education programming, thereby ensuring alignment with their relational and spiritual place-based literacies, and for enhancing the potentialities of youth to take up their responsibilities in response to current sociopolitical and cultural realities. Writing about Native youth as beings with agency, something their ancestors were denied for much of the twentieth century, is a politicized response to the sustained racial and colonial violence perpetrated against Indigenous people in Canada to the present day. As with youth in other contexts (Fine, et al., 2003, p. 188), Indigenous youths' social locations are varied and important, and so too does it matter that we see this particular constituency as *more than* independently knowing individuals, as epistemologically connected across time and space. North American Indigenous peoples recognize epistemological agents as individuals connected to communities, and knowledge as constructed by 'knowing' beings that are in relationship to one another. Thinking in terms of communities of knowers is crucial to producing an important counter-narrative that can serve to disrupt whitestream curriculum, and it also makes possible the linking of lived experience to larger social, cultural, and spiritual processes in Indigenous societies.

Going beyond the term's literal definition then, we should understand orality as traversing space and time, and in this, retaining much relevance for fostering broad notions of solidarity, in the process restoring what it means to be Nêhiyawi (Cree) and Âpihtawikosisân-Nêhiyawi (Métis-Cree). Against a backdrop of Idle No More, and a widespread Indigenous resurgence across North America, the push back now occurring in education requires a contemplative, culturally centered analysis that can understand tribal-oriented resistance in ways that enable us to comprehend youth actions as linking an expansive Indigenous reality. The voices of the young people cited here "serves as a reminder that exclusive, exclusionary systems of meaning are forever haunted by those who are written out and erased" (McLeod, 2000, p. 43). Youths' adapted manner of learning in the context of imperialist nostalgia in outdoor education should be read in ways that go beyond conventional ideas about youth resistance. As "everyday practices of renewal and responsibility" (Corntassel, 2012), youth actions in this context serve as an entryway for seeing beyond a reaction to discriminating depictions of "Native," and towards centering notions of kinship, responsibility, freedom, and deep cultural connections in the context of place. In this, Indigenous youth exhibit an intensely constituted complex of knowing that for the most part has tended to be overlooked in educational research.

Works Referenced

Alfred, T. (1999). *Peace, power, righteousness: An Indigenous manifesto*. Oxford: Oxford University Press.

Alfred, T. (2010). What is radial imagination? Indigenous struggles in Canada. *Affinities: A Journal of Radical Theory, Culture, and Action, 4*, 2, 5–8.

Altamirano-Jiménez, I. (2004). North American first peoples: Slipping up into market citizenship? *Citizenship Studies, 8*, 4, 349–365.

Anderson, K. (1998). Science and the Savage: The Linnean Society of New South Wales, 1874–1900. *Ecumene: International Journal of Culture, Environment and Meaning, 5*, 2, 125–143.

Armstrong, J. (1996). Sharing one skin: The Okanagan community. In J. Mander & E. Goldsmiths (Eds.). *The case against the global economy*, pp. 460–470. San Francisco, CA: Sierra Books.

Battiste, M. (2002). *Indigenous knowledge and pedagogy in First Nations education: A literature review with recommendations*. Ottawa, Ontario: National Working Group on Education and Indian and Northern Affairs Canada.

Belanger, Y., Barron, L., McKay-Turnbull, C., & Mills, M. (2003). *Urban Aboriginal youth in Winnipeg: Culture and identity formation in cities*. Winnipeg: Canadian Heritage.

Berkhofer, R.F. (1978). White conceptions of Indians. In W.E. Washburn (Ed.). *Handbook of North American Indians*, Vol. 4, pp. 522–547. Washington, D.C.: Smithsonian Institution Press.

Bird, E. S. (1996). Introduction: Constructing the Indian, 1830's–1990's. In S.E. Bird (Ed.). *Dressing in feathers: The construction of the Indian in American popular culture*, pp. 1–12. Boulder, CO: Westview Press.

Canadian Council on Learning (2009). *The state of Aboriginal learning in Canada: A holistic approach to measuring success*.

Chrisjohn, R., Young, S., & Maraun, M. (2006). *The circle game: Shadow and substance in the residential school experience in Canada*. Penticton, BC: Theytus Books Ltd.

Corntassel, J. (2012). Re-envisioning resurgence: Indigenous pathways to decolonization and sustainable self-determination. *Decolonization: Indigeneity, Education & Society, 1*, 1, 86–101.

Cruikshank, J. (2005). *Do glaciers listen? Local knowledge, colonial encounters and social imagination*. Vancouver: UBC Press.

Deloria, Jr., V. (1999). "If you think about it, you will see that it is true." In B. Deloria, K. Foehner, & S. Scinta (Eds.). *Spirit & Reason: The Vine Deloria, Jr Reader*, pp. 40–60. Golden, CO: Fulcrum Publishing.

Deloria Jr., V. (2001). American Indian metaphysics. In V. Deloria, Jr. & D.R. Wildcat, *Power and place: Indian education in America*, pp. 1–6. Golden, CO: Fulcrum Resources.

Denis, C. (1997). *We are not you: First Nations and Canadian modernity*. Peterborough: Broadview Press.

Duran, B. (1996). Indigenous versus colonial discourse: Alcohol and American Indian identity. In S.E. Bird (Ed.). *Dressing in feathers: The construction of the Indian in American popular culture*, pp. 1–12. Boulder, CO: Westview Press.

Edwards, E. (1992). (Ed.). Introduction. In E. Edwards (Ed.). *Anthropology and photography, 1960–1920*, pp. 3–17. London: Royal Anthropological Institute.

Fine, M., Weis, L., Weseen, S., & Wong, M. (2003). For whom? Qualitative research, representations and social responsibilities. In N. Denzin & Y. Lincoln (Eds.). *The handbook of qualitative research*, pp. 167–207. Thousand Oaks, CA: Sage Publications.

Fixico, D. (2003). *The American Indian mind in a linear world: American Indian studies & traditional knowledge.* New York: Routledge.

Francis, D. (1992). *The Imaginary Indian: The image of the Indian in Canadian culture.* Vancouver: Arsenal Pulp Press.

Friedel, T.L. (2010). The more things change, the more they stay the same. *Cultural and Pedagogical Inquiry, 1*, 2, 22–45.

Friedel, T.L. (2011). Looking for learning in all the wrong places: Urban Native youths' cultured response to Western-oriented place-based learning. *International Journal of Qualitative Studies in Education: Special Issue—Youth Resistance Revisited, 24*, 5, 531–546.

Friesen, J.W., & Friesen, V.L. (2002). *Aboriginal education in Canada: A plea for integration.* Calgary, AB: Detselig.

Furniss, E. (1999). *Burden of history: Colonialism and the frontier myth in a rural Canadian community.* Vancouver: University of British Columbia Press.

Giroux, H. (1994). Slacking off: Border youth and postmodern education. *Journal of Advanced Composition, 14*, 2, 347–366.

Harris, C. (2004). How did colonialism dispossess? Comments from an edge of empire. *Annals of the Association of American Geographers, 94*, 1, 165–182.

Hart, M.A. (2002). *Seeking Mino-Pimatisiwin.* Halifax: Fernwood Publishing.

Hebdige, D. 1979. *Subculture in the meaning of style.* London: Methuen.

Henderson, J.Y. (2000). The context of the state of nature. In M. Battiste (Ed.). *Reclaiming Indigenous voice and vision*, pp. 11–38. Vancouver: University of British Columbia Press.

Hermes, M. (2005). "Ma'iingan is just a misspelling of the word wolf": A case for teaching culture through language. *Anthropology & Education Quarterly, 36*, 1, 43–56.

Ignas, V. (2004). Opening doors to the future: Applying local knowledge in curriculum development. *Canadian Journal of Native Education, 28*, 1/2, 49–60.

Jojola, T. (2004). Notes of identity, time, space and place. In A. Waters (Ed.). *American Indian thought*, pp. 87–96. Malden, MA: Blackwell Publishing.

King, T. (2003). *The truth about stories: A native narrative.* Toronto, ON: House of Anansi Press.

LaRocque, E. (2004). When the "Wild West" is me: Re-viewing cowboys and Indians. In L.W. Felske & B.J. Rasporich (Eds.). *Challenging frontiers: The Canadian west*, pp. 136–154. Calgary, AB: University of Calgary Press.

Li, V. (2006). *The neoprimitivist turn.* Toronto, ON: University of Toronto Press.

McLeod, N. (2000). Plains Cree identity: Borderlands, ambiguous genealogies and narrative irony. *Canadian Journal of Native Studies, 20*, 455–486.

Moreton-Robinson, A. (2004). *Whitening race: Essays in social and cultural criticism.* Canberra: Aboriginal Studies Press.

Newhouse, D., & Peters, E. (2003). *Not strangers in these parts: Urban indigenous people.* Ottawa: Indian and Northern Affairs Canada.

Office of the High Commissioner for Human Rights. n.d. Indigenous children and youth. Leaflet No. 9.

Okri, B. (1997). *A way of being free.* London: Phoenix House.

Raibmon, P. (2005). *Authentic Indians: Episodes of encounter from the late-nineteenth century Northwest coast.* Durham, NC: Duke University Press.

Redford, K.H. (1990). The ecological noble savage. *Orion Nature Quarterly, 9*, 3, 25–29.

Richards, J., & Vining, A. (2004). *Aboriginal off-reserve education – time for action.* Toronto: CD Howe Institute, Author.

Rosaldo, R. (1989). *Culture and truth: The remaking of social analysis.* Boston, MA: Beacon Press.

Silko, L.M. (1977). *Ceremony*. New York: Signet Books of New American Library.

Skutnabb-Kangas, T. (2000). *Linguistic genocide in education—Or worldwide diversity and human rights?* Mahwah, NJ: Lawrence Erlbaum.

Smith, A. (2005). *Conquest: Sexual violence and American Indian genocide.* Cambridge, MA: South End Press.

Statistics Canada (2008). *Aboriginal Peoples in Canada in 2006: Inuit, Métis and First Nations, 2006.* No. 97-558-XIE. Ottawa: Minister of Technology.

Tarrant, M.A., & Green, G.T. (1999). Outdoor recreation and the predictive validity of environmental attitudes. *Leisure Sciences, 21,* 1, 17–30.

Tuck, E. (2009). Suspending damage: A letter to communities. *Harvard Educational Review, 79,* 3, 409–428.

Vizenor, G. (1994). *Manifest manners: Narratives on postindian survivance.* Lincoln: University of Nebraska Press.

Weber-Pillwax, C. (2001). Orality in northern Cree indigenous worlds. *Canadian Journal of Native Education, 25,* 2, 149–165.

15

LGBTQ STREET YOUTH DOING RESISTANCE IN INFRAPOLITICAL WORLDS

Cindy Cruz

A misplaced gesture or a misspoken word can have terrible consequences. (James C. Scott, 1990, p. x)

We are also other than what the hegemon makes us be. (Maria Lugones, 2010, p. 746)

When feminist philosopher and popular educator Maria Lugones (2010) talks about a *resistant sociality*, I recognize this way of being in the world with others; one in which lesbian, gay, bisexual, transgender, and queer (LGBTQ) street youth share with each other gossip and information about jobs, teachers, social workers, the police, and their security guard agents. These spaces *away* from the scrutiny and examination of those in power, when queer street youth compare their experiences and analyze power, become locations of creativity and possibility. A resistant sociality also makes space for the queer youth to rest without harassment, smoke and laugh with friends, dress provocatively with new-found clothes, dance to publically taunt onlookers, but also dance to enjoy their own and each other's bodies. It allows youth to release the "muscular tension" (Fanon, 1963, p. 17) accrued from constant negotiations with teachers, police, and medical personnel.

When I first began working with queer street youth, I didn't recognize the infrapolitics, the dissident offstage practices that resisted the everyday humiliations, degradations, and experiences of exclusion that make up the daily fabric of LGBTQ youth lives. The young people I worked with often hung out together outside of the gates of the schoolyard and in front of the youth drop-in center. I often saw young people assembled at the bus stop or standing together on the sidewalks smoking cigarettes, joking around, and talking loud with each other—and often talking dramatically at other passersby. Despite a strong police presence in the public sites where my research takes place, as well as security guards at community and youth social service centers, it becomes helpful to think about youth resistance in these spaces as offstage practices (Scott, 1990) that take place just underneath the surveillance of authorities. Offstage practices are important in how we can think about resistance by LGBTQ street youth.

Maria Lugones (2003) writes about resistance in "tight spaces"—the fragile spatiality produced in such off-stage practices. This spatiality is constricted in that it is not concrete. "You are concrete. Your spatiality, constructed as an intersection following the designs of power, isn't" (p. 10). In this chapter, I engage a rethinking of resistance to capture the embodied agency of LGBTQ street youth. It is in the careful observations of the often violent intersections of the body, race, gender, and sexuality, where the "tight spaces" of youth resistance are engaged. This essay interfaces Lugones' theorizing of resistance with those by James C. Scott (1990), and Robin D.G. Kelley (1993). Everyday acts of resistance in tight spaces describe "how oneself and others violate this spatiality or inhabit it with great resistance, without willful collaboration" (Lugones, 2003, p. 10). This chapter posits ways we can reframe youth experiences that extend traditional notions of resistance, where the daily and seemingly spontaneous acts of resistance performed by LGBTQ street youth are important. Lugones' (2010) notion of a resistant sociality is particularly important in an examination of the off-stage practices that may create the breathing spaces, however tight, for LGBTQ street youth—life for otherwise disposable lives. Resistance in these instances is not about changing or intervening in the life circumstances of LGBTQ youth, nor is it about the destruction of a system of oppression. It is a deviation from the overwhelming logic of domination, a fissure in the monolithic space of oppression. These gestures and maneuvers by LGBTQ street youth movements represent departures from these logics, however small and imperceptible they may be. In spaces where the queer youth body is perceived as infected, contaminated, and often expendable, their talking back must be attended to.

Thinking Infrapolitically with Youth

> What one did was turn away smiling all the time, and tell white people what they wanted to hear. But people always accuse you of reckless talk when you say this. (James Baldwin, *A Talk to Teachers*, 1963)

Throughout my tenure as a teacher with LGBTQ students, I observed youth "talking" back to teachers, administrators, and social service workers in bodily ways. It was the exaggerated snap of fingers in someone's face, or the slow swagger of a student turning their back on an authority figure. Schools, even those places whose mission emphasized the educational experiences of LGBTQ adolescents, were the spaces where the "daily confrontations, evasive actions, and stifled thoughts" (Kelley, 1993) of an *infrapolitics* was in place. Infrapolitics, defined as the space of offstage practices (Scott, 1990, p. 4), and "dissident political cultures that manifest itself in daily conversations, folklore, jobs, songs, and other cultural practices" (Kelley, 1993, p. 77), are strategies of resistance created by subjugated communities to negotiate the continuous scrutiny and containment by the powerful. To illuminate resistance in the tight spaces of youth infrapolitics can counter deficit models, and culture of poverty models. It moves away from discourses of criminalization and poverty that haunt educational policy and research.

A deficit approach to research is often about "fixing" pathologized people. Under this rubric, change is forced upon "degenerate" bodies. Such research models attempt to enact a theory of change within a model of normality. Countering such research models requires another kind of infrapolitics. To delink or to divest oneself from the research models of radical othering requires educational and social science researchers to reframe the dialectics of domination and submission between youth and police, doctors, teachers, and other authorities.

Thinking about LGBTQ youth practices and small acts of resistance through an infrapolitical framework offers invaluable insight into the economic, political, and cultural patterns of power and resistance. Scott (1990) defines the *public transcript* (p. 45) as the public performance of deference and humility by the powerless. Further, the powerful uphold this public transcript through the maintenance of the symbols of a hierarchical social order. These *on-stage* practices of a public transcript maintain the illusion of the social order. These performances in the public sphere reveal little information, if any, of how power is wielded between communities.

> A skeptic might well ask at this point how we can presume to know, on the basis of the public transcript alone, whether this performance is genuine or not. [. . .] The answer is, surely, that we cannot know how contrived or imposed the performance is unless we can speak, as it were, to the performer offstage, out of this particular power-laden context, or unless the performer suddenly declares openly, on-stage, that the performances we have previously observed were just a pose. (Scott, 1990, p. 4)

If on-stage performance is the public transcript, the *hidden transcript* is the narrative that takes place off-stage and beyond the direct observation of powerholders (p. 14). The hidden transcript is the space of rest and leisure; a place to gossip about your bosses, teachers, caseworkers; and a place to exchange valuable information about the inner working of institutions, organizations, worksites—in this case schools and youth centers.

At the youth drop-in center where I did some of my primary observations, I often hung out with the LGBTQ students who congregated on the sidewalk, or on the roof (where there were tables and chairs). These were places to smoke cigarettes out of range from surveillance by the center security and staff. In this off-stage space, youth often shared stories, gossiped, and complained about their treatment from caseworkers and center staff.

At one point I overheard a young African American transgender woman complaining to a group of youth outside the drop-in center about her demeaning treatment by center staff, saying, "that bitch in the office called me a man." The imposition of rigid categories of gender on trans-youth who came in for services became a point of contention for many of the youth clients seeking assistance. Because they often depended on these services from the drop-in center, it necessitated a public transcript of civility between youth and staff. It might be that the sidewalk and rooftop were some of the few secure places where youth could share information, complain, and talk back about their mistreatment—out of the sight and hearing of center staff and security.

The hidden transcript helps us understand non-attendance as resistance. With the emphasis on security, more guards were hired, less training required. Youth stayed away in such numbers that some community centers were forced to cut hours and staff, if not close operations altogether.

Agency, in a resistant sociality, needs to be rethought not as an individual act but one with histories and communities that contribute to the thinking, the weighing of options against other people's experience, the discussions that happen in these off-stage spaces. Lugones (2010) names this not as agency, but as an "active subjectivity," one that recognizes a "peopled sense" of the world. In other words, a resistant sociality is collective, peopled, and intersubjective.

Access to offstage spaces is not so easily granted to researchers, whose questions and observations are perceived by youth as informing the powerful. Coded languages, like Chicana/o *caló* or the queer languages of youth, may be indecipherable and inaccessible to some. Furthermore, the frontier between the public and the hidden transcript is a "zone of constant struggle" (Scott, 1990) where our recognition of subordinate/dominant narratives and resistant/conformist behaviors is not so clear. A researcher may not even recognize, or worse, misrecognize or misinterpret certain kinds of behavior as resistance. As social scientists, we are positioned mainly to recognize a public transcript.

Researching Resistance

There is a certain stance a researcher must take when working with youth of color, homeless youth, and LGBTQ students. It is a belief that youth have something to say about their own experiences with oppression that is important, that their insight is enlightening and survivor-rich, and that you have as much to learn from youth as they from you. Sometimes the narratives that youth put forth elicit emotions that are not ones of solidarity or even empathy. This stance is not one of pity. Pity is a diversion from a deeper engagement with the issues that are central in a young person's narrative. Once you have put pity between you and the young person, there can be no bridge. Pity turns an individual into an object. She can no longer be a subject.

To research resistance is to take the stance that youth are not victims, but are often witnesses and survivors of great trauma and oppression. In order to recognize their resistance later, I have to first recognize the stories that students tell me *on their own terms*. For instance, one 18-year-old, Eastern European, queer youth told a story of meeting an older American photographer "friend" online. This friend later sends him a plane ticket to the United States so that they can meet. (The youth was 16 years old at the time of the story):

> When I got to [large East Coast city], I lived with this photographer who said that maybe I could work for him, as photography is my passion. But after a little while, things weren't going to work between us and I left him, with the cash that he had given me. I stayed with new friends for a while, crashing on their couches as I looked for work. Nobody was going to hire me—young, and now illegal, as I had already overstayed my visa. I did back work at a bar, but I didn't make enough to really live on, and slowly I found myself at the shelters.

I had to acknowledge that this was a story of youth trafficking, a queer youth lured by a potential job in photography and a plane ticket, that was reframed by the subject as a relationship. The youth then leaves the short-lived relationship with cash in hand, and soon finds himself homeless in a large East Coast city. But it was in the way that he framed the story to me that was important. In his telling, the ending of the relationship is mutual for both the youth and the photographer. The youth "leaves" the older man on his own terms. His re-casting of events is significant, from being a youth caught in the traffic of queer bodies, to a novice photographer yearning for a new life in the United States. In this zone of constant struggle, my reading of the trafficking of a young gay man becomes intimately tied to my recognition of his refusal to be defined as a victim.

What is helpful in thinking about these multiple interpretations of a narrative is Lugones' (1987) conception of "world"-travelling. "World"-travelling is the agentive negotiation of mainstream life in the US, where queer youth and women of color (and others from non-dominant communities) occupy and move through multiple worlds in their daily existence. Lugones recognizes that much of "world"-travelling is done unwillingly, within often hostile worlds. A key insight is that the self is multiple too, where the self constantly changes in its movements across multiple worlds. In a "world" of trafficking, a young person's self is exploitable, powerless, and utterly victimized. The youth refuses that "world," and instead reframes his story in a "world" where his self is ambitious and entrepreneurial. Nonetheless, a researcher also recognizes this other "world" of trafficking. In these multiple and contradictory "worlds" that exist in this example, we must attend to the conflicts between how the youth sees himself, how a researcher might see him, and how the youth sees the researcher. We must attend to "what it is to be them and what it is to be ourselves in their eyes" (Lugones, 1987, p. 17). The researcher's role becomes vital in this negotiation of multiple frames, selves, and worlds. To create different interpretations of experience, and to create new knowledges that are outside of the usual frames of pubic performances of power, is a risking together. It often means challenging both subject and researcher to see what meaning can be made. To recognize and validate the multiple narratives of this example is a critically important methodological move, where this queer street youth's story can be reclaimed as resistant, agentic, and sometimes liberatory, even when risky.

LGBTQ street youth take many calculated risks, such as the youth mentioned earlier, who weighed the chances of immigrating to the US, for a commitment of intimacy, with the costs of exploitation. In contrast to the moral panics that rationalize withholding information about safe sex, contraception, and HIV, the youth here is well-aware of the unequal transaction between a 16-year-old foreigner and an older American professional. Despite guarantees of anonymity in the research interview process,[1] it may be that the youth's testimony is still deliberately designed to have multiple meanings, to shield the identities of the actors in this story. To make sense of explicitly ambiguous narratives, we must also consider the resistant sociality in those tight spaces where meanings are developed.

Learning to be Together in a Resistant Sociality

In his study of the Black working class in the Jim Crow South, Robin D.G. Kelley (1993) discusses how workers in Birmingham, Alabama, organized their time and space with others in a way that reinforced a collective identity. It was in these spaces of Black working-class culture where workers "take back their bodies, to recuperate, to be together" (p. 84). Kelley theorizes that in places of rest and recreation—family organizations, churches, dance halls, parties, and bars— were where Black workers learned to be together outside of the institutions of white supremacy. Coming together for a dance, a party, or church reinforced the sense of shared community, knowledge, and cultural values for Black workers. I find this idea helpful in thinking about LGBTQ youth sociality, where spaces like a continuation school for LGBTQ students or a youth drop-in center, despite their problems, offer the possibility of mutuality and sociality. What happens in these youth spaces helps to explain the solidarity that queer street youth have shown in times of duress. In this case, the theory of change is not only about countering oppressive systems, but of building infrapolitical worlds that are essential for survival for LGBTQ street youth.

The Black workers in Kelley's study not only made these spaces to unmask themselves of the disguises of deference and humility, they also practiced kinships and relationships outside of racist or classist constraints. Both Lugones (2010) and Kelley (1993) suggest that these socialities can only be practiced in spaces where communities are able to define themselves outside of the frameworks of their oppressors. In off-stage spaces where youth create, define, and rehearse more egalitarian ways of relating with each other, there is an implied pedagogy.

A Pedagogy of Faithful Witnesses

To bear faithful witness is to be completely present with people. It is about listening deeply with intention. It is also about making public a commitment to interpret other people's experience "against the grain of power" (Lugones, 2010, p. 7), a commitment to documenting experience as social memory. In researching LGBTQ street youth, it is also about making public a commitment to recognizing resistance in all of its complex and intermeshing/intersecting ways. However, these experiences of both youth and researcher are always from power-laden contexts. Despite Scott's (1990) assertion that the infrapolitics of subordinate groups cannot be known unless we can speak to the performer off-stage, the presence of outsiders / ethnographers must put into question, when can researchers, even those committed to pedagogies of faithful witnessing, claim that our presence does not disrupt the resistant sociality of youth?

In one of my last engagements in my ethnography, I met Tommy, an 18-year-old gay street youth. In this excerpt from my interview fieldnotes, he turns from telling a story about his body to a critique of power, representation, and research:

> I was just thinking that maybe it was time to go home, to take care of some shit that I need to deal with. I've been here in [large city] for over nine months and it's been hard. This body can tell you a story that nobody will want to believe. Right now I can't even think about tomorrow. But I was thinking that maybe testing positive is a good thing, because nothing else seems to motivate me when it comes to taking care of myself, my body. I've lost so much weight, I'm just a bag of bones, and my arms. These sores never seem to heal. But you, this is your job, huh? Making me think? Let me show you something—
>
> *(Tommy stretches out full length on his chair.)*
>
> This body's made hundreds, thousands of dollars. Tell me, what do you think this body's worth now?

Equating a body to its in/ability to produce wealth is a discourse directed at immigrants, homeless women and men, teen mothers, and youth of color. Likewise, these same bodies are assessed on their cost to the state. Tommy implicates the research process as part of the mechanism for these neoliberal discourses. As a researcher, I was attempting to compile experiences of violence, homelessness, and the body. Tommy's response talks back to how the process of knowledge production about the queer body is reductive and predatory. He challenges the appraisal of a body's net worth in terms of dollars accumulated in a lifetime of earnings. He is also critical of the implied pedagogy in my research ("making me think") and its disciplinary effect on the research subject's own appraisal of his self.

Being present as a faithful witness is inadequate if it is reduced to only acknowledging the narratives that describe the trauma and perils of LGBTQ street youth insubordination. Researchers know very little about a homeless queer youth, if we only notice that he is homeless and hungry. We might know that he is particularly desperate to find a place to sleep that night, we might know the limited availability of beds, we might know that he may be HIV positive, and we might know he has suffered at the hands of his family or schoolmates or partner. We might have learned something about the shape of his oppression. These are certainly important understandings of the conditions facing LGBTQ street youth. However, it is critical that we challenge a social science theory of change that surmises "once we know" about LGBTQ street youth, then this knowing offers something. We must challenge the idea that things supposedly "get better" with better research. Perhaps faithful witnessing has revealed to me how a resistant sociality is necessary in the lives of queer street youth. To survive these often hostile worlds, to negotiate cooptation, youth have to resist. In the tight spaces of their resistance, we might witness the opening of new creative strategies for organizing life.

Conclusion

In *Ideology, Culture, and the Process of Schooling*, Giroux argued that resistance is the translation of a critical or political understanding of collective experience into political struggle that contests the hegemonic practices of schools. Part of that contestation is an understanding by students that political struggle is also tied to the larger struggle against the concentration of power in the capitalist state itself (1981, pp. 92–8).

Resistances in the form of traditional politics, such as mobilizing for public action and civic engagement in formal organizations, do not often work for LGBTQ street youth. What I witnessed were small yet deliberate acts by youth towards their social service workers, police, and medical personnel (Cruz, 2011). A theory of change that based on a resistant sociality may be as simple as creating "a new story of the self" (Lugones, 2000, p. 180) for LGBTQ street youth, whether in the tight spaces of the hidden transcript or the sidewalk, which in turn offers the possibilities to create ways of being and acting in the world outside of the parameters of power.

Note

1 My work with LGBTQ street youth had strict protocols for anonymity under IRB, which did not allow for any names, places, or information collected that could be linked

back to the identities of the youth I talked with. I never asked for names and coded my data by asking youth to give me two letters and two numbers, along with other demographic information. My original fieldnotes are strictly redacted. This may have freed youth to talk openly, yet the politics of the public/hidden transcript seemed a part of every public observation and every interview.

Works Referenced

Baldwin, J. (1963/1988). A talk to teachers. In Simonson, R., & Walker, S. *Multi-Cultural Literacy. The Graywolf Annual Five. Opening the American Mind*, pp. 3–12. Saint Paul, MN: Graywolf Press.

Cruz, C. (2011). LGBTQ street youth talk back: A meditation on resistance and witnessing. *QSE: International Journal of Qualitative Studies in Education, 24*, 5, 547–558.

Fanon, F. (1963). *The Wretched of the Earth*. New York: Grove Press.

Giroux, H A. (1981). *Ideology, Culture & the Process of Schooling*. Philadelphia, PA: Temple University Press.

Kelley, R. (1993). "We are not what we seem": Rethinking Black working-class opposition in the Jim Crow South. *The Journal of American History, 80*, 1, 75–112.

Lugones, M. (1987). Playfulness, "world"-travelling, and loving perception. *Hypatia, 2*, 2, 3–19.

Lugones, M. (2000). Multiculturalism and publicity. *Hypatia, 15*, 3, 175–181.

Lugones, M. (2003). *Pilgrimages/Peregrinajes: Theorizing coalition against multiple oppressions*. Lanham, MD: Rowan & Littlefield.

Lugones, M. (2010). Toward a decolonial feminism. *Hypatia, 25*, 4, 742–759.

Scott, J.C. (1990). *Domination and the Arts of Resistance: Hidden transcripts*. New Haven: Yale University Press.

16

OUT FOR IMMIGRATION JUSTICE

Thinking through Social and Political Change

Daysi Diaz-Strong, Christina Gómez,
Maria Luna-Duarte, and Erica R. Meiners

Illegal aliens, DREAMers, wetbacks and criminals—these are some of the terms still used to describe the approximately 1.8 million undocumented youth that currently reside in the United States. Most of the youth came to the United States with their parents, guardians, and in some cases arrived by themselves. They have grown up in the United States, attended elementary schools, high schools, and often lived their lives as though they were "American" except that they are not. Many of them now attend colleges and universities across the country and challenge the status quo of what it means to be one of the 11.1 million undocumented people who live in the United States (Passel & Cohn, 2012).

According to the Migration Policy Institute, approximately 140,000 undocumented students attended institutions of higher education across the United States. Another 80,000 already have a college degree—about 48 percent from two-year programs, 43 percent from four-year programs and 8 percent from graduate schools. The majority of these students, 85 percent, come from Latin America and the Caribbean; approximately 9 percent come from Asia and 6 percent from other countries (Batalova & Mittelstadt, 2012). These undocumented students lack the legal status to have a "normal life" in the United States; they do not possess official social security numbers, visas, resident alien cards, or other documents that would allow them to reside or work legally in this country. Only recently (June 2012) has a new program, Deferred Action for Childhood Arrivals (DACA), given these youth the ability to apply for legal employment, but no option for obtaining citizenship and no guarantees for permanent legal residency.

Building on our research and advocacy project with undocumented youth, this chapter examines how undocumented youth struggle to resist dehumanization and, consignment to low-wage work, redefine and negotiate their identities, and with an awareness of social justice frameworks generate new and unique ways to circumvent oppressive environments. Centering the resistances of undocumented youth, this chapter explores how "coming out" worked to redefine what it means to be "undocumented" in the United States from an invisible or negative image to a story of people who struggle to flourish within a punishing and unjust environment.

Our Locations and Work

This research evolved from our outrage with the escalating anti-immigrant and anti-Latino climate that many undocumented immigrants faced in the United States in recent years. The media coverage further exacerbated this condition by routinely depicting Latino immigrants as "illegal aliens" while offering little historical context to the nation's immigration policies and trends. Chavez (2008) presents several arguments regarding the public discourse on Latinos as a group that has been "plagued by the mark of illegality, in which in much public discourse means that they are criminals and thus illegitimate members of society undeserving of social benefits, including citizenship" (p. 3). This threat narrative outlines the debate over immigration policies, and shapes public discussions that reframe access to human rights into questions about who does and does not deserve certain privileges. Our research and organizing project occurred during this oppressive context for immigration "reform" where all proposed federal legislation has floundered. As a team of people composed of formerly undocumented people and non-U.S. citizens, and all of us with loved ones without status, we knew the mainstream public representation of those without legal status in the U.S. was harmful and erroneous.

Over a two-and-a-half-year period (2007–2010), we interviewed 40 currently and formerly undocumented youths and collected their oral histories, centering on educational experiences while addressing other issues, including family, border crossings, relationships to U.S. identity, and future plans.[1] In addition, our project included our participation in many public meetings, campaigns, and gatherings related to immigration justice. This component of our work continues.

In particular, the site of the university or college and the figure of the student emerged as a contested site of social movement development. The Latina/o youth we interviewed were denied access to most avenues of support for postsecondary education, to social assistance benefits, and to legal employment, and many learned to live in constant fear of visiting public spaces and travel. Despite the stigma, legal and political risks, and potential implications for family members and loved ones, several of the youth participants in our project (and many in our communities) organized with advocacy groups, participated in marches, engage in civil disobedience, and some "came out" publicly to classmates, teachers, and to media sources as undocumented. These activist demonstrations took place from California to Georgia on radio stations and in local papers, in church basements and on the steps of city halls. Our interviews, observations, fieldwork, and participation in social movements also suggest that young people active in immigrant justice organizing understand how their lives are linked to wider social inequalities and how their tactics are partial and temporal.

Political Contexts

Access to education for undocumented students has been controlled in part by federal and state policies. In the 1982 U.S. Supreme Court case *Plyler v. Doe*, the court held that states could not discriminate against students enrolling in K–12 public schools in the United States on the basis of their legal status; the decision, however, did not address public education beyond high school. In the absence of federal guidelines for higher education, states have created their own rules. Although undocumented students can apply to most colleges, they are not eligible for federal or state financial aid. As of July 2012, only 12 states allow undocumented students who meet specific requirements to receive in-state tuition rates at public postsecondary institutions (National Conference of State Legislatures, 2012).

This uneven landscape facilitated organizing at college and university campuses across the United States. In particular, this context supported the only piece of legislation that has had any traction in Congress related to immigration in the last decade. First introduced in 2001 by Senators Richard Durbin of Illinois and Orrin Hatch of Utah, the DREAM Act (Development, Relief, and Education for Alien Minors) attempted to provide a potential path to legal residency for select undocumented students; as of October 2012 the DREAM Act has not passed. The last iteration of this legislation (2010) would have provide undocumented students who arrived in the United States before the age of 16, have lived in the country for at least five years, and are of "good moral character," temporary residency for six years during which time they must obtain at least an associate's degree or complete two years of military service. After satisfying these requirements, a young person *could* be eligible to receive permanent residency. Those who do not meet the requirements would be subject to deportation. While the DREAM Act could help undocumented students enrolled in postsecondary education, it would not help their families. The military-service provision must also be questioned as Latinos (the majority of undocumented students) have low rates of college entry and college completion.

Given the failure of the DREAM Act in 2010, and new political conditions in 2012 (mainly due to elections, the increasing Latino electorate, and the need for politicians to cater to specific actors to gain political support), President Obama announced on June 15, 2012 potential reprieve from deportations for the 1.8 (according to recent estimates) million undocumented youth residing in the United States, through the Deferred Action for Childhood Arrivals (DACA). This change in policy came as a memo directive from the Obama Administration through Janet Napolitano, Secretary of Homeland Security (2012), indicating the following:

> I am setting forth how, in the exercise of our prosecutorial discretion, the Department of Homeland Security (DHS) should enforce the Nation's immigration laws against certain young people who were brought to this country as children and know only this country as home. As a general matter, these individuals lacked the intent to violate the law and our ongoing review of pending removal cases is already offering administrative closure to many of them. (Napolitano, 2012)

This new policy opened the door for undocumented youth to potentially halt their deportations and obtain a work permit to seek legal employment. This policy is a presidential directive that allows undocumented individuals who are under 31 years of age and came to the U.S. before 16 years of age, to apply for employment authorization. However, it is not a "direct path to lawful permanent residence or to citizenship and can be revoked at any time" (Immigration Equality). DACA permits some undocumented individuals to apply for the ability to work "legally," but it also opens up the possibility of removal proceedings, and even if deferred action is granted, it can be revoked at any time. The cost for applying is a minimum of $465 and is prohibitive for many. As of December 2012, 367,903 applications for DACA had been received; 102,965 applications had been approved and 12,014 were rejected (U.S. Citizenship and Immigration Service, 2012). For many undocumented students DACA has opened up the possibility for legal work, but the situation is little changed. There is still no pathway to citizenship, and their family members who do not fit the narrow requirements under DACA have no options. It is a temporary fix to a major issue that affects millions of undocumented youth, and only those eligible fit the stereotype of the "good immigrant," while leaving their parents and siblings behind.

Beyond DACA, the most recent significant change since the November 2012 elections is the turnaround by many Republicans who are now publicly voicing some measure of support for legalizing the status of undocumented individuals. Even Senator Rand Paul of Kentucky has been on record as more sympathetic toward a liberal immigration policy (Parker & Shear, 2013). By "coming out" as undocumented students might have indirectly helped with the Republican Party's 2012 election losses, which blamed "immigration" and the "Latino" voting bloc, which was estimated to have been 10 percent of the electorate. This leads some to believe that a comprehensive immigration reform bill might be possible in the near future, as occurred in 1986 through IRCA, the Immigration Reform and Control Act under President Ronald Reagan (Preston & Santos, 2012).

The failure of the passage of the DREAM Act, which would have granted undocumented youth a pathway to U.S. citizenship if they met specific requirements, forced undocumented youth to "out" themselves and resist possible deportation. The credit for DACA must be given to the undocumented students that have chosen to fight and not remain silent in their quest for dignity and legalization in the U.S. In the words of Ginwright, Cammarota and Noguera (2005, p. 32), "youth collective action is a rational response to state control and repression." By resisting the shame imposed on them for being undocumented and naming who they are in public spaces, undocumented youth refused isolation and built networks of solidarity and worked to educate key stakeholders in political and educational arenas about immigration. This form of organizing and resistance also shaped a national debate about how to support these students.

Outing as Resistance

Starting in 2007, students across the nation began to hold "Coming Out of the Shadows" rallies to testify before friends, family, and strangers that they are undocumented. Their testimonies often included their experiences of crossing the border, struggles to secure living wage work, and/or being arrested or witnessing the arrest or deportation of family members. With the failure to pass the DREAM Act in 2010, undocumented students felt there were few options to raise awareness of their situation. The first big "Coming Out of the Shadows" rally was in Chicago in March 2010, and media coverage of these youth, was largely sympathetic in mainstream papers, as in this coverage of a rally in New York:

> She was tiny and trembling and looked so very vulnerable. Barely 15, having already experienced a lifetime of hardships since losing her mother at 5 and crossing the desert with her father, she clutched a microphone before a crowd in New York's Union Square. "My name is Diana," she said. "I am undocumented and unafraid." (O'Neill, 2012)

The stories told at these rallies are often tear-filled and frequently detail horrendous journeys across borders. While these public "coming out" events participated in reshaping the landscape for immigration in the U.S. they developed as a direct result of years of organizing that failed to secure even a sliver of immigration reform.

In Chicago, the Immigrant Youth Justice League (IYJL), an organization led by undocumented activists, has been at the forefront of organizing "coming out" events. This strategy of "coming out," along with the slogan "undocumented, and unafraid" was first proposed by IYJL members in May 2010, and has been replicated nationally each year (IYJL, 2011). While many of the first gatherings were held at universities, since 2010 rallies have been held all over the country in public spaces. Instead of remaining quiet, or "passing" as youth with citizenship, these speech acts bring attention to themselves and name who they are— *undocumented, unafraid and unapologetic.* These students have decided to "come out" as *unafraid* because they could no longer live in fear, thus advocating for change and reform, and reasserting the sense of fear to become fearless. They are also *unapologetic* because they feel that they should not apologize for their families—mainly their parents—who brought them here in search of a better life and educational opportunities.

Through public counter-storytelling, undocumented youth have struggled to deliver varied messages to different communities. The impacts of their counter-storytelling are diverse. Youth have functioned to shame unfamiliar audiences into understanding a reality that many have refused to incorporate into our historical memories and current reality, to reclaim lives and families from the frontal assault on immigration by media and politicians, and to signify solidarity with a wide range of people experiencing trauma and punishment from immigration policies. Solórzano and Yosso (2002, p. 32) suggest that counter-story is a method of telling the stories of those people whose experiences are not often told—those on the margins of society. These stories or narratives about the realities of life for these undocumented youth destroy and reconstruct the preconceived notions about undocumented individuals. The activism of this immigrant youth and their counter-storytelling pushed many in power, including the President of the United States, to react and begin a dialogue about immigration and devise solutions that could lead to immigration reform.

"Coming out" as undocumented, of course, does not just happens at rallies and other public political events, but in many intimate settings including classrooms. As educators, students "come out" when we teach, particularly during classes that include discussions of immigration, identity or race. These speech acts are complex. In our experiences, sometimes students feel empowered and free of the burden of keeping this secret. For others "coming out" is an opportunity to speak publicly about deep feelings, anger, frustration, and sadness. These acts allow young people to claim their identities as undocumented, but they can also make others, including people who are undocumented, feel uncomfortable. Interestingly, sometimes in this difficult space a solidarity is formed; the act of coming out brings the group together and attracts others who might have similar stories, but are not quite ready to reveal their stories. Not all undocumented students are ready or want to publicly "out" themselves.

In addition to the marked increase in the number of youth "coming out" as undocumented, a smaller number have also "come out" as non-heterosexual. Many of these individuals (and sometimes related organizations) explicitly state that their tactic of "coming out" as undocumented comes from, or is intimately linked to, their experiences of the power of "coming out" as non-heterosexual and the trajectory of "coming out" as a political act within lesbian and gay liberation movements. In cover articles for the *New York Times* magazine and *Time Magazine* successful journalist Jose Antonio Vargas "comes out" as gay and undocumented and explicitly links these trajectories. Vargas describes both experiences of "coming out" and writes:

> Tough as it was, coming out about being gay seemed less daunting than coming out about my legal status. I kept my other [immigration] secret mostly hidden. (Vargas, 2011)

In his cover article in *Time Magazine*, which includes portraits of men and women who also out themselves as undocumented, Vargas explicitly makes the connections between gay liberationists "coming out" and the tactics of the contemporary (youth) undocumented movement. These speech acts have highlighted tense relationships between the state, access to citizenship, race, and compulsory heterosexuality. Potential pathways for legalization almost always include and reify "family" reunification or heterosexual marriage, and lesbian, gay, and transgender lives do not have legal access to these legitimatizing and capital-producing institutions.

This tactic of outing has been used at mass rallies as a form of popular political education, but it has also been used to shift particular cases and to provide protection for individuals facing deportation. For example, Rigo Padilla, a University of Illinois at Chicago student who was scheduled to be deported in December 2009, was able to stay in the country after his deportation was deferred. There was strong public support for this student from various constituencies that included student organizations, university faculty members, community leaders, and state and federal legislators. Rallies, letter-writing campaigns, and petitions quickly circulated to help stay his deportation. Padilla became "a symbol to immigration activists yearning for passage of the DREAM Act" (Olivo, 2009).

The landscape for self-identifying as undocumented publicly has shifted dramatically in a short time period. One of our respondents in our project, Jorge, a student interviewed in 2008, reflects how cautious he is when speaking or revealing to others about this undocumented status:

> I think most people are afraid of revealing their status. I don't disclose this to others unless I trust them, but I personally never let nobody know anything, it can always come back to hurt you and so forth, so I don't trust them, I don't tell them anything period. (Jorge, age 22)

Jorge's comments highlight the shifting contexts of immigration policies and how young people who publicly identify as undocumented (plus years of immigration justice organizing) have altered the affective landscape for many.

While the sociopolitical contexts surrounding public disclosures of immigration status for select groups of young people may have shifted, our interviews highlighted the reality that parents, especially, warned their children about being careful and not divulging their undocumented status. Despite these parental concerns and a widening culture of increasing surveillance and punitive actions towards those undocumented, according to Immigration and Custom's Enforcement's data, the annual number of deportations has been stable in the last few years: 370,000 in Fiscal Year 2008, 390,000 in FY 2009, 393,000 in FY 2010, and 397,000 in FY 2011. Other estimates indicate that close to 1,500 people per day have been deported (Lerner, 2012).

As the number of undocumented students entering or wanting to enter the legal workforce or higher education continued to grow, the pressure to find other possibilities for survival and mobility increased. This act of resistance, of naming oneself publicly, even though there exists possible dangers—arrest, deportation, social distancing by friends, and loss of trust—became a strong and available option to build a social movement. Prior to these rallies many undocumented were silent about their status for fear of being deported. Silence about being undocumented signaled the "wrongness" or "shame" of the situation. It also did not allow for knowing who actually was undocumented and consequently a difficulty in organizing. Public naming contributed to consequently was unable to build community, producing an important form of social capital.

As the most "protected" category of an immigrant subject tended to be the figure of the child and the student, and because the only piece of immigration legislation that has had any traction over the last decade is the DREAM Act that centered students, college and university campuses have emerged (and continue to be) as pivotal sites of organizing and change. As more undocumented students "come out," these students began to collectivize and to push back on how their colleges and universities work with and support undocumented students.

One of the positive things that has come about as a result of undocumented students' advocacy is that some colleges and universities across the nation have listened to the needs of these students, and their support for policy reform around the issue of undocumented students has been rather public. For example, the Illinois DREAM Act, signed by Governor Pat Quinn, on August 1, 2012, gained support from a number of Illinois college and university presidents from state and private institutions. The Illinois Dream Act serves undocumented students to gain access to private scholarships, and college savings, and to educate high school counselors about educational opportunities for undocumented students (Illinois General Assembly, 2012). As more students came out, and the federal government continued to stall on a response to immigration, activists mobilized within states to shift educational policies to improve access for undocumented students. They also pushed hard within their institutions to change discriminatory policies and practice, and to offer visible services to support undocumented students, and expanded work to include those in mixed-status families including the barriers faced by students who are U.S. citizens, but whose parents are undocumented.

Yet as these colleges/universities offer their open support, there are individuals in high-level positions who are not in favor of policies benefiting undocumented students, and who have the power to create policies that will hinder the funding of these institutions of higher education if they favor immigrants. South Carolina and Alabama offer examples of states that do not allow undocumented students to apply to public universities.

Building Social Change

As we reflect back on our almost five years of work together and alongside many others working for immigration justice, we conclude not by drawing any broad conclusions about social movements or social change, but rather our collective points of learning from our work and our engagement. These points of learning, or forms of social movement analysis, point to possible ways to understand how political shifts, always dynamic, happen. We conclude by offering four interrelated observations from our ongoing work that frame our ideas about the work of social change.

First, we highlight how *self-determination*, or the right of people to shape their own political and personal pathways, is central to all social change movements, and leadership and analysis by those most impacted facilitates the development of self-determination. We started this project as extension of political work that impacted our lives and the lives of people we loved because we rejected the narratives, representation and the dominant political frameworks that were made available to new migrants. Our participation in immigration justice social movements shaped us to both recognize the importance of the *principle* and the *right* of self-determination. When people in movements have the time and space and claim the right to self-determination, radical transformations are possible. This is hardly a new observation. Black power, queer liberation, and disability justice activists (and many others) have long championed that stigma and dehumanization is made possible through the isolation and shame that is produced and circulated through oppressive forces that seek to violently suppress self-determination. Sometimes, the act of claiming self-determination and "coming out" (as queer, as undocumented) is the most radically transformative act. Although a full path to citizenship was not achieved by the undocumented youth that "came out," this movement did achieve short-term reforms, such as DACA, that could make a difference in the lives of some, and could lead to a more permanent solution.

Second, *collectivization* is vital for social and political change. In our own project we learned both to support one another and to work across our differences, and these practices created stronger work and deeper analysis. Beyond our team, through collectivization individuals became stronger, potentially able to address their own harm, and develop vocabularies and strategies for personal and political transformation through collectivization.

Third, while we doubt that the "no borders movement" (Anderson, Sharma, & Wright, 2011) will see any traction in the immigration platforms that will arrive in 2013—we are enlivened and inspired by *radical movements and analysis* that push beyond the norm. Radical analysis—from prison abolition to no borders—expands our imaginations and widens the possibilities of what constitutes a response to injustice. While all too often these radical demands are dismissed as not pragmatic or trivialized as utopic, we see clearly in immigration justice work how, for example, young people's radical critique of the militarization of immigration embedded the DREAM Act functioned, not to dismantle the military or to senselessly fracture social movements, but to politically educate millions about role(s) of the military in the lives if new migrants. The "unapologic and unafraid" campaigns of many groups of young people across the Unites States, almost unthinkable initiatives only a few years earlier, remade the terrain for immigration politics. The shift of young people to come out as queer and undocumented, to ask for more than what was offered—full legalization for all, not just students—changed the game. These demands ignite radical imaginations that force us to leave no one behind, and to challenge responses to injustice that prioritize select communities over others, or offer a small number the promise of more access to rights while conferring civil death on too many others.

Finally, in our work within and alongside immigration justice movements we also observe the strong recuperative and co-optive power of oppressive systems and forces, reminding us that power and oppression are not static, but rather are dynamic forces. Justice is not something to achieve, a set of goal posts to pass, but is something we must continually build, together. Social change work is *intellectual* and *dynamic* work. Thirty years from now, even if we have closed our immigration prisons, and allowed gays the right to marry, what forms of punishment will be in place, what systems of stigmatization and isolation will be in practice, and which bodies will be targeted for this capture? How can our work anticipate and intervene in these shifts? How will "normativity" and race, particularly anti-Blackness, still be central to these forms of capture? The work of social change is to keep our eyes on the prize and collectively build liberation that leave no one behind.

Note

1 We accessed formal and informal networks, and interviewed youths through snowball sampling. Our participants are self-identified Latino students (at least 18 years of age) already enrolled in high school or college and working to be academically successful. This is a select sample and not representative of the total population of undocumented youth in the Chicago region or the nation. In total, we interviewed 27 female and 13 male students.

Works Referenced

Anderson, B., Sharma N., & Wright, C. (Eds.). 2011. Special Issue on "No borders as a practical political project." *Refuge, 26*, 2 [dated Fall 2009].

Batalova, J., & Mittelstadt M. (2012). *Relief from deportation: Demographic profile of the DREAMers potentially eligible under the deferred action policy*. Washington, D.C.: Migration Policy Institute.

Chavez, L. (2008). *The Latino threat: Constructing immigrants, citizens, and the nation.* Stanford, CA: Stanford University Press.

Diaz-Strong, D., Gómez, C., Luna-Duarte, M., & Meiners, E. (2012). Undocumented Latino youth: Strategies for accessing higher education. In P. Noguera, A. Hurtado, & E. Fergus (Eds.). *Invisible no more: Understanding the disenfranchisement of Latino men and boys.* New York: Routledge.

Fordham, S. (2010). Passin' for Black: Race, identity, and bone memory in postracial America. *Harvard Educational Review, 80,* 1, 4–30.

Ginwright, S., & Cammarota, J. (2002). New terrain in youth development: The promise of a social justice approach. *Social Justice, 29,* 4, 82–95.

Ginwright, S., Cammarota, J., & Noguera, P. (2005). Youth, social justice, and communities: Toward a theory of urban youth policy. *Social Justice, 32,* 3, 24–40.

Illinois General Assembly. (2012). Full Text of SB2185, Illinois Dream Act. Retrieved from http://www.ilga.gov/legislation/fulltext.asp?DocName=&SessionId=84&GA=97&DocTypeId=SB&DocNum=2185&GAID=11&LegID=58384&SpecSess=0&Session=0

Immigration Equality. (2013). Deferred Action for Childhood Arrivals (DACA). Retrieved from http://immigrationequality.org/issues/immigration-basics/daca/

Immigrant Youth Justice League. (2011, February 24). Coming out of the shadows: Undocumented, unafraid, unapologetic. Retrieved from www.lyjl.org/?p=1914

Jones, M. (2010, October 21). Coming out illegal. *The New York Times Magazine.* Retrieved from http://www.nytimes.com/2010/10/24/magazine/24DreamTeam-t.html?pagewanted=all

Lerner, G. (2012, October 21). How many people have really been deported under Obama? *New York Times.* Retrieved from http://www.huffingtonpost.com/2012/03/01/deportation-numbers-obama_n_1314916.html

Muhammad, K.G. (2010). *The condemnation of Blackness: Race, crime, and the making of urban America.* Cambridge, MA: Harvard University Press.

Napolitano, J. (2012, June 15). U.S. Department of Homeland Security, Washington, D.C. Retrieved from http://www.dhs.gov/xlibrary/assets/s1-exercising-prosecutorial-discretion-individuals-who-came-to-us-as-children.pdf

National Conference of State Legislatures. (2012, July). Undocumented Student Tuition: State Action. Washington, D.C. Retrieved from http://www.ncsl.org/issues-research/educ/undocumented-student-tuition-state-action.aspx

Olivo, A. (2009, December 6). Rigo Padilla: Support grows to fight UIC student's deportation. *Chicago Tribune.* Retrieved from http://articles.chicagotribune.com/2009-12-06/news/0912050311_1_uic-deportation-top-students

O'Neill, H. (2012, September 16). Teenage undocumented immigrants coming out of the shadows. *Huffington Post.* Retrieved from http://www.huffingtonpost.com/2012/05/20/teenage-undocumented-immigrants_n_1530923.html

Parker, A., & Shear, M.D. (2013, March 19). GOP opposition to immigration law is falling. *New York Times.* Retrieved from http://www.nytimes.com/2013/03/20/us/politics/gop-opposition-to-immigration-law-is-falling-away.html?pagewanted=all&_r=0

Passel, J.S. (2005, March 21). Estimates of the size and characteristics of the undocumented population. *Pew Hispanic Center.* Retrieved from http://www.pewhispanic.org/files/reports/44.pdf

Passel, J.S., & Cohn, D. (2011, February 1). Unauthorized immigrant population: National and state trends. *Pew Hispanic Center.* Retrieved from http://www.pew hispanic.org/2011/02/01/unauthorized-immigrant-population-brnational-and-state-trends-2010/

Preston, J., & Santos, F. (2012, November 7). A record Latino turnout, solidly backing Obama. *New York Times.* Retrieved from http://www.nytimes.com/2012/11/08/us/politics/with-record-turnout-latinos-solidly-back-obama-and-wield-influence.html

Solórzano, D., & Yosso, T.J.. (2002). Critical race methodology: Counter-story telling as an analytical framework for education research. *Qualitative Inquiry, 8* (1), 23–44.

UCLA Center for Labor Research and Education. (2007). Undocumented students, unfulfilled dreams. Retrieved from http://www.labor.ucla.edu/publications/reports/Undocumented-Students.pdf

U.S. Citizenship and Immigration Service. Deferred Action for Childhood Arrivals Process, August 15–December 13, 2012. Retrieved from http://www.uscis.gov/USCIS/Resources/Reports%20and%20Studies/Immigration%20Forms%20Data/All%20Form%20Types/DACA/DACA%20MonthlyDEC%20Report%20PDF.pdf.pdf

Vargas, J.A. (2011, June 22). My life as an undocumented immigrant. *New York Times, Magazine.* Retrieved from http://www.nytimes.com/2011/06/26/magazine/my-life-as-an-undocumented-immigrant.html?pagewanted=all

Wilderson, F. (2003). The prison slave as hegemony's (silent) scandal. *Social Justice, 30,* 2, 18–27.

AFTERWORD

Ruth Wilson Gilmore

Scholarship at its best is mind-expanding[1]

The scholarship in the 1980s on social movements pushed to locate the resistance in every part of everyday life. The mind-expanding part of that scholarship alerted us to the fact that there are many more things that we can do, and that we *already* do, to resist than we might otherwise recognize.

However, to some degree the work that flowed from that work became a caricature of itself, and started representing everything that anybody did to "the man" as resistance. It seemed to say that anything and everything was resistance. The task that we face now is to bring the good thinking of *resistance is everywhere* back, without falling prey to the notion that all you have to do is point at something and say, "it's resistance" and be done. Because if we don't get that richness of resistance in many aspects of life back into the front of our consciousness, then the situation can feel so dire that many people will feel hopeless, think narrowly, and check out rather than step up.

The central contradiction of modernity is freedom. One of the things that makes me a Marxist in the radical tradition shaped by thinkers such as Amilcar Cabral, Claudia Jones, Angela Y. Davis, and many others is that we must understand the relationship of how a certain kind of freedom is linked to the possibility of capitalist expansion, and therefore the necessity of undoing that, so that a greater freedom can be realized by everybody. Thinking about capitalism—which is actually the problem that most demands our attention in these times, and demands we develop the ability to imagine alternatives to it—connects with problematizing resistance—clarifying our understanding that resistance is everywhere but not everything is resistance. In the last few years, we have seen a kind of resurgence in consumer activism. For example, certain manufacturers now have a label called (RED)™. If you buy whatever thing, (PRODUCT)^RED, ten cents of the profit will go to some starving or oppressed person or cause somewhere. These campaigns that promote a kind of foolish optimism that we can buy our way, shop our way to a post-dispossessed world, are kind of silly. But with that said, there still are possibilities in consumer activism that have been born out of necessity.

The boycott, for example, is a type of engagement with capitalism. It is a tool that people in different places are trying to think through very carefully; a tool that Laura Pulido examines beautifully in her first book, *Environmentalism and Economic Justice: Two Chicano Struggles in the Southwest*. She works through how the United Farm Workers (UFW) figured out a number of different ways that different kinds of people could participate in the farmworker movement. Some might send a check; other people might hang up a *no uvas* sign. Still other people could participate by not buying the boycotted product. The UFW successfully developed what used to be thought of as an invincible weapon—the boycott—to create all these different ways to get people at various removes from the farmworkers and the fields to become involved in a labor action that needed a concerted effort. An example from today would be the people working to develop Boycotts, Divestments, and Sanctions (BDS) with firms that do business in the Occupied Territories of the West Bank and Gaza. And others who put the same keen focus on Occupied Kashmir.

So, having noted the problem as well as the promise of boycotts in the work of resistance and liberation, I continue to worry about the extent to which some people participate in and believe that boycotts are the answer *because* they cannot imagine alternatives to capitalism. There are limits to the kinds of freedom made possible through capitalist expansion. And yet it is also true that resistances to and through capitalism should make us pause and think systematically how it is that the central contradiction of modernity is freedom. What do we wish freedom could be, and how do we recognize the entanglements and engagements happening all over the world, including in the United States, to expand or contract what freedom is and how we live it? I realize that the word freedom can seem jingoistic. But it should not: Just as we must imagine a world beyond capitalism, and a world beyond cages, so too must we imagine freedom that is not an export of U.S. imperialism but rather something made through the persistent efforts of many people on behalf of themselves and an unknown future. Remember, there were three great revolutions at the end of the eighteenth century, but only one, Haiti's, ended with all the people in the territory free. Let me give an example of what I mean.

So Too With Me

I recently got to talk about resistance, scholarship, and imagination with Laura Pulido as part of a Participatory Open Online Course (POOC) called *Inq13: Reassessing Inequality and Reimagining the 21st Century, East Harlem Focus* facilitated by Wendy Luttrell, Caitlin Cahill and other faculty at The Graduate Center,

The City University of New York. In that conversation, Laura told us that as a young person, she was profoundly influenced by stories of Harriet Tubman. She connected Harriet Tubman to imaginations beyond slavery, beyond capitalism, beyond apartheid, beyond occupation. I share this with Laura, having also been inspired by Harriet Tubman.

Harriet Tubman tells a great story about freedom: The what and the how and the who of it. She says she once knew a man who was sentenced to prison for a very long time, decades and decades. While in prison, all he could think about was going home, and seeing his old people, and getting back there. Eventually, the time came when he was free. He left the prison and he went back to the old home, to the town where he lived. His house wasn't there. And his family wasn't there. When he got back to the place he was from, *there was no one there to take his hand, and welcome him back to the world.*

So too with me, Harriet Tubman said. *I achieved freedom, I achieved that thing that I always dreamed for myself. And then, when I got to the North, there was no one there to take my hand.* So she realized, *I can't do this just for myself.* She decided, *I have to go back and do it over and over and over and over again.*

So too with me is a wisdom cultivated in living a life of resistance, in living along lifelines of resistance. Being there to take your hand, is a way of living that Cedric Robinson called the Black Radical Tradition, a tradition that has accumulated since the first instant that chattel slavery came into being. The work of those who forged that tradition has always been to figure out a way to make freedom meaningful for somebody they didn't know and might never see. This work does not just take place between two people who are family, as in "This is my child, this is my relative, and therefore I'm going to take care of them," or even between friends. They're *strangers*, actually. Some people just live this way. It's a way of being in the world. One need not be of African descent—although all humans are—and be of a tradition in which the principle of freedom is the greatest motivation, and the survival of the collective is the purpose of life. The Black Radical Tradition has a compelling energetic sense that the central dynamic or narrative of our lives should unroll as a narrative of freedom. Further, we have the *obligation* and the *ability* to figure out how to make that happen. So too, as Harriet Tubman says, so too with me, I will be the someone there to take your hand.

Some people may feel that academic scholarship on injustice and resistance is beside the point—maybe because it is too intellectual and not activist enough. I want to remind readers that whenever extreme repression takes over in any place, its agents become really organized about getting rid of the intellectuals. They slaughter them, they defund research, privatize schools, dismiss professors. They crush the capacity—which is the power—to learn and teach, so that we can't use our time and skills to learn so that other people can learn. Being a public scholar, or a scholar-activist, or anything that has "scholar" in name, means that *you are a scholar*, that you are engaged in critique. Studying the injustices that we also want to change often means going back and forth between despair—of the statements, the archives, the government data that are so painful to read—and the joy in getting glimpses of resistance, of patterns of resistance, of the emergence of freedom over and over from the ground up. There are times that this work fills me with me with the most joy I can imagine, just from figuring stuff out, and figuring it out well so that other people can use it.

Returning to the wisdom accumulated in resistance: Harriet Tubman went South, time after time after time, first working in the Underground Railroad, then as a spy for the Union Army during the Civil War. She was learning things and figuring out things that other people were going to have to rely on to live. I take really seriously that if I do something badly in my scholarship, it could hurt people. I don't really care about my career—it's turned out to be a nice career—but I don't care about my career; I care about somebody picking up my book and saying, "Oh, this is how things work," and then going off and being bamboozled because I didn't do a good job.

We as public scholars have the obligation—as well as a kind of joyful responsibility—to do a fantastic job figuring things out—a fantastic job on the scholarly part, so that we can help make tools that will be weapons for change. Figuring out resistance and theorizing change only for the academy won't help, but doing it well so that many people can use it, can make an enormous difference in the world.

The work in this volume is a wonderful example of what I mean. The scholarship is careful, it's committed, and it shows us what can be done on the ground. It deals with difficult subjects but refuses despair. In other words, it follows the narrative arc of freedom as something that we make over, and over again—in the face of disappointment, outrage, and systematically produced and reinforced vulnerability. Mostly, the chapters in this book assure me that the capacity to make freedom, imaginatively and energetically, prevails, especially among young people. So too with all of us . . .

Note

1   This Afterword is in part built upon a May 7, 2013 livestream discussion between Ruth Wilson Gilmore (in Lisbon at the time) and Laura Pulido (in Los Angeles) (see the recorded discussion at this link, http://inq13.gc.cuny.edu/module-12/).

Works Referenced

Pulido, L. (1996). *Environmentalism and economic justice: Two Chicano struggles in the Southwest.* Tucson: University of Arizona Press.

LIST OF CONTRIBUTORS

Aekta Shah is a Student/Research Associate at Harvard Graduate School of Education, Co-Founder of the Big Green Bus, and Student Director for Enrichment at Dartmouth (SEAD).

Allison Scott is Director of Research and Evaluation at the Level Playing Field Institute where she conducts and manages empirical research related to hidden bias and barriers in K–12, higher education, and the workplace.

Antwi A. Akom is an award-winning educator, scholar, writer, a leading expert on the Green Economy, participatory action research, and climate change and co-founder of the Environmental Sustainability Planning Network (ESPN), a national learning and climate change action network.

Christina Gómez is Associate Professor of Sociology, and Latino and Latin American Studies at Northeastern Illinois University.

Cindy Cruz is an Assistant Professor in the Department of Education at the University of California, Santa Cruz.

Daysi Diaz-Strong is a graduate student in Social Service Administration at the University of Chicago.

Erica R. Meiners is Professor of Education and Women's and Gender Studies and a faculty affiliate in Latino and Latin American Studies at Northeastern Illinois University.

Eve Tuck is Assistant Professor of Educational Foundations and Coordinator of Native American Studies at the State University of New York at New Paltz.

Gerald Vizenor is Distinguished Professor of American Studies at the University of New Mexico and Professor Emeritus of American Studies at the University of California, Berkeley.

Greg Dimitriadis is Professor of Educational Leadership and Policy at the Graduate School, University at Buffalo, The State University of New York.

J.I. Albahri is a student at the University of California, San Diego, and a principal member of Students for Justice in Palestine.

James C. Scott is the Sterling Professor of Political Science and Professor of Anthropology and is Director of the Agrarian Studies Program at Yale University.

K. Wayne Yang is Assistant Professor of Ethnic Studies at the University of California, San Diego.

Lisa (Leigh) Patel is Associate Professor of Education at Boston College.

Maria Luna-Duarte is the Interim Director of NEIU-El Centro Campus, and an educational policy studies doctoral student in Policy Studies in Urban Education at the University of Illinois at Chicago.

Michelle Fine is a Distinguished Professor of Social Psychology, Women's Studies and Urban Education at the Graduate Center, CUNY and is a founding faculty member of the Public Science Project (PSP).

Monique Guishard is an Instructor of Psychology at the Bronx Community College, The City University of New York (CUNY) and doctoral candidate in the Social-Personality Psychology program at The Graduate Center, CUNY.

Pedro Noguera is the Peter L. Agnew Professor of Education at New York University, the Executive Director of the Metropolitan Center for Urban Education, and the co-Director of the Institute for the Study of Globalization and Education in Metropolitan Settings (IGEMS).

Robin D.G. Kelley is the Gary B. Nash Professor of American History at University of California, Los Angeles.

Rocío Sánchez Ares is a community researcher and doctoral student in Curriculum and Instruction, Lynch School of Education, Boston College.

Ruth Wilson Gilmore is Professor of Geography in the Doctoral Program in Earth and Environmental Sciences, The Graduate Center, CUNY.

Signithia Fordham is a public intellectual and cultural anthropologist at the University of Rochester, where she also was the Susan B. Anthony Professor of Gender and Women's Studies (2001–2006) in the Susan B. Anthony Institute for Gender and Women's Studies.

Tracy Friedel is Assistant Professor in Indigenous Education in the Department of Curriculum and Pedagogy at the University of British Columbia.

INDEX

Blassingame, John 105
Bloomberg, Michael 75
board games 184–185
body 215–216
Boggs, Grace Lee 30, 74, 84
Bourdieu, Pierre 49–50, 102
Bourgois, Philippe 103
Bowles, S. 37, 47
Boycott, Divestment, Sanctions (BDS) campaign 123, 168, 169–171, 231
Bradley, Matt 129, 135, 139
Brayboy, Bryan 14
Brokaw, Tom 90
Brooks, R. 188
Brown v. Board of Education (1954) 41, 66, 105, 147
Buras, Kristen 128–129, 132, 137
Burma 63
Bush, George W. 11, 12

Cahill, Caitlin 41, 129, 135–136, 139
calcification 8, 30, 34, 122, 177, 191
California 134–135
Cammarota, J. 42, 222
Camus, Albert 31, 101
Canada 13–14, 130, 196, 198–201
capitalism 30, 32, 50, 80, 141, 155; entrenchment of 83; racist politics 142; resistance to 230, 231
Castañeda, Justice 136–137
cell phones 15–16
Central America 72, 74, 79
Cesaire, Aime 37
change 13, 41, 44, 103–105; building social change 226–227; colonial theory of 190, 204; disruption as precondition for 66; Kelley 35, 37; local 93; Noguera 43; Palestine 173–174; radical empathy 94; revolutionary 93; system-compatible resistance 64–65; theories of 17, 18–19, 92, 119–123, 125–138, 216; undocumented immigrant youth 142, 144, 150
charter schools 3, 53, 55, 132
Chavez, L. 219
Chicago 2, 3, 179, 222, 227n1
Chicago Seven 62–63
chispas 127
choques 127
circuits of dispossession 55
citizenship 89, 144–145, 219, 221–222, 226
Civil Rights movement 12, 65, 66, 67, 74, 85, 89, 104, 105
class 47, 105–106, 157, 163

class reproduction 33, 37
Clinton, Bill 53
Cloward, R.A. 64, 65, 66
Cold War 30–31, 66
collaboration 31, 63, 91–92
collective consciousness 78–79
collective identity 36, 98, 214
Collective of Researchers on Educational Disappointment and Desire (CREDD) 181, 184, 185
collective unconscious 16
collectivization 226
Collin, M. 126
"colonial cosmology" 200
colonialism 2, 3, 7–8, 94–95; colonial theory of change 190, 204; Palestine 167–168, 170, 171; racial domination 198; surveillance of Native youth 199; white settler 141–142, 146, 150
coming out 142–145, 149, 179, 219, 222–226
commodification 53, 54
communism 30–31, 82, 83
community 158
competition 100
conformity 46, 77
consent 188, 189
consumer culture 90
containment, youth development as 89–90
Cooper, Ana Julia 2, 122
corrientes 127
Corrigan, Phillip 87
counter-stories 223
"counter-topographies" 56, 131, 184
crazy glue theory 135–136
criminal justice 131–132
criminalization 64, 88, 140
Criollo, Manuel 88
critical consciousness 191
critical education 47, 54
critical ethnography 182–183
critical participatory action research 56
critical pedagogy 74–75
critical race theory 47, 156–157, 159
Cruikshank, Julie 203
Cruz, Cindy 178–179, 209–217
cultural resistance 62
cultural studies 32, 83, 90
culture 32, 34, 86, 200, 203
curriculum 196, 200, 201, 203, 204, 205

Davis, Rennie 62–63
decolonial participatory action research (DPAR) 187–188